Duct-tape Community: Hope for Neighborliness in an Unequal World

Jim Herbst

Published by Jim Herbst, 2024.

DUCT-TAPE COMMUNITY: HOPE FOR NEIGHBORLINESS IN AN UNEQUAL WORLD

First edition. November 11, 2024.

Copyright © 2024 Jim Herbst.

ISBN: 979-8230813002

Written by Jim Herbst.

Table of Contents

Dedicated to my nieces and nephews: Brynn, Isaac, Dylan, Jordynn, Josiah, Ben, Maggie, and Rhyann. Since I suck at sports and anything requiring physical coordination, the least I can do is dedicate a book to you.

Front Cover Pictures

The center picture on the front cover is my mom (left) and her friend standing in front of mom's trailer.

The bottom cover picture is graffiti along the Eliza Furnace Trail in Pittsburgh when I lived there.

Back Cover Picture

Corn day at the Ringgold Ruritan sometime in the 1950s, Ringgold, Maryland.

Introduction
Duct-tape Neighborliness

Key Idea: "Its not where you live, but how you live."

This book is about neighborliness. A professor once told me that I told interesting stories, but he couldn't determine the point. To avoid repeating the mistake, *Duct-tape Community* is a declaration that community takes two resolves: one to make the world a fairer place and a second to be neighborly in one that isn't.

The idea of writing a book all started when I was thinking about Ms. Pearl Willis. If you, the reader, could have been in the car with Ms. Pearl the same day I was, you would have witnessed the same force I did. Ms. Pearl was driving a few of us college-age volunteers in an old mini-van during the Chicago gang wars of the mid-1990s. We had helped a retired pastor pull up a basement carpet in their Roseland neighborhood. As we approached an intersection, two teens on the corner caught her attention as probable gang members dealing drugs. "When they see this van, they'll clear the corner. They know I'll get out of this car and tell them about Jesus. You watch," she said.

Sure enough, the van turned the corner, and the teens split. There was no squad car. No flashing lights, and no siren — just Ms. Pearl in an old mini-van.

In the many years since that ride, I have sat in hundreds of community meetings—the kind of community meetings in rooms with cement block walls, uncomfortable stacking chairs with little or no padding, and echoey acoustics—listening to community members frustrated with crime. In one of my early meetings working for the City of Norfolk, I sat in the back of a room with a divided audience. Half wanted the police to be more aggressive and remove groups from street corners. The other half wanted them to be less aggressive. I thought of Pearl. No guns. No badge. No powers of arrest. No calling the police. Yet she had the force to clear the corner.

What did Pearl have that could clear crime without violence or police? She wasn't an expert who headlines expensive conferences at luxury hotels. She didn't sit in fancy conference rooms setting policy. She had no Ph.D. in public policy. She had no trappings of power, wealth, or title. No, it was something different.

She earned her credibility by changing diapers, maybe thousands of them. After dropping out of school as a pregnant mom, she dedicated herself to helping other women in the same situation. Pearl started a daycare for teenage moms in her Roseland neighborhood. When the other students and I volunteered with her program, she ran the daycare out of her house's lower floor and lived upstairs. She has since expanded into a formal center. She cared for hundreds of neighborhood babies and their moms. The two teens on that corner knew Ms. Pearl loved them or their families. I often wonder how communities would be different if more police officers and community members were more like Ms. Pearl.

Pearl was among the first standouts in a long line of people who don't command armies, sit at the head seat of government conference rooms, or come from neighborhoods with perfect social indicators. Still, they have an undeniable force of character derived from something else.

Consider another example: Lorene Stokes. In the world's hierarchy of status, Lorene Stokes didn't rank very high. She was a custodian for the Newport News Redevelopment and Housing Authority, where she had been a public housing resident. Ms. Stokes was a mother to one daughter and three sons. Her daughter, Michelle, spent part of her childhood in public housing after her father left. Michelle was required to make her bed, fold her clothes, and not leave dirty dishes in the sink. Her home was immaculately clean, and life was orderly. Their apartment was always a home to take pride in, whether someone else owned it or not. Her mother raised four children with humble confidence, faith, steadfast morality, a genuine love of others, and a commitment to their community.

I never met Ms. Stokes but was honored to attend her funeral. Her daughter, Michelle Johnson, was my boss, the Director of Norfolk's Department of Neighborhood Services, before retiring. Michelle lives with incredible integrity and has a beautiful marriage and two stellar children.

Given the same disturbing set of circumstances that trap so many others in poverty, how did Michelle escape? Although many factors aligned, including Michelle's intelligence and people skills, I suspect the strongest had something to do with the character of Lorene Stokes.

When I heard Cynt Marshall's story, I instantly thought of Michelle, who loves basketball. Cynt Marshall, the first Black woman C.E.O. in the N.B.A., explains concisely, "Its not where you live, but how you live."

After leaving a senior executive job at AT&T, billionaire Mark Cuban hired Cynt Marshall to transform the culture of the Dallas Mavericks. She told her story in her book *You've Been Chosen: Thriving Through the Unexpected* and subsequent interviews. If there is a checklist for failure, she could nearly check them all.

Racism? Check. She started life in Birmingham, Alabama, before her mother moved their family to escape segregation in the South.

Superiors instructed her to change her hair, dress, and mannerisms to advance in the corporate world.

Poverty? Check. After Alabama, they settled into a four-bedroom townhouse near San Francisco in Richmond, California's public housing projects. Her mom worked two, sometimes three, jobs and occasionally went without eating to support the family.

Broken Family? Check. Her mom eventually divorced her dad.

Childhood Trauma? Check. Her father was a self-described hustler and a domestic abuser. Although in self-defense, Marshall once saw her dad shoot a man in the head. After her mom filed for divorce, her father later pointed the gun at the teenage Cynt.

Marshall credits her faith and community. Public school teachers saw her value, encouraged her, and made school enjoyable. Neighbors bought clothes and school supplies one summer after Marshall's bitter father burnt their clothes.

Most of all, Marshall credits her mother, Carolyn Gardner, and her unshakable spirit, structure, faith, sacrifice, goal setting, discipline, and emphasis on education. When Marshall was young, her mother placed a Bible in one hand and a math book in the other, promising that those two books would be the ticket to a better life.

Oddly, Marshall claims to have never felt poor: "Her love and her faith in us were unshakable, and because of her, we never felt poor. 'It's not where you live, but how you live,' she would tell us. And more than that, 'It's who you live for.'"[1]

There are other success stories from what we call the underprivileged. President Dwight Eisenhower parents raised him in a house he later calculated to be about 833 square feet.[2] Michelle Obama grew up in an apartment in her aunt's house in a modest Chicago neighborhood. Howard Schultz, of Starbucks fame, spent time in New York's public housing. After Juan Sotomayor died of a heart attack, his wife, nine-year-old daughter Sonya, and her younger brother moved into modest but well-kept city-owned housing in the Bronx. Sonya became an Associate Justice on the Supreme Court; her younger brother became a physician and professor.[3]

There are thousands of books about how to be successful. This isn't one of them. This book is more concerned with the people who helped the successful get there, like the Carolyn Gardners of the world. Millions of people fight over power's acquisition, use, and maintenance. I'm more interested in the immense influence of the seemingly powerless.

Abraham Lincoln

Duct-tape Community is about this moral force entirely independent of our best social and economic indicators. Abraham Lincoln's biographer gave this mysterious force a name: neighborliness. Lincoln's secretary and biographer, John Nicolay, identified character attributes Lincoln acquired in his early pioneering days—values like equality, liberality, modesty, charity, and sympathy. Nicolay narrowed them down to one word: "neighborliness."[4]

Lincoln's early community environment defies all modern social-indicator standards. Harsh winters in a one-room cabin, his mother's premature death, clearing land, tilling the earth, and laying rail defined his early life. The frontier elements created a sense of community and dependency on neighbors that superseded appearances and could not be purchased. It wasn't the quality of the housing stock, amenities, or architecture but his community's ability to overcome adversity that shaped the future president.

Perceptions of Inequality

We have more computational power than ever before to compare big data across every census tract in the United States. That data reveals startling disparities and destructive, vulgar inequality.[5] There are people on a sold-out waitlist to buy $600,000 Lamborghinis and other families struggling to pay $1200 in monthly rent for a one-bedroom apartment.

One thorny complication is that claims of inequality get convoluted. Stefanie Stantcheva and her colleagues have written about perceptions of inequality. Views about inequality and fairness tend to be relative to position in life: "people's fairness views are strongly related to their social position and change when their positions change."[6] According to their research, those with lower incomes tend to underestimate the extent of inequality.

Robert Putnam's writings support her suggestion. When interviewing classmates from his 1959 high school graduating class from Port Clinton, Ohio, Putnam heard a familiar reframe: "We were poor, but we didn't know."[7] One classmate said he didn't realize a sense of deprivation until taking an economics course in college.

When Barack Obama first visited family in Africa, he contemplated the idea of poverty as both absolute and relative. Rural villagers without indoor plumbing or the ability to eat meat daily didn't view themselves as poor until outsiders changed their perception: "Perhaps the idea of poverty had been imported to this place, a new standard of need and want that was carried like measles...."[8]

This ever-changing set of wants and needs makes pinpointing inequality and its sister equity difficult. Low-income neighborhood

A, which had no community center, gets a new one with a rock-climbing wall and an extensive fitness studio. Neighborhood B then feels dissatisfied with their older community center. Neighborhood C, whose residents can mostly afford private health clubs, claims inequality because they lack any center. Claims of inequality are as straightforward as asking who the best N.F.L. team is.

About the Title

Stantcheva's point holds true in my experience. I grew up in what might be dubbed "The Duct-tape Class" on the lower rungs of the middle class. Although we were high enough on the privilege ladder by my teen years to make a pilgrimage to Disney World in the mid-1980s, my parents did so by sitting through time-share presentations (which they never bought) for discounted tickets and complimentary breakfast. We ate baloney sandwiches in Disney's parking lot out of the rear of our second-hand, 1979 Dodge Aspen station wagon and stayed at budget motels when we traveled. One motel where we stayed charged extra for the T.V. remote; another had a rocking toilet. At home, we had generic clothes and extruded every last milligram of toothpaste from the tube before throwing it away.

As a child, I knew others had superior cars, newer computers, and didn't stay at motels with rocking toilets. If life is a big comparison contest over who has the best material stuff, I knew I wasn't winning. Yet, it never stopped my family from having fun or having rich relationships with family, church members, neighbors, and the community. I was also aware that others had it worse.

I was jealous of other kids whose family vehicles were new and had that new car smell. Until some point after I had gone to college, my parents' cars were always used, and my dad's car always smelled like sweat. They smelled the way they did from hauling sweaty kids from our little clan, neighborhood kids, Cub Scouts, the church, the basketball team, the football team, or the volleyball team. Kids who were rough around the edges had a special place in my parents' hearts. Mom's used 1983 A.M.C. Eagle bore the brunt of their youth taxi service. One kid kicked out the rear speakers. Another neighborhood kid pulled off the hood ornament. I was embarrassed to take that car on a date. I was further mortified when I came home from college in the early 90s, and the rear lift gate was duct-taped together.

My attitude about my parents' cars changed during another trip home from college. The good people of Winifred Road Church of Christ in Cumberland, Maryland, where my dad was minister, had given an appreciation dinner for my parents. Cookies, chocolate cake, apple dumplings, cards, and other gifts of appreciation covered the dining room table and the kitchen counter. I came to appreciate my parents' smelly cars as a badge of honor for those whose lives they had influenced.

The quality of community life wasn't measured in nice material possessions but the value placed on others. Moreover, it wasn't the outward appearance of those cars that mattered but how they were being used. Admiration for the values behind their duct-taped, stinky cars replaced jealousy.

It was near the end of my freshman year at college when I was trying to decide on a career. I decided that whatever I chose, I wanted a career I could love and be loved like my parents. Since then, my career has transitioned from being a church minister like my dad to starting a neighborhood-based non-profit to over a decade of neighborhood work for local government. Two college degrees, multiple certifications, thirty years, hundreds of books, hundreds of hours in training, and three cities later, I have immense respect for knowledge experts in community development. Despite all the knowledge, knowledge experts aren't always the value experts. I keep returning to simple values from people like my parents. I've developed a great affection for duct-tape communities that may not look like much to outsiders but are full of neighborly people.

Later, after meeting Ms. Pearl, something felt incredibly familiar. Her urban neighborhood looked completely different from my rural upbringing. Her skin color and ancestry were different, but her values bore a striking resemblance to my parents'. They shared many of the same values. I set out to write a book about those people and those values.

Why Duct-tape Community?

Today, as inequality widens, it has become a hot topic. What to do about it is an even hotter debate. This book deals with three specific problems related to an unequal world.

First, it is often assumed that those better at making money are better at life and that wealthy celebrities have more desirable values. I intend to argue those points. What may be suitable for economics may not be good for community.

Second, the ancient Greek word for zeal was the same word for jealousy. Fiery zeal for a more equal world can become green jealousy. Concern over inequality is healthy. Jealousy is corrosive. I've struggled with it my whole life. It wreaks havoc on relationships.

Aleksandr Solzhenitsyn, a Nobel Prize winner, observed how prison tormentors skillfully used jealousy and competition to wear down souls during his time in the Soviet Gulag.[9] He warned that class warfare can become all-encompassing until everyone is an enemy.

Rebalancing economic policies can alleviate inequality, but they can't fix community where jealousy and greed are the root problems.

The third problem is that individuals and families still must go on living while social engineers debate how to achieve equality and justice. I am concerned that younger generations fighting so hard for a perfectly equal world are missing coping skills for one that isn't. Expecting perfect equality might be compared to shuffling a deck of 10,000 Uno cards, by hand, on a moving roller coaster and expecting a perfectly distributed deck. Many in duct-tape communities can't stop living while waiting for policymakers and philosophers to figure it out. Duct-tape communities provide insight into how to live meaningful lives in an unfair and unequal world.

Duct-tape Community is first a declaration that community takes two resolves: one to make the world a fairer place and a second to be neighborly in one that isn't. It is a challenge to all communities that neighborliness and the values herein are accessible to you regardless of your appearance or your median income. Neighborliness is never a substitute for justice, good schools, economic opportunity, or needed infrastructure. At no point do I argue otherwise. The weight of research papers about neighborhood effects on social and physical well-being could crush a library table. It would be a mistake, though, to assume that the absence of adversity builds a stronger community.

In a 2017 opinion piece first for the *New York Times*, Yale professor and Nobel Laureate Robert Shiller challenged the modern notion of the American Dread as "excessively lustful about homeownership and wealth, to the detriment of our economy and society."[10] He traced the phrase to 1931 when it was more about the value we place on each other than about materialism. Shiller said the housing industry took it over in the late 1970s and 1980s as a marketing gimmick.

Like Shiller, a partial purpose behind this book is to challenge materialistic assumptions. Can neighborhoods that price out anyone below a certain income level be considered neighborly? Does being an expert on neighborhoods equate to being a skilled practitioner of neighborliness? Can policymakers allocating millions of dollars in programming funds incentivize neighborliness? Should less attractive communities with lower property values always want to be more like their wealthier counterparts? Is neighborliness restricted to neighborhoods with manicured lawns, mini-mansions, and a high enough percentage of the median area household income?

Suppose you live in less attractive places, whether inner-city Chicago or the Appalachian Mountains. Commentators may describe your community as disadvantaged, underprivileged, under-resourced, devalued, and powerless. These may be true of economics, education, and other outward circumstances, but those words harm community when neighbors internalize them and believe those words about themselves. They siphon off a sense of pride, an awareness of gifts they can contribute, and interdependence on each other. Neighborliness becomes conditional on outsiders.

In the conclusion, I offer evidence from formal studies that levels of narcissism are rising. To most, this is self-evident without formal studies. It is evident from how we communicate on social media, drive, and spend time. Even unselfish volunteering is self-centered if the fundamental orientation is making yourself feel good. We elevate appearances over substance and are raised, whether rich or poor, to compare ourselves to what others have, and we don't. Neighborliness, on the other hand, requires other-centeredness. *Duct-tape Community* is a call to stand against the great American comparison contest and rediscover neighborliness.

Duct-tape Community is first a declaration but second a ledger of gratitude. Some of the most neighborly super-heroes I am grateful for are from places not associated with neighborliness. They have blessed my life, demonstrated the power of caring, and taught me how to live a fulfilling life regardless of place. They are people who turn places into communities.

Neighborliness is harder to see and quantify than other social indicators. In a matter of minutes from my work laptop with the City of Norfolk, I can calculate the assessed monetary value of any neighborhood in Norfolk, but those numbers don't tell the whole story. When London desired a new airport, they surveyed residents near where they wanted to place it. They asked residents to estimate the value of the neighborhood over and above its literal market value. Residents were so attached to their neighborhood that they placed the value of their attachment at 40% over the market rate.[11] It was a strong indicator that the dollar figure of a home's sale price doesn't capture a given neighborhood's relationships, sense of community, and memories. For all the technological savvy to measure things, numbers never tell the whole story. I haven't found a way to measure the invisible force of influence that I witnessed in Ms. Pearl and others like her. *Duct-tape Community,* therefore, offers an accounting of unlikely heroes who have shifted my view of community.

My chief qualification for writing a book is these extraordinary people whom I've met while doing neighborhood work and whose stories are intriguing, inspiring, and worthy of more recognition than they usually receive. My advice in the book is from trial and error, not any genius or mastery on my part. The book contains my observations, but, as with most people, perceptions are subject to significant flaws. I provide some advice but do so hesitantly. It is up to you, the reader, to determine whether the advice contained herein is good advice.

Duct-tape Community is next a confessional. My parents raised me in Cumberland, Maryland. Cumberland is located inside Allegany County and was a comfortable small town in which to grow up. Allegany County is a rural, post-industrial, blue-collar county familiar with the ghosts of its manufacturing past. Shuttered plants like Celanese, P.P.G., Kelly Springfield, and others testified to its faded manufacturing might. Today, Cumberland has a median income 57% of the national median. Allegany County is higher at 81% of the national standard. West Virginia—a state with the third-lowest median income—is about 1500 feet away on the other side of the Potomac River from where we lived. I started life in a trailer, am familiar with rural poverty, and rode my bike by the "projects" when we lived in town.

The catch is that Allegany County was 98% White and far from the surroundings that shaped so many of my future friends, coworkers, and acquaintances. I could never have imagined what I later learned about slavery, Jim Crow laws, and their ongoing effects.

I had never paid attention to George Washington Carver until I stood over his grave. It was an unusually pleasant August day under the Alabama sun on the beautiful campus of Tuskegee University. Born into slavery and poor health in 1865, his mother's owners raised him as their child in Missouri after his mother was kidnapped and presumably murdered by bushwhackers during the Civil War. After leaving home in grade school, he worked to further his education by doing laundry, cooking, gardening, and other odd jobs. Carver fled Fort Scott, Kansas, after watching the brutal lynching of a Black man by a fanatical White mob. He graduated with his master's degree from Iowa State Agricultural College.

Booker T. Washington recruited Carver to join the Tuskegee Institute specifically to help formerly enslaved people and other poor farmers barely existing in the South. He lived on a $1000 yearly salary during his 47-year career at Tuskegee. Being a thrifty saver, he gave most of his savings away near death. The year Booker T. Washington died, he gave half his salary to scholarships on top of his tithe to his church. At students' request, he taught a Bible study for 30 years. He provided practical lessons to farmers on how to switch to better crops than cotton, such as peanuts and sweet potatoes. He invented new uses for their products, provided training, risked his life traveling through the South in a mobile training unit, and testified before Congress. Carver spent most of his career living in a dormitory near his students and ate in the cafeteria. Though an adviser to U.S. Presidents, he wore a suit for fifty years because it was a treasured gift, and he hated waste. He turned down better-paying jobs by Henry Ford and Thomas Edison. Most of his research he gave away for free. An epitaph written in stone over George Washington Carver's grave reads, "He could have added fortune to fame, but caring for neither, he found happiness and honor in being helpful to the world."

Stories like his had never been part of my education. My first attempt to listen to W.E.B. Du Bois's 1903 book, *The Souls of Black Folk*, failed. I lacked the historical context to understand it. Now that it makes sense, it is one of my most valued books. Studying neighborliness has brought uncomfortable conflict with race issues and our country's treatment of those different or poor. In the pages hereafter, I confess my awkward, stubborn wrestling with these issues. The call for neighborliness is not a call to return to a nostalgic 1950s.

To Whom is *Duct-tape Community* Written?

Publishers ask annoying questions like, "What is your writing style," and "Who is the book's audience?" To theirs and my frustration, I have never been able to pinpoint either. I try to write as a couth, educated person should write, but sometimes my rural crudeness breaks through. Nor have I ever been able to identify a specific marketing demographic like Gen Z students or Millennial suburban homemakers. I can only describe who I had in mind when writing.

This book is for those below average in the great American comparison contest. It offers reassurance that great values don't always come in attractive packages.

This book is for those who feel like they are driving from Ocean City, Maryland, to San Diego, California, on a riding lawnmower. They are moving, just not very fast.

This book is for those who have learned healthy grief and who can hold a hospice patient's hand without blabbering false promises. It is not for the dangerously optimistic who fart rainbows and whose utopia is always around the corner with the next election.

This book is for activists skilled at building bridges, not burning them.

This book is for a certain kind of academic. It is for authentic learners who see the residents of duct-tape communities as having something valuable to learn. It isn't for know-it-all critics who see residents as problems that need fixing.

This book is not for the overly spiritual. It is for those, as Brennan Manning put it, whose "cheese has fallen off their cracker."[12]

This book is for those suffocating in the smog of bitterness and want to breathe deeply from the fresh air of grace and forgiveness.

This book is for younger generations in the U.S. who have known nothing but yelling and screaming in public discourse and long for something more.

In the sports world, lucrative contracts, name recognition, and endorsement deals are reserved for the talented few. Sportsmanship is not. It is as accessible to kids at the neighborhood sandlot with paper-plate bases as it is in the most grandiose stadium. The two should not be confused. In the world of neighborhoods, trendy restaurants, weedless lawns, private security, and top-notch schools are usually reserved for those who can afford them. Neighborliness is not. *Duct-tape Community* is my way of shouting to America's beautiful, wonderful, quirky, duct-tape communities that community is as accessible to you as to anyone else.

Wouldn't it be wonderful if more people shared Carver's epitaph? What if neighbors found more happiness and honor in helping their communities and less in winning some comparison contest? Ultimately, I hope that the unlikely heroes who have influenced me to be more neighborly will have the same influence on you and that you, the reader, will summon the power of neighborliness in your community.

Who is Duct-tape Community?

Key Idea: "Not much money but a whole lot of love."

Who is Duct-tape Community?

Who is Duct-tape Community? Two of my favorite songs help visualize what I mean. The first is John Conley's "Domestic Life" [select verses and chorus].

Cruising in my station wagon

Trying to keep my muffler from dragging

Sometimes it seems so defeating

As I'm hustling to make it to the Cub Scout meeting

I dream about Mexico

Where all the pretty people go

But we're on a budget that just won't budge

Not much money, but a whole lot of love

See me mowing my domestic yard

Lord, I owe my soul to Master Card

But it seems to suit me to a tee

That domestic life's all right with me

I'll never be president

And we never seem to save a cent

But things are looking better everyday

Hell I'm Sergeant At Arms of the P.T.A.

[Chorus]

Living that domestic life

Happy children and a pretty wife

Our cocker spaniel's always having puppies

How could anybody be so lucky?

The other is Evvie McKinney's "Bring the Whole Hood", [select verses and chorus]

I come from Memphis, Tennessee

Little small house, big family

Seven kids, and I'm the baby

But I'm grown now

And I'm like praise the Lord

Cause everything I've been praying for

Is finally knocking on my door

And it's so so loud

[Chorus]

I'ma bring the whole hood with me

They say, girl what you talkin about

I'ma bring the whole hood with me

Then I'ma buy my mama a house

And my mama done worked her butt off

Make sure the lights don't cut off

Made sure we never went hungry

So now I gotta make that money

And I'm making my daddy so proud

That's where I got my sound

I know that he can hear me now

Putting on for my town

A car with a dragging muffler, tight budgets, a big family in a small house, and a mother working her butt off are perfect images. Those from duct-tape communities presently or in their past identify with everyday struggles that cut across lines usually used to divide people like race, religion, or political affiliation. The songs also demonstrate involvement in community: Cub Scouts, the P.T.A., or caring about the hood.

Who makes up Duct-tape Community? They are mostly defined by shared struggles and grit. However, they are not one, big, happy family but have significant divisions.

Shared Struggles

Financial Football

Duct-tape communities' most recognizable indicator is a financial football game of gaining and losing yards in a constant patchwork of trying to pay bills and save for the future. Duct-tape community members know the struggle of working hard, scrimping, doing without, eating tuna noodle casserole, keeping the thermostat low in the winter, air drying clothes in the summer, and taking staycations. When they feel a sense of progress, their water heater quits, their car's alternator needs to be replaced, a kid needs braces, or their taxes go up.

In his book *The Future of Capitalism,* Paul Collier, an Oxford economist and former Director of Research Development at the World Bank, addresses the economic fault lines that many of us feel. For one, the world economy has grown more complex, leaving more significant divisions between educated, technologically skilled labor and the less educated, less technologically proficient class. There was once a near-equal pride in professions and work identities. There is now an imbalanced pride with a new educated class that feels a sense of superiority over the less educated. This has left a resentful, less educated class who can sense a smug sense of superiority over them.

Another fault line Collier names is the "greed is good mentality" propagated by popular economists and business schools of the 1970s and 1980s. This greed gutted corporate ethics and widened the disparities between the haves and the have-nots. In some cases, C.E.O.s are compensated 200 times more than the lowest-paid workers.

Collier further addresses the rise in lawsuits. The average citizen's and employee's autonomy was lost to increasingly complex legal mechanisms to govern every possible behavior and protect against every imagined liability. Group identities multiplied while a shared identity disintegrated. Shared values, a shared identity, and a shared sense of reciprocal obligations have broken down. Citizens became consumers demanding more rights.

The most egregious example of rights without reciprocal responsibilities is Canadian Geese. Federal law protects them, but they have no reciprocal responsibility. They are not responsible poopers. They blanket playgrounds, parks, church parking lots, or any open field with their mines. They cause vehicle accidents and block traffic. Rights without responsibilities leave people frustrated and angry. If it were up to me, Canada could have their geese back. Collier wasn't referring to geese, but he accurately summarized the frustration many of us feel.

Others' Leftovers

A second shared struggle of duct-tape communities is others' leftovers. For the first half of the twentieth century, inner cities shoved industrial businesses that no one else wanted into Black and poor White neighborhoods. A picture from 1940s Norfolk shows a giant multi-story gas container wedged right into an area designated for "Negros."

After the collapse of manufacturing, Allegany County was the proud recipient of new prisons and landfills to accommodate overflow from east coast cities. The state created Rocky Gap State Park to open beautiful western Maryland scenery to public enjoyment and conservation. Then, they added a golf course. Now, it is a casino. Casinos, after all, are the solution to all financial problems.

In West Virginia, coal companies mined the money out of West Virginia hills, closed, and left entire mountain tops blown off. The latest gift to West Virginians is high-powered transmission lines that transverse farms and neighborhoods to feed data centers in northern Virginia.

USA Today and other news outlets covered the story of the "poop train" from New York City left to sit idle in the small town of Parrish, Alabama.[13] Since a federal ban on dumping it in the ocean, sewage sludge from the Big Apple went to wherever had the weakest zoning regulations to prevent it. In this case, it sat on a train next to a Little League field. People with the least political power are frequently handed what others don't want.

Feeling Screwed

Closely related is the feeling of being abused by the greedy. The absurdity of the healthcare system is a prime example. After shopping for a mammogram, Eileen Anderson wrote an excellent 2006 editorial for the *Pittsburgh Post-Gazette* aptly named "The Adventures of a Health Care Consumer" that accurately expresses the opinion of most lower and middle-class Americans. She writes

> Maybe your idea of fun is putting together a 1,000-piece jigsaw puzzle of a snowy scene. Health Care is that complicated. Now, imagine trying to put together the puzzle in the dark. Shopping for health care is like that.

> ...My overriding impression is that no one who helped to create the healthcare system—providers, insurers, administrators, politicians—has used the system as a self-paying customer and gone through the experience of shopping for any healthcare service.

She described the adventure almost everyone has experienced: making phone calls, navigating phone trees, being transferred from one person to another, leaving voicemails, and waiting on return phone calls, many of which never come.

Loss of Culture and Status

As part of urban renewal in 1950s Pittsburgh, the civic arena displaced 8000 residents in the Hill District when it was built. The Hill District was Pittsburgh's "Little Harlem" and the hub of African American culture. Forty years later, it was still very much in the memory of the Black community. Many displaced people settled in places like Hazelwood, where I lived. I remember hearing people talk about traditions that originated in the Hill District. Old heads from those neighborhoods lament the loss of culture.

The South Armour Square neighborhood fought a losing battle against Comiskey Park in Chicago. The Eisenhower Expressway and the University of Illinois displaced West Side neighborhoods in the 1960s.

People in the country also know a bit about threatened culture. Between 1974 and 2017, 513 counties were reclassified from non-metro to metro.[14] This expansion is evident from Ringgold, Maryland, to the disappearing farms in Virginia Beach and Chesapeake, Virginia. They are long gone in Norfolk.

Sprawl is a rural form of urban gentrification. Newcomers to the area gradually saturate local organizations, and long-standing traditions disappear. Those brushed to the sidelines feel displaced by "progress."

These shared struggles unite Duct-tape communities regardless of race, religion, urban or rural.

Duct-tape Divisions

To shed any suggestion that Duct-tape communities are one big, happy, unified family locking arms and singing Garth Brooks', "Friends in Low Places," let me dispel any false inferences. If my friends in the city and my friends from the country were to sit down in a focus group about government policy, they would be deeply divided.

Policy Wedges

A policy's proponents and opponents often use moralistic language to politicize a position. Complex policies and different approaches to fairness are painted as us. vs. them, good vs. evil when, in many cases, it is not so cut and dry. What may be fair to one group may be unfair to a different group. What corrects one injustice may cause another. A zoning change that may be good for the city may not be beneficial to an individual neighborhood. Environmental regulations that are good for the planet's future may kill jobs in the present. Sadly, many laws exist because people cannot be relied upon to do the right thing. The many become penalized for a few.

Policy becomes a wedge for at least five reasons: 1) Policymakers are political and must satisfy constituents to pass legislation. 2) Many policies are incredibly complex. Most of us and many lawmakers don't understand them. 3) How policymakers market a policy to win support often departs from reality. 4) Policy is a value judgment of what, or rather who, is important and less important. 5) Building political will depends on good storytelling to fire the public up emotionally. It becomes theater. Naomi Eisenstadt captured popular sentiment well: everyone believes in local democracy until it is their issue, and then it is ok to tell other people what to do.[15]

When the name "The Farm Bill" is mentioned, one might imagine helping a person in overalls, a plaid shirt, a John Deere hat, boots, and leaning against a pitchfork with a red barn in the background. Somehow, images of multinational food corporations, energy companies, environmental activists, the Defense Department, educators, foreign governments, international relief organizations, and more do not come to mind. Yet, they all have a stake in the far-reaching Farm Bill. For years, agricultural policy based crop commodity payments on acreage, so naturally, the largest farms received the most government payments, not the small farmers. When policies are so complex, the average person is left scratching their head about who benefits.

The Patient Protection and Affordable Care Act (ACA) of 2010 and all the changes since its original passage are a hotly contested issue. On the one hand, it has genuinely helped large segments of the population who needed help. On the other hand, those who watched their health insurance deductibles and premiums increase didn't feel like "The Affordable Care Act" was making health care more affordable. Policy becomes a wedge between those receiving something and those having something taken away. Having different opinions on a policy doesn't make anyone morally deficient.

The Language of Take

The competition for resources expresses itself through the language of take. In Virginia, a ritual called public budget hearings occurs annually for local governments. State law requires a public hearing before a vote by the city council. At the public hearing, petitioners go before their elected representatives for about two hours. It feels like an adult version of kids lining up to see Santa Claus. Occasionally, one or two crazies want to be on camera and say nothing related to the budget. They keep it entertaining.

A few things strike me as sad. First, few ever return to say anything positive. Second, only some petitioners offer suggestions for paying for their requests. Raising taxes is unpopular, so the demand is usually to take from someone else. Third, most leave after petitioning for what they want. The majority do not listen to others' concerns. Most petitions are worthy causes, yet few people are concerned with the painful choices of balancing those causes with limited resources.

Intentional Division

By General Ulysses S. Grant's estimation, census figures, and other sources, most men fighting on the Confederate side of the Civil War didn't own slaves.[16] Even so, Southerners saw a threat to slavery as a threat to themselves. Grant attributes the war to the political fear and fervor stirred up successfully by the small minority of wealthy, White, slave-holding aristocracy, many of whom did not take to the battlefield themselves.

Former slave Louis Hughes's account concurs with this description of the planter class. While Hughes was a slave on a Mississippi plantation, his owner claimed that he could take six Yankees with just a pocketknife at the outbreak of the war. Hughes noted, however, how his master fell ill on the couch and called for a poultice every time the Yankees came anywhere near: "He and many like him were especially valorous only when the bluecoats were far away."[17]

While a planter class may not exist today, some enrich themselves by sowing division and fear. Media titans, academics, politicians, entertainers, and businesses build their brand by feeding an us vs. them mentality.

Duct-tape Grit

The last characteristic of the Duct-tape Community is grit. James McBride's book, *The Color of Water: A Black Man's Tribute to His White Mother,* has connections to Hampton Roads, Virginia. I saw the approximate site of his grandparents' grocery store and visited the Cedar Hill Cemetery, where McBride's mother played as a child. When I visited in 2016, Confederate flags and a Confederate general's memorial still celebrated the Confederacy as a just cause for states' rights. The monument said nothing about slavery.

James McBride's family story has all the identity intersections that intellectuals opine over. His mother, Ruth McBride Jordan, was born in Poland before immigrating to the U.S. at age two. Her parents gave her the name Ruth Shilsky by the time they settled in Suffolk, Virginia. Her father was an orthodox Jewish rabbi who owned Shilsky's Grocery Store during the Great Depression.

Within her family, her mother was disabled from polio. Her father was abusive, cold, and openly unfaithful to his wife. Though discriminated against as a Jew, her father enriched himself by selling goods to Black people at inflated prices.

Outside her family, young Ruth Shilsky was teased as a "Christ killer," "Jew baby," and "Dirty Jew." She only had one real friend who accepted her. As a little girl, she once asked what the parade going up the street was and why all the Black people disappeared. It was the K.K.K.

She fell in love with a Black boy and became pregnant at age 15. In the 1930s South, that was a death sentence for the Black boy, so she quietly had an abortion in New York.

After high school graduation, Ruth Shilsky escaped Virginia in 1941 for New York. There, she married a Black pastor, Andrew McBride, and converted to Christianity. Her father and extended family disowned her and treated her as if dead.

After 16 years of marriage and eight children, Pastor McBride died unexpectedly. After an extended period of depression and raising eight children by herself, Ruth McBride married another Black man, Hunter Jordan. They had 14 years of marriage and four children before Ruth McBride Jordan was widowed a second time.

Despite the challenges, Ruth McBride Jordan raised a who's who of children. She produced two doctors, two professors, two engineers, two teachers, a social worker, a nurse-midwife, a financial director, and a best-selling author. She completed her own Bachelor's degree at age 65.

Ruth McBride Jordan experienced abuse, rejection, discrimination, poverty, housing projects, depression, the deaths of two husbands, a quadruple bypass, a minor stroke, and the deaths of a son and two great-grandchildren. Why would anyone with that life story wake up every morning and say, "I'm blessed," or frequently tell her children, "I'm blessed beyond measure."[18]

Why? Because the Ruth McBride Jordans of the world live by a different set of rules.

The words "not much money but a whole lot of love" ring true for her family. Inner character transformed her adversity into a grit that drove her to rise and take her family and community with her.

The Carolyn Gardners and the Ruth McBride Jordans stand out in a whiney, entitled, self-absorbed culture. They demonstrate duct-tape-community grit and that you can have a whole lot of love without much money. They leave a legacy to future generations on how to live meaningfully in an unfair, unequal world.

Two Resolves

Key Idea: Money doesn't buy community.

Equality is a human invention. We imagine it and aspire to it, but it is not natural. The natural world is neither fair nor safe. The natural world favors a hierarchy: the biggest bull elephant, the most muscular lion, and the fastest shark. The natural world favors golden genetics, not people with Down Syndrome, low IQs, or genetic disorders. Michelle Obama described "a strange and cruel randomness to it all."[19] This book is about the struggle between striving for a more equal world and being neighborly in one that isn't.

In the West, equality is considered a legal right because it is inscribed in the Declaration of Independence from 1776 and the 14th Amendment to the U.S. Constitution from 1868. Yet, we dare not assume it is the natural order because it says so on two old pieces of paper.

Community life takes two human resolves to overcome the natural order. The first is the resolve to make the world a fairer place. It takes intentional and ongoing effort. Howard Fineman names 13 arguments the nation has debated since it began. Questions like "who is a person," "who is American," and "what is a fair, 'more perfect' union" are perpetual hot topics. They are worthy debates stemming from our resolve to impose equality in an unequal world. This first resolve is the one that keeps lawyers, legislators, activists, academics, and op-ed writers employed.

Civil rights attorney and Supreme Court Justice Thurgood Marshall epitomized this resolve in his 1988 speech accepting the American Bar Association's Jurist of the Century award.

> What is important is a goal. A goal that is the basis of true democracy. You must pray for it. And work for it. And that goal is very simple. That goal is that if a child, a negro child, is born to a Black mother in a state like Mississippi or any other state like that, born to the dumbest, poorest sharecropper, just by merely drawing its first breath in a democracy, there and without any more is born with the exact same rights as a similar child born to a White parent of the wealthiest person in the United States. No, it's not true. Of course, it's not true. It never will be true. But I challenge anybody to take a position that that is not the goal that we should be shooting for.[20]

Although his focus was racial equality, the same resolve applies to other areas of equality and fairness.

Marshall, however, also points to the need for a second resolve. There will never be perfect equality. If the first resolve is to make the world a fairer place, the second is to remain neighborly in one that isn't. Whether in the African jungle or driving to work, nature is weighted toward speed and aggression, not kindness. This second resolve, being neighborly, is the subject of this book. It is a search for neighborliness in a neither fair nor safe world.

This book is about true neighborhood character—kindness toward others—not appearances or architectural styles. Simply put, money doesn't buy community. David Brooks's 2015 *The Road to Character* made the *New York Times* bestseller list. He describes the inner conflict between our two natures. The résumé side of our nature wants to succeed, achieve, gain status, and self-promote. It is the economic logic of inputs and outputs. The other side of our nature, the eulogy side, follows moral logic. It is more about serving, humility, and loving others. He describes this lifelong self-confrontation between the two sides as the road to character.[21]

Looking back in history, we see a conflict between Booker T. Washington and W.E.B. Du Bois. Washington emphasized personal responsibility and character. Du Bois emphasized correcting structural deficiencies. *Duct-tape Community* assumes that their conflict is not an either/or proposition. It balances the two resolves to make the world a better place.

The Great American Comparison Contest

If inequality is one threat, the great American comparison contest is a secondary threat. Because equality is a human invention, there is no constant in nature to measure it against, like earth's gravity or the boiling point of water at sea level. It thus becomes a comparative competition.

In 2007, *The New York Times* had an article about a suburban neighborhood of millionaires in Silicon Valley. Neighbors didn't feel rich, even as millionaires. One neighbor worth $5 million summarized it, "Here, the top one percent chases the top one-tenth of one percent, and the top one-tenth of one percent chases the top one-one-hundredth of one percent."[22]

Many not in Silicon Valley's tax bracket may scornfully judge their oblivious privilege as raw jealousy. This judgment would seem warranted if I had not seen residents in lower-income neighborhoods tear each other apart in a similar comparison contest. It may be a comparison contest over individual wealth, or it may be over status or recognition. Inequality is one battle. The Great

American Comparison Contest is a hidden second battle. We judge others and ourselves by measuring neighborhoods, community, love, happiness, joy, relationships—nearly everything in life—against what someone else has or some idealized standard. Social media thrives on the Great American Comparison Contest.

To draw a fine line of distinction, the threat is the contest part. Comparison is part of life. The threat that does collateral damage to community is turning everything into a contest. The dangers of the comparison contest are well established. By 1835, Alexis De Tocqueville observed the envy, weariness, and bitterness generated by the gap between America's promise of equality and its unattainable fulfillment.[23] However hard society tried to make community equal, human pride had the opposite effect.[24]

Two thousand years before De Tocqueville, Aristotle wrote about inequality. After studying 158 constitutions, he observed different forms of government produced different forms of justice and equality. Revolutions were an inevitable result of jealousy over one group's perceived advantage over another, regardless of government's form.[25]

Nordic countries warranted their own chapter in the 2020 World Happiness Report for their consistently high ratings of life satisfaction. The research into the correlation between income inequality and well-being had mixed results. What was more telling was other factors associated with income inequality, like perception of fairness, status anxiety, and economic opportunities.[26] Frank Martela, one of the contributors to the report, wrote separately about three things Norwegians never do. Number one was that they don't compare themselves to their neighbors.[27] More recently, however, Norwegians' sense of well-being dropped when individual tax returns became available online, and they could compare incomes.[28] U.S. surveys demonstrated similar results. Neighbors showed less happiness when comparing themselves to neighbors with higher incomes.[29]

The comparison game is dangerous. It trades intangible human values for tangible market values. It substitutes relational models of community with materialistic models. As in the Silicon Valley neighborhood, the attitude that someone else has more becomes an excuse to be more self-centered.

Having a higher income reduces survival's stress, but is love—life's fundamental source of fulfillment—tied to income? Do the residents of a high-income neighborhood love their grandmothers more than lower-income residents? For every percentage increase in income, does someone experience an equal increase in laughter and robust joy? The research says, "No!" Money adds no further emotional well-being at a certain point around the median income. [30] The appendix provides further research on the relationship between money and happiness.

Duct-tape Community says that neighborliness comes from something inside the heart that is not tied to something material. Economics is competitive. Neighborliness isn't. Money doesn't buy community.

Life as a Game of Monopoly

For the last 14 years, I've worked as a city employee in Norfolk, Virginia's neighborhoods. When I started working for government, I had the highest hopes of doing my part to make city neighborhoods fairer, better, and more equitable places to live, work, and play. To that end, I'm very proud of the City of Norfolk. It has increasingly diversified its economic base beyond the military. It has invested billions of dollars in schools, infrastructure improvements, housing, flood prevention, poverty reduction, Diversity, Equity and Inclusion initiatives, libraries, parks, and public art. Yet, after 14 years, I can't say confidently that residents behave any better.

The relativity of inequality is evidenced regularly. Vocal residents in every neighborhood claim neglect relative to other neighborhoods. Neighborhoods may receive new parks, housing grants, tens of millions of dollars in infrastructure improvements, new schools, new indoor pools, new affordable housing, new libraries, or city-subsidized businesses. Some will still claim that the City never gives them anything whenever another neighborhood gets something they don't have. Affluent neighborhoods claim low-income neighborhoods get better treatment. Low-income neighborhoods claim the same about affluent neighborhoods. Residents in the same neighborhood will complain that another part of the neighborhood gets better treatment.

Making places nicer is no guarantee that people are nicer. Installing speed tables, driver feedback signs, landscaping, and new intersections has not made drivers more considerate. The City of Norfolk received $154 million from the American Rescue Plan Act, and Norfolk Public Schools received another $113 million. Groups competed over how it was spent. Activist organizations began paying people to disrupt public meetings.

Covid and its economic setback provided a convenient excuse for bad behavior. Covid is now mostly in the rear-view mirror. The economy is thriving, yet shoplifting is so bad that Walmart started locking up its men's underwear and its toothbrushes. Shopping at our crowded Walmart was never pleasant, but I now have to find an associate and announce that I need a pair of size 38 Fruit of the Looms.

My work can feel shallow. Some elected representatives stand up to bad behavior; others feed it. I sometimes feel like a game piece in Monopoly that others move around in their conquest to beat others for more stuff. I'm not alone. The solution to teachers being mistreated has been to give them more money. The solution to police resigning in mass numbers has been to pay them more money. The solution to retail workers being treated poorly by the public has been to give them higher wages. At what point will we be unable to buy our way out of poor behavior, overblown expectations, and toxic entitlement?

Something is missing. I think of William Kamkwamba (from *The Boy Who Harnessed the Wind*) living through famine in Malawi, a family member from Nigeria, and immigrants who have come through far more trauma than most Americans. Why are Americans so depressed, anxious, angry, and perpetually dissatisfied? The Great American Comparison Contest is wearing people down. America has a character problem separate from Covid or economics.

If Columbus's journals weren't such a tragic history, it would read like a Monty Python skit.[31] Cruelty was first and foremost, but it was also a disdain for anything simple. It was a belief that anything they touched could be made bigger and better. He looked at what, by his admission, was the most beautiful place he had ever seen and thought to himself, "What would make it better is if we had some revenue-generating settlements, towns, ports, and if these people could labor for us."

Five hundred years later, we still view community through a market lens. We love nature but want to make it perfect-er by generating revenue. In the perpetual chase of the novel and Columbus's gold, we exhaust resources in one place and move on to the next.

The debate about rising inequality is vital to justice. Still, it may have the psychological side effect of causing us to constantly compare ourselves entirely by wealth and the stuff it buys.

Another avenue for neighborhood change is government enforcement. Neighborhoods that rely too heavily on enforcement are not warm and inviting. Rather than meet a new neighbor or inquire if a senior needs help to mow a yard, they report them to the city. Nothing says "Welcome to the Neighborhood" like a Notice of Violation from local government because of a code crusader neighbor.

The more important force, human character, requires the least dollar amount but costs the most in human transactions. Teddy Roosevelt said a healthy nation needs good laws, the best people in office to enforce those laws, and private character. Of those three, he concluded that the character of the average citizen is ultimately most influential in shaping the former two.[32]

Character impacts neighborhoods daily and forms community through simple acts of caring about others. The neighborly are a force in the most physically attractive neighborhoods to what some would consider imperfect, duct-tape communities. Paul Grogan of the Boston Foundation cites a South Bronx neighborhood that hasn't solved poverty or unemployment. For all the effort, the numbers haven't moved on those issues. It isn't the idealized picture of a middle-class neighborhood. Nevertheless, it is a safe, affordable, livable neighborhood where residents are active citizens and participants in their neighborhood.[33] I suspect it is because the South Bronx has neighbors like Ms. Pearl. It takes neighbors who are resolved to make the world fairer but are equally resolved to remain neighborly in one that isn't. The community that people want can't be bought.

Goals of the Book

I have the following goals for influencing you, the reader. First and foremost, I ask the reader not to judge a neighborhood's character by outward appearances or economics but by its people. Second, I ask the reader to value the small, humble, and kind. There are many well-written books about big movements and public policies. This book in no way intends to counter them. It is instead to place the importance of the small, humble, and kind on a parallel and equal plane. It is sometimes helpful to look for people behind the scenes, not in carefully selected publicity photos. A third goal is to comfort the confused. If you find the current state of politics and identity wars confusing, I offer encouragement that you're not alone. A fourth goal is to encourage the middle—both middle voices and middle neighborhoods. Fifth, I seek to elevate the language urban and rural dwellers use to describe each other. Having been raised in the country and having made a career in the city, how people talk about each other deeply grieves me. Finally, the sixth goal is a call for humility in the gap between our stated values and actual behavior.

I divided the book into four sections. Section one is specifically about community life and leadership. Section two is about the positive impact public servants have on government-neighborhood relationships. Section three is about the urban-rural divide, the complicated convolutions of race, class, education, and the importance of honor in understanding each other. Finally, section four covers the impact of the faith community. The sections are independent of each other, so you won't hurt my feelings by skipping ahead. But first, let me say a little more about a few goals.

Beyond Appearances: Character vs. Curb Appeal

When people talk about neighborhood character, they usually refer to a neighborhood's physical appearance and features like architecture, green space, set-back distances from the street, density, or curb appeal. Is it more urban or suburban? Are homes clad in brick, vinyl, or stucco? Is the neighborhood townhouses, single-family homes, or apartments? A great deal of literature covers the physical properties of neighborhood character. What is the human character of a community.

In 2011, I set up a table at Norview Community Center, placed out two sets of cards and markers, and asked kids to finish two sentences. The sentence on one set of cards was "I like [my neighborhood] because...." The other cards asked them to complete the sentence, "A good neighbor...." Of the 67 cards that I retained, none mentioned physical appearance beyond "clean." Housing stock, housing tenure, economics, proximity to a grocery store, condition of the roads, curbs and gutters, and street layouts didn't seem to matter to a child's experience. Nearly all the responses were behavioral, such as how they were treated and felt in their neighborhood. The pop-out box contains a few of the responses.

Good design, planning, architecture, and sound economics are all critical. I can show you ample bad examples to demonstrate why. Nevertheless, Neighborhood appearance and economic measures can be deceptive as a measure of human character. Some neighborhood leaders, regardless of income levels, overflow with love, welcome newcomers with open arms and would give up their last $20 to help someone else. Other neighborhood leaders are self-absorbed, whiney, snobby, and

What I Like about My Neighborhood from the Perspective of Children

I once sat up a table at Norview Community Center, placed out two sets of cards, markers, and asked kids to finish the two sentences below. These are a few of their answers. I have preserved them as written fully aware that the spelling and grammar are not entirely correct.

I like [my neighborhood] because ...
> They have a corner store/and they have Almost cookouts Every day
> clean, Big Field, no smell babies in front of the school
> I like my playgroud
> We play every day
> It's more quite now and I love my friends
> They are not load
> Every day I go to say hi to them
> He's quiet and he don't bother us
> It's quiet and peaceful and no kids
> Peace full lot of dogs
> There is no shooting no getting taken to jail
> Mr. nick let us come in and play with her kids give us anything we want to
> [I like] Nelly [because] she helped me do my work
> It's quite at night time.
> I like the comuty.
> It has friend and people I can count on.
> There is a lot of kids

A good neighbor...

> Is nice they are swite and kind
> A good neighbor to me is mr. nicks because anything my mother want she will get it and she lets us come in her house too
> Ms. Woods let us use the the phone and when my mommy is gone she let us stay over there 4a little bit

entitled. Periodically, dictatorial HOAs will make the news for some rigid rule over paint colors, yard flags, or parking RVs.

When I think of what has made my neighborhood a community, it is Ms. Foca's pickles, Ms. Avis' chocolate cake, Ms. Susan's honeybees, Ms. Wonder's roses, Vernon and Gina's BBQ ribs, feeding dog treats to Ms. Ramirez's dachshund Vita. It is watching my neighbor's daughter graduate high school and college and become an engineer. I think of my late neighbor Milton, the plumber, redoing my plumbing at a substantially lower cost than a company. They make my neighborhood a community, not how many houses have dormers.

Appearances aren't everything. The South has magnificent, historic, architecturally significant mansions. They called them plantations. The Greek columns, grand entrances, balconies, and manicured gardens hid the wretched cruelty of slavery and Jim Crow. One of the justifications for the removal of Native Americans was that they didn't build good English homes with hedges and fences to enclose workable land. European settlers viewed them as nomads incapable of holding title to land.[34] They forcibly removed natives so that they could establish proper English neighborhoods.

In his prophetic role, Cornel West calls out the damage done to American community by a market-inspired way of life. Seductive images edge out all other "non-market values — love, care, service to others—handed down by preceding generations."[35] Elsewhere, popular home remodeling shows give the impression that if you don't remodel your home every other year, a homeowner is out of touch with the market. Branding, messaging statements, and projecting the right image become proxies for neighborliness. This book attempts to return "neighborhood character" as a reference to shared community values and behavior, not landscaping and color palettes.

Small Things by People Not in the Pictures

While celebrities, academics, and government executives capture headlines, many neighbors make a difference through unrecognized acts of love. This is especially true of people not in the pictures at groundbreakings, ribbon cuttings, and events that attract power players. I think of Lois Tevis in the Hazelwood neighborhood of Pittsburgh. Lois spent most of her 80 years in Hazelwood and raised four kids in their house on Flowers Avenue. Her street was the location of many shootings and a major drug bust involving SWAT and the capture of a pet alligator.

Lois's kids have encouraged her to leave. She doesn't because she loves her neighborhood. She volunteered for Meals on Wheels, picked up neighborhood litter, attended neighborhood meetings, planted flowers in public spaces, and volunteered at her church. When it snowed, and we attended the same church, it was a rush to beat her to the sidewalks to shovel snow. In the February 2010 blizzard, she let my wife and I stay with her when we lost power for two days during temperatures in the single digits.

How many tons of trash has Lois picked up over a lifetime? How many cumulative meals has she delivered? How deep would the dust and dirt be in her church building if someone reversed all the years of her cleaning? Yet she is never the person with the giant scissors or the gold-painted shovels in the pictures that make the news.

Next to our home in Hazelwood was a vacant lot with a picket fence and a sign that read "Project Picket Fences" with the City of Pittsburgh logo and a former mayor's name. I bet Lois wasn't in any of the pictures or the fanfare to launch that program. Three mayors later, the fence was faded and decayed, but Lois was still picking up litter and volunteering. Badly deteriorated concrete stairs from a "greenway" trail project from years earlier were scattered throughout the neighborhood. The trails were mostly non-existent. Concrete stairs with broken, rusted railings and missing steps lead nowhere. There was probably a big ribbon-cutting for that program, too. It is a hallmark of governments to fund splashy upfront projects but not long-term maintenance.

Many place their faith in big policy changes. An article in a leading academic journal from a reputable sociologist outlined fundamental problems in modern American neighborhoods: increasing job specialization, racial and immigrant integration, increasing mobility for employment, the upbringing of neglected children, the need for social recreation for young adults, and public health.[36] He optimistically called on neighbors, neighborhood leaders, public schools, and churches to take up their patriotic and civic duty to renew neighborhoods as the instrument for curtailing society's ills. The article was published in March 1914. A century later, we are still wrestling with the same list. A few months after the article, World War I broke out. Neighbors did come together, but not in the way he could have foreseen.

Similarly, in his 1928 acceptance speech, Herbert Hoover declared, "We in America today are nearer to the final triumph over poverty than ever before in the history of any land."[37] Thirteen months later, the U.S. entered the Great Depression. President Lyndon Johnson later said the U.S. would eliminate poverty within 30 years. *Duct-tape Community* places more faith in people than in policies.

Comforting the Confused

You're not alone if you strive to be a genuinely good person but are confused by ever-changing us-versus-them labels, political correctness, and the latest isms. Nine Supreme Court justices rarely agree on legal issues. Nobel prize-winning economists disagree. Social scientists argue with each other. You're not alone if you are confused.

Trying to be a good, inclusive person on my job, I began referring to Latinos as Latinx. Then I read an NPR article that cited a Pew Research Center survey that only 3% of Latinos in the U.S. refer to themselves as Latinx.[38] We later hired a Puerto Rican who doesn't like the term. It raised the question. Who is the moral authority who decided that Latinos should start calling themselves Latinx? Among so many subjects, the questions are not only what is just or unjust, or what is equality, but who gets to decide.

Michael Sandel's course on justice is one of Harvard's most popular courses. Tens of millions worldwide viewed the free online version. Because of its popularity, Sandel turned the class into a book, *Justice: What's the Right Thing to Do?*. Sandel demonstrates the complexity of topics like justice, equality, fairness, and the general arbitrariness of life by posing complex problems. He identifies three different approaches to justice that are in tension with each other: public welfare, individual rights, and personal values. For example, if equality is valued, he asks if doctors should be paid more than bus drivers.[39] If so, how much, who decides, and by what principle? Justice itself is subject to the great American comparison contest over who is just-er. It is refreshing to hear someone honest about complexity in a culture that popularly distills topics into highly concentrated, made-for-mass-media soundbites and snarky us-versus-them tweets.

Mathematician Francis Su describes people's political views as geometric, yet in the United States, political viewpoints are flattened into a linear, two-party political system between two poles.[40] This flattening of diverse perspectives into two major coalitions can be odd, illogical, and even entertaining. Sometimes, the only seeming connection between an otherwise circus of groups is the old maxim, "An enemy of my enemy is my friend." The United States has survived, but it might be more convivial if its citizen-participants were humbler about their inconsistencies.

A goal of *Duct-tape Community* in approaching the subject of inequality is to offer neighborliness as a pathway for navigating the confusion that many of us feel.

The Importance of the Middle

Another theme and reason for writing about neighborhoods is the importance of the middle. At the neighborhood or national levels, people at the extremes tend to be the loudest. Neighborhood character is occasionally more readily found in the silent and sometimes invisible middle.

One of life's harsh realities is that a few can destroy the work of many. It takes dozens of skilled tradespeople weeks to build a house. It only takes one person with a bulldozer to destroy it. It takes years for good cops to build credibility and trust in a neighborhood. It only takes one lousy cop to destroy it. Good neighbors volunteer countless hours doing cleanups, planting flowers, helping neighbors with repair work, and working with officials to build a better reputation. All it takes is one hot-button issue to draw out fanatics that reporters love to interview. In 30 seconds or less, a neighborhood's reputation is dragged through the mud. The few's destruction overshadows the excellent work of many.

Confronting the Character Gap

Duct-tape Community's declaration may seem like an uncontested dud of a proposition. Of course, neighborliness is more critical than comparisons over curb appeal, real estate values, median incomes, or the price tag of the cars in residents' driveways. Who would argue the contrary? In our theoretical values, maybe. The reality is questionable. The conflict within *Duct-tape Community* is not in the face value of the proposition but the tension between our stated values and the way we behave. Economists Richard Thaler and Cass Sunstein call it "dynamic inconsistencies."[41]

If I knew more about sports, I might write about sportsmanship. If sportsmanship is the highest value, athletes or coaches with $100 million-plus contracts should theoretically exhibit an exponentially better quality of sportsmanship than a little league team. Teams with the most wins should have higher ethical standards than their counterparts. Cities and universities that invest in expensive stadiums should be kinder and gentler because of the model superstars who play in them. In our theoretical values, maybe. In reality, we know better. The stated value might be sportsmanship. The more realistic values are talent, ticket sales, entertainment taxes, and endorsement deals.

Then again, I don't know much about sports. I only know about neighborhoods. The stated value might be neighborliness. The more frequent priorities are power, curb appeal, property values, property taxes, trendy businesses, amenities, political concentration, and keeping up with the Jones.

Christian Miller, a philosophy professor at Wake Forest University, wrote a book on the subject: *The Character Gap: How Good Are We?* He shares formal studies documenting the gap between our stated values and behavior. Or, you could ask a traffic cop. I hear residents complain about a lack of speeding enforcement in their neighborhood with the rationale, "I got a ticket on Thole Street; why aren't police ticketing here." Why is it ok to speed through others' neighborhoods, just not their own?

Google's N-gram tool shows that the word "neighborliness" peaked in popular literature around 1943 before a steep decline. Robert Putnam notes that at the same time the word "neighborliness" was declining, the word "identity" was on an upward climb as Americans became more focused on themselves.[42]

Over a decade ago, Charles Buki, a neighborhood consultant, gave the neighborhood engagement team one of the most honest, valuable quotes about neighborhood development. He went beyond touchy-feely platitudes and addressed the gritty reality.

> "When work is needed, there is resistance and work avoidance. There is a gap between what they say they believe and the way they actually conduct their lives. Your job is to find that gap and find a gentle way to rub their nose in it. ... In this process, they will be disoriented (pissed off). This produces heat and distress. Your job is to modulate it, not get rid of it."

What is true at the neighborhood level is true at the national level. The nation is awash in touchy-feely platitudes from John 3:16 to "Love Wins" posters. The hard work of neighborliness isn't in making posters but in the heated friction practicing it. This book attempts to gently rub our noses in some of the gaps between our stated values and the way we behave.

Character, however, doesn't always come in a sexy wrapper. The best pee wee football coach isn't the dad with the Escalade who fantasizes about his five-year-old playing for the NFL. It may be the dad with the mismatched hubcaps who wants his kids to have fun and grow into responsible, caring spouses, parents, and citizens.

In addition to the purposes above, I want to honor all those like my parents who have stinky, duct-taped cars and the values they contribute to duct-tape communities. The imperfect can be a profound source of character. Those neighborhoods and those people are worth the attention. They teach us that we can strive for a fairer, more equal world while remaining neighborly in one that isn't.

Section 1: Community Life and Leadership

Seeing - Imperfect Beauty and Bad Assumptions

Key Idea: Meaning comes from seeing other people, not trying so hard to be seen.

Psychiatrist Curt Thompson says that every baby born into the world is looking for someone looking for them.[43] For my first six years, I alone enjoyed being the center of my parents' and paternal grandparents' gazing attention. Then, early one November morning, I was cast off my throne as an only child by a baby brother who made unsightly, noxious, green diaper deposits and later peed on my Lincoln Logs, my Star Wars X-wing Fighter's box, and me. The transition from being the sole center of attention to being one among others provoked early feelings of uneasy downward social status.[44] The comparison contest had begun.

We enter the comparison contest early, and I quickly realized I was below average. As a child, I felt it being chosen among the last for kickball and every other sport. I felt it taking piano for three years and not advancing. I felt it having thick glasses and not being gifted or talented. I felt it wearing generics instead of Jordache Jeans or KangaROOS shoes when they were popular in the 80s. The pressure to be seen only intensified during my teen years, but not to much avail. Though my parents fought against a culture that grooms us to compete, achieve, and be seen by others, the conflict reached a turning point only after I moved to the Uptown neighborhood of

Chicago for graduate school. Uptown was a duct-tape neighborhood that rejected the comparison contest. Uptown forced me to choose between wallowing in self-pity over not being seen or redirecting emotional energy into seeing other people.

When I lived there in the 1990s, Uptown was a picture of a neighborhood still stuck in the Great Depression 40 years after it ended everywhere else. If neighborhoods were ranked by appearance, Uptown would have ranked closer to the bottom. Many patriotic songs emphasize the beauty of America's bucolic landscapes: rocks and rills, woods and hills, purple mountains, waves of grain, and shining seas. I appreciate all of them. Urban landscapes with soot-covered buildings, grimy sidewalks, and urine-soaked alleys don't provide the same sentimental material. Uptown, though, introduced me to a bigger, more beautiful America than I knew. Uptown demonstrated that community happens anywhere there is the capacity to love. Uptown upended many of my assumptions about community and neighborhoods.

The only sign of Uptown's former opulence was its architecture. It boomed with wealth in the Roaring Twenties. Charlie Chapman filmed his early films at Essanay Studios there during the teens. The Green Mill Cocktail Lounge was a famous jazz lounge and hangout for Al Capone. I had my first and last martini there. The Wilson El stop opened in 1923. By its appearance when I lived there, it hadn't changed much since then until a 2014 reconstruction. The ornate, Spanish Baroque, 4000-seat Uptown Theatre opened next to the Green Mill in 1925 and featured a lavish lobby, childcare with a merry-go-round, and a nurse on duty.[45] The Aragon Ballroom followed in 1926. Tall hotels and apartment buildings sprang up, increasing Uptown's density and transient nature. Then came the Great Depression and a World War when wealth waved goodbye to Uptown.

Its hotels and apartments were converted to rooming houses during the Depression and a worker housing shortage during World War II. The film industry had long since moved to the milder climate of Hollywood. Over the years, the Uptown theatre sold off its interior accessories until it closed and sat in disrepair. The high-brow Aragon Ballroom became a roller rink, boxing arena, disco, and rock concert venue.[46]

I am quietly amused when I hear residents in Norfolk talk about their neighborhoods as "diverse" because they have one or two ethnic families. My bank in Uptown offered transactions in 30 different languages. Low rents attracted transients, immigrants, and refugees. So many Appalachians migrated to Uptown that the Council of the Southern Mountains, headquartered in Berea, Kentucky, opened an Uptown center in 1963.[47] Marty Hansen and Sam Hong tracked the influx of refugees and immigrants into Uptown. During the 70s and 80s, Uptown was home to 10,000 Guatemalans and Salvadorans, nearly 8,000 Vietnamese, 4000 Cambodians, 3,000 Ethiopians, and almost 1,000 Laotians.[48] According to Hansen, a study by Chicago Public Schools showed that 60 different languages were spoken.[49]

The super of my second apartment building, Kenny, was a young Vietnamese man who was reliable and very friendly but spoke limited English. We talked briefly here and there. I would ask about his story, but language was a barrier. As far as I remember, he was alone in the U.S., separated from his family. From across the hall, I would hear long conversations in Vietnamese with his family overseas. As an aside, I wasn't sure what was worse in that apartment: the roaches or the pesticide coating on everything. The roaches were so bad I once made a game out of it with my Super-soaker water gun.

During the de-institutionalization of mental facilities, patients were deposited in Uptown, further concentrating poverty and social problems. I remember one middle-aged woman sitting on the sidewalk outside Truman College in her urine. Her dirty, darkened, scaly ankles stretched across the sidewalk clearly indicating that it had been a long time since she had a safe bed in which to spend the night and a bathroom of her own.

Like millions of new college graduates before and after, youthful exuberance to make a difference, make money, and build a successful career was intoxicating. After college, I decided move to Chicago for graduate school. The initial thrill from the sights, riding the elevated train, having lunch on the 95th floor of the John Hancock Tower, tasting new food, experiencing world cultures, and the rush of exploration deepened the initial high. Unfortunately, time brought with it the less exhilarating experience of mundane life.

As we were unloading the U-Haul at the rear door of my first Chicago apartment after moving from small-town Cumberland, at least three Chicago police cars swarmed the building opposite the alley and lined up several young men. The following morning, before Dad left for the airport, we watched out the kitchen window as the scenario repeated. As he prepared to leave, dad instructed, "If you get in trouble, call me at the office. Do not call your mother. Let me tell your mother." Those were the only words that hinted at a father's concern that his son was not moving to a dream location.

In that same building, I had a friendly neighbor across the hall named Sylvester, who was genuinely a good neighbor to me. As an ex-felon, however, he had job and financial troubles. He and his wife rented out the bedroom of their one-bedroom apartment for additional income. He had fallen behind on his electric bill and once asked to borrow an extension cord. I obliged until he plugged it into my outlet and prepared to run it across the hall to his refrigerator. He had just purchased a bunch of meat, which he didn't want to lose. I instead helped him find an outlet in the rear hallway.

Having lived with other people all my life, I had no clue about the time and expense involved in living independently. My head knowledge was worthless on the street. This was most apparent when I inadvertently gave a prostitute my address. Determined to make the streets friendlier, I greeted passers-by as I walked with a smile and a nod. I suppose this signaled to one woman, not especially attractive, that I was interested in getting to know her better. She struck up a conversation and asked where I lived. With all the sophistication of Gomer Pyle, I blurted out my address. She then asked if she could come over. When she asked a second time with increased pressure, it finally dawned on me that she was a drug-addicted hooker in need of money to score a hit. I politely excused myself should the reader ask any questions.

On another occasion, in my first apartment building on the 4500 block of N. Malden Street, I noticed that the residents of one apartment were extremely popular. They were receiving short visits from people all the time. "I should get to know them," I thought to myself. After the police gave them and a security guard an alternative dwelling, I realized that they were dealing drugs.

One Mile of Neighborliness

Most importantly, my youthful arrogance greatly underestimated the vast network of compassionate individuals already pouring love into the neighborhood. Take, for instance, the roughly one-mile stretch of W. Wilson Avenue from Montrose Beach to N. Malden Street from 1995 to 1999. On the lakefront from Clarendon Avenue east to Lake Michigan was postcard material: expansive green space in the park, Weiss Hospital, Montrose Beach, and beautiful Lake

Michigan. Tall, attractive apartment buildings lined Clarendon with a view of the lake. Unfortunately, the postcard scenery ended.

Moving West was a health clinic that provided services to the poor. I once had a T.B. test there for a volunteer mentoring program in a public school. It was clean and orderly but noticeably busier than Dr. Bolino's office in Cumberland—the only doctor I had ever been to besides E.R. visits. Next was Jesus People U.S.A. They reminded me of Jesus hippies who lived in their own apartment building but cared deeply about the community. They were doing micro-enterprises before micro-enterprise became trendy. They had a printing business and a screen printing shop, if I remember correctly, among other businesses. Near them was a ministry to male street prostitutes.

Next was Uptown Baptist Church, which was a unique church. Jim Queen started the church. The Chicago Bears had drafted Queen but so did the U.S. Army. By the time he returned to the Bears, an injury prevented him from ever playing. He later started Uptown Baptist in an old congregational church building. By the time I moved to Uptown, Uptown Baptist had seven different language congregations meeting in their building: Nigerian, Bulgarian, Spanish, African fellowship, Russian, Vietnamese (with 250 members), and Cambodian. They served a weekly meal to the homeless and had outreach programs to a low-income, seniors' high rise across the street. They had an active sports program. They had to shuttle in teens from different parts of the neighborhood, so they didn't have to cross gang boundaries on foot. They also screened them before entering. They had an art ministry responsible for several murals in the neighborhood. One was visible from the Wilson El stop. During a visit to one Sunday School class, on one side was a Ph.D. candidate at the University of Chicago. On the other side was a homeless man with body odor. I'll return to Uptown Baptist later.

Crossing Broadway on Clifton Avenue Cornerstone Community Outreach had a new women's and family shelter. Here, I learned one of the most important lessons about race relations. As part of the work program at school, I would host out-of-town volunteer groups. I took a group of volunteers to the shelter to provide activities for children. After playing ball, one young African American boy struck up a conversation with us, "When I grow up, I want everything to be white. I want a white house, a white car, a white ball, and white clothes."

I first looked around at our all-White group. I then looked at all the staff. The staff who were there at that particular moment were all white. Then I looked at the guests, who were all Black. Sadly, the little boy's comments suddenly made me understand why fairer representation is essential.

On the other side of Wilson was Harry S. Truman College, part of the city college system. I incorrectly assumed that the low cost correlated to low quality. I was arrogantly mistaken. I took a Spanish course and had the best language teacher in my career. At the next corner at Racine was a fire station. In addition to saving lives, they attached sprayers to the fire hydrants for kids during hot summers. The next corner was Magnolia Avenue. A thrift shop occupied the southeast corner at the time. It provided low-cost and convenient options. The alternative was catching the bus to pay full retail prices every time we needed something. I bought some clothes, serving spoons and glasses there. On the Northeast corner were our school offices. For a time, a Vietnamese family had a restaurant in the building. Chicken-fried rice became a staple of my diet then. On the northwest side was a Lebanese woman who opened a small falafel shop, which began my love of chickpea and parsley patties. I enjoyed hearing her story. I assumed, incorrectly, that she was Muslim. She was, instead, an orthodox Christian. On the southwest corner, an always cheerful African immigrant managed the Subway restaurant. The blocks north between Wilson and Lawrence had the Magnolia Malden Neighbors Association. In the late summer of 1995, they dedicated a flower bed in the Lawrence-Magnolia Triangle to Ms. Gladys Tomlinson. Although not based in Uptown, a ministry bus came through regularly with medical help, condoms, and other services.

On the next block was the Inspiration Cafe. It was a cafe-style diner that served the homeless meals as regular customers only without paying. It was an alternative to the sometimes demoralizing traditional soup-kitchen-style meals. Lisa Nigro, a Chicago police officer, started it. She wanted a more humane response to homelessness than she often saw. It has since moved and expanded its programs. Near the cafe was the Uptown Center of the Jane Addams Hull House Association on Beacon Street. It provided child care, economic development, counseling, senior services, an art gallery, and a highly reputable theatre.

Such was the fabric of just a one-mile stretch in one neighborhood of Chicago: clinic, homeless shelters, art programs, churches, immigrants beginning a new life, neighborhood groups, educational institutions, and a firehouse. Vietnamese were living next to Vietnam veterans. Ph.D.s sat next to the homeless in Sunday School. A former felon lived next to a seminary student. Ethnic groups who were enemies overseas had kids on the same sports teams. It was far from the utopian ideals of either liberals or conservatives, but people weaved themselves into communities and made life work. People have a remarkable ability to adapt to their surroundings. Anywhere there is the capacity to love, there is community. Except for diversity, it failed most social indicators when stacked against neighborhoods like Lincoln Park or the Gold Coast. Yet, it was a wonderful neighborhood to live in.

What is Community Worth?

While living in Uptown, my college credit card provided airline discounts, so I made several trips to New York for an anthropology project. The Bay Ridge area of Brooklyn in the 1990s was about as charming an urban neighborhood as I can imagine. It was far different from Uptown. Bay Ridge had those wonderful, six-step, walk-up brick and brownstone row houses on narrow New York tree-lined streets. It was easy to imagine myself back in 1940s New York at the well-preserved Anopoli Restaurant and Ice-Cream Parlor. Since my first visit in 1997, I've failed to find a bagel as good as the bagel I had in Bay Ridge.

The human transactions there took Bay Ridge from aesthetically pleasing to truly beautiful. While doing research, I contacted Howard and Kathy Taylor, who let me stay with them at their rented duplex on 73rd Street. They volunteered at a church building at 345 Ovington Avenue, where three churches used one building. The host church was a traditional Norwegian Lutheran Church whose numbers had dwindled. The most fascinating of the three churches was Salam Arabic Lutheran Church. Although officially Lutheran, the universe of Arabic-speaking Christians is not large, so the church contained Arabic-speaking Christians from all different backgrounds. Most came from countries undergoing dangerous political upheaval or where authorities persecuted them. As they assembled in Arabic unmolested in a simple Brooklyn church building, they were living, breathing evidence of the magnitude of freedom, security, and safety of the U.S. Constitution envisioned by our founders.

The Taylors belonged to the third small church renting the building for services. The Taylors ran children's programs and ESL classes. Howard was a retired accountant, and Kathy was an English teacher.

Howard was an Army Air Corps Captain during World War II. One of the trip's highlights was sitting on the Taylor's couch with Howard looking at his photos of airplanes and his time in the service. While some spend their retirement buying Winnebagos, on the golf course, or hanging out at Costco for hot dogs, the Taylors moved to Bay Ridge as a mission project. They put me to work volunteering with their children's program while I was there. I still have pictures of over a dozen toddler-size kids around a table resembling a mini-United Nations. When we were in public, they never seemed to make it very far without someone knowing them. When they took me to buy shoes, a child came up to Kathy and gave her a big hug. When we stopped in a deli, a Russian woman started talking to her. Other kids and students from her ESL class would say hello as they showed me around.

How do you measure the economic value of those interactions? Howard and Kathy later moved back to Ohio, and the Salam Arabic Lutheran moved locations. The church at 345 Ovington was demolished and replaced with condos. How do you establish the value to new immigrants of having people like Howard and Kathy greet them with a hug and love on their children? What is it worth to have Pastor El-Yateem offer hope and community to Arabic Christians persecuted in their own countries and then viewed with suspicion in the U.S. after September 11? I have no recollection of whatever I put in the anthropology paper, but I remember walking down the street with the Taylors and seeing the value it was to the people they had helped.

We attach dollar values to nearly everything. An expensive engagement ring or an over-the-top wedding equates with more love. Weedless yards and three-car garages equate with better neighborhoods. Yet, when consideration is given to all those trying to come to the U.S., it isn't for the architecture or weedless yards.

I can't think of better role models who embodied our good habits and the American spirit more than people like Howard and Kathy or Pastor El-Yateem.

In an almost ten-year-long ethnography, Martín Sánchez-Jankowski formally documented the rich community fabric in poor neighborhoods despite rundown appearances[50]. There is something about shared adversity significant to community. Adversity forces people to look beyond themselves and be interdependent on others. Adversity in places like Uptown draws out the worst in a few but the best in many others.

Uptown and Bay Ridge upended many of my assumptions about life and community. I saw people living a different but fulfilling American dream, more about people and less about a modern homestead with a two-car garage. There was beauty in Uptown's imperfection, and adversity could strengthen community bonds. I found people like me whose SAT scores were underwhelming, who weren't being recruited by top universities or corporate headhunters, and who didn't make the adult gifted and talented list. Still, they lived meaningful lives by directing their emotional energy into seeing other people rather than being seen. I didn't have to wait for others to look for me; I could look for other people. It is what my family, professors, and others had been trying to teach me all along. I witnessed people making the world a fairer place and being neighborly in one that isn't. The same character traits that empowered neighborliness in rural Maryland worked in inner-city Chicago despite wildly different contexts. Meaning comes in seeing other people, not trying so hard to be seen in the big comparison contest.

Resolute - More Important Than Vision

Key Idea: It doesn't matter what the community was, nor what it will be; resolute neighbors make the present the best it can be.

In duct-tape communities with no easy fix to long-standing systematic problems, there is still the power of the resolute. It doesn't matter what the community was in the past, nor what it will be in the future; resolute neighbors fiercely determine to make the present the best it can be. I saw this take two forms in the Hazelwood neighborhood of Pittsburgh.

First was Memorial Day and the Perris family. Memorial Day was a lower-tier holiday for my family growing up. It meant American flags in the church driveway and service members leading a flag ceremony during Sunday services. We didn't have any particular traditions on Memorial Day itself, except maybe visiting the auction at my grandparent's Ruritan Club. What could be more patriotic than watching hoarders and bargain hunters compete for hidden treasures in boxes of junk?

After Chicago, I moved to the Hazelwood neighborhood of Pittsburgh. Memorial Day was a huge deal at the corner of Elizabeth and Lytle Streets. On the Northwest corner sits the Lytle Street Cafe, and next to it is a long-standing War Service Honor Roll memorial to those lost in World War II, Korea, and Vietnam. Each year, a respectable crowd from an area known as "below the tracks" gathered at that corner to honor veterans. Before he died in 2005, Joe Dugan, a Hazelwood hero, decorated Vietnam-era Marine, detective, and fireman, presided over the services. A resident sang the national anthem. One or more local politicians spoke. Some official placed a wreath on the memorial. The honor guard did a gun salute. Politicians sped off to other events. The crowd lingered and eventually departed for cookouts.

When I lived there, the last honor guard was a biker group, most weighing over 180 pounds, wearing leather or jean vests, standing next to their motorcycles. Its location is far from touristy downtown Pittsburgh, where few outsiders dare to venture after dark. Instead, what makes it significant is the effort that goes into the memorial before the service. Since 1974, the Perris family has run the Lytle Cafe, the last bar left in Hazelwood. It is an old steel mill bar where steelworkers and others getting off work went for a drink. Since 1974, they have made that corner a bright spot below the tracks, including the war memorial. DeDe Perris is the owner. A few years ago, cancer took DeDe's husband John, Joe Dugan's uncle. I think of John every time I eat pistachios. He introduced me to the green goodness.

Every holiday, big and small, was an excuse to decorate the Lytle. It was a great place to get a hot sausage on Wednesday or authentic Pittsburgh pierogies on Thursday. The Lytle is a place for old-time, gritty Pittsburghers. Oakland and Southside are hotspots for trendy new-tech Pittsburghers driving Teslas. The Lytle is for old blue-collar Pittsburghers driving Chevy pickups.

DeDe, her daughters, and her grandkids keep the memorial spotless. First, they paint the sidewalk red, white, and blue on their hands and knees. After the paint dries, they stencil on tanks, ships, and planes. The many veterans from the neighborhood it represents are a source of pride in an otherwise challenged neighborhood.

A once thriving, 178-acre steel mill sat abandoned two blocks away. A railroad terminal was at the other end. A vacant lot across the street from the Lytle Cafe was once a cheap apartment building, drug haven, and widespread crime spot. Around the corner was a makeshift community garden with old tires painted as repurposed planters. There were a few rusty-roofed commercial buildings, but most of the neighborhood was narrow row houses, some selling less than an average car in the early 2000s. The nearest ball field was in shambles. Only one end of the park sign still hung on the graffitied scoreboard. The cement block restroom/concession stand had a big hole in the wall, and vandals decorated it with spray-painted, anatomically exaggerated scrotums and breasts.

It is safe to say there weren't any one-percenters living in Hazelwood. There was no schmoozy shellacking over America's economic or racial problems in full view of everyone in attendance. However, it would be a huge mistake to think they were any less patriotic. I've heard combat veterans say that they weren't fighting as much for the country as their friends-in-arms on the front lines. That same camaraderie struck me at Hazelwood services. However unequal to wealthier parts of the city, what surrounded them was something they could call their own—their homes, families, bar, neighborhood, and piece of America. The emotion wasn't in some abstract ideal of a utopian country but in their family and friends' real lives.

Since working for the City of Norfolk, I have been privileged to attend official city Memorial Day services. They are formal affairs with Navy admirals and City officials carefully choreographed by professional staff. The honor guard is active duty in cleanly pressed uniforms and in combat-ready physical shape, mostly weighing under 180 pounds. The U.S.S. Wisconsin, a battleship from World War II, is the background. It is an affair appropriate as an official function in a city that hosts the world's largest naval base. Yet the Lytle Street service is closer to my heart. The picture of young people like Eddie, Keke, Biz, Johnny, Billy, Bean, Bobby, Jimmy, and Savannah, along with Dede on their hands and knees painting the sidewalks, tells me something meaningful about America and neighborhood pride.

The Jones and Laughlin Steel Corporation (J. & L.) had been part of Hazelwood since its first presence in 1884. Builders built hundreds of row houses in and around the formerly suburban neighborhood to house thousands of employees within walking distance. J. &. L. sold to L.T.V. in 1974. L.T.V. eventually filed for bankruptcy and closed the Hazelwood plant in 1997. The Pension Benefit Guarantee Corporation, a U.S. government agency, had to take over the pensions for 82,000 workers and retirees, the largest takeover up to that time.

The neighborhood declined with the steel mill. In the 1960s, Hazelwood was home to over 200 businesses, including a theater, clothing shops, bakeries, bars, and grocery stores. When I moved there, there were only a few legitimate, sustainable businesses. Instead, there were dozens of shops here today and gone tomorrow. The last grocery store, Dimperios, closed during my decade there. A convenience store remained; people like Ms. Dorothy Savage walked there every morning for coffee and socializing.

A recycling plant and a junkyard didn't add much to the neighborhood's aesthetics but provided a few jobs. Early when I moved there, a brown 1980s model Ford Taurus, minus wheels and any glass, sat on a vacant cement pad near the main entrance to Hazelwood at 2nd Avenue and Hazelwood Avenue. Further back, hanging over a small embankment, was an old Buick in a similar shape.

The City of Pittsburgh wasn't doing much better financially at the time. It requested state assistance to avoid bankruptcy in 2003. Open sewage ran down the street from the vacant house across from me after my neighbor died. I reported it. Inspectors theorized the sewer was backed up in the house's basement causing a blockage further up the hill. All the neighborhood schools closed one by one and remained vacant: the middle school, the elementary school, and the Catholic school.

City government struggled to keep up with the vacant lots, abandoned housing, and boarded-up businesses. Entire streets were closed off and reclaimed by nature. They demolished 50 abandoned Hazelwood houses in one year alone, but it was barely noticeable.

The housing authority placed 127 public housing units in the far end, known as Glen Hazel, and a 97-unit high rise. With low rents came the struggling class, those living on Social Security, people with disabilities, and part-time employees trying to make ends meet. Predatory landlords brought additional crime and social problems. Street art adorned many of the buildings. The wall along the rails-to-trails path was a giant canvas: "Life is Made for Playing," "Class War, Sell Out Society, Oil War," and "Bleed the Poor."

Below the Tracks is so named because it sits below the tracks on one of Pittsburgh's few relatively flat planes. Railroad tracks bound it on three sides. The abandoned steel mill bounds the fourth with a chain link and barbed wire fence. It was never a Mayberry, but an influx of drugs and the loss of jobs in the seventies and eighties made it a challenging place to live. I always felt like I was passing into the Wild West when I crossed those tracks. I heard stories about mob involvement before a crackdown.

People like DeDe and her family, though, resisted the call to give up. Instead, they fought to keep their corner clean and safe. Like many bars in Pittsburgh, the logos of the Steelers, Penguins, Pirates, and Pitt Panthers adorn the exterior wall. Sports teams are another source of pride, even for many who can't afford to attend Steeler games in a stadium built with public funds. Connected with the bar was a cast of likable and interesting characters. Many locals who grew up there had nicknames like Fly or Pus-head.

John and DeDe raised three daughters who still love the neighborhood. One daughter lives across the street and married a fireman. Another daughter manages a train unloading terminal down the street. The oldest daughter lives within easy walking distance. The family's compassion runs deep. John and DeDe lent or gave money to people in a bind. Their bar stools were a refuge for people others had forgotten. When an old neighborhood friend showed up at their doorstep, beaten up, their daughter Denise Provident spent the entire next 24 hours getting him a bed in a hospital and calling around to find him a rehab bed for a more extended solution. Her husband, Ed, was from the neighborhood and lived the hardscrabble street and drug life. After reaching a breaking point and turning their life around through faith, their door and kitchen were always open to friends struggling in the neighborhood. Their mini-van accumulated hundreds of miles, driving people all over Allegheny County.

People like the Providents, DeDe, and John carved out a happy place in a challenged area. Like many in her situation, years of neighborhood struggles hardened DeDe's personality. She reminds me of many I've met in tough neighborhoods: hard, colorful, and sweet at the same time, like Jawbreaker candy. Characters like hers form from years of disinvestment, government politics, crime, family struggles, neighborhood division, and the false starts of outsiders passing through the neighborhood promising change. DeDe and many like her have held their ground. It may be a single house. It may be a corner. It may be a block, but they have held their ground. They have kept it from blight, drugs, and nuisances that have plagued other parts of the neighborhood. She and others typify the word "resolute": "marked by firm determination, bold, steady."[51]

The second example is Tim Smith and the Center of Life. Tim Smith's superpower is stretching 30 hours out of a day. When I lived there, Tim was a father, husband, pastor, founder and executive director of Center of Life, Chair of Hazelwood Initiative, jazz pianist, and attached to several other organizations. While many, like the extended Perris family, worked at the block level to make their neighborhood a home, Tim worked on systematic issues.

His father had been a pastor in Hazelwood at the Keystone Church of God in Christ, but Tim first chose a career in banking before feeling a call to return to work in Hazelwood. Recognizing the need for investment, he worked tirelessly to advocate for educational, economic development, housing, and health resources. In addition, he fiercely made sure city leaders didn't forget about us. Having presided over too many funerals for youth, Smith's Center of Life resolutely determined to provide better opportunities for youth: a jazz group, the K.R.U.N.K. Movement, performances in public schools, sports, art, and summer programs.

I most appreciated Smith's willingness to support anything good for Hazelwood. I've worked with countless pastors; many of which don't support anything outside their control. Tim was different. If the library was doing something for the neighborhood, Tim supported it. If other churches did something beneficial, Tim showed up in his old Mercedes station wagon and lent his resources. If it was picking up trash, Tim was there. A man of his talents could have easily kissed Hazelwood goodbye and ascended in the ranks of the comparison contest, but Tim lived above it.

Vision, Dreams, and Hope

The Perris family and Tim Smith illustrate this "resolute" characteristic, which may be more critical to neighborhood health than vision, especially bad vision. In the mid-90s, as I was finishing college, all the famous, successful leadership gurus talked about having a big vision. It seemed to be the faddish thing to do. During the real estate boom of the mid-2000s, I received letters from various organizations requesting money for big building campaigns spurred by their big, bold vision. When the bubble burst, the same organizations asked for help to bail them out. Over and over, government, non-profits, businesses, and churches promise Big Gulps and deliver Dixie Cups.

When I moved to the neighborhood of Hazelwood in 2000, I was drawn into a series of charrette meetings to form a master plan for Hazelwood's redevelopment. I left a decade later with the neighborhood looking nearly the same. During those ten years, I watched a parade of programs and professionals pass through the neighborhood with their visions to stimulate Hazelwood's revitalization. They came and went in their careers.

As far back as the late 1950s, state, and Pittsburgh leaders began discussing a Mon-Fayette Expressway that would cut through the neighborhood and provide another connector to downtown. For sixty years, the neighborhood and the central business corridor were held hostage by the big vision. It was the kind of big vision people who didn't live there could afford to make. The vision was there; the money was not. Fortunately, people like DeDe didn't wait on big visions to improve their corner.

This is not to deny the importance of dreaming or vision. Our office in Norfolk helped our mayor and city executives facilitate discussions in three public housing communities. Residents didn't know it, but Ray Gindroz, a world-renowned urban designer who had retired to Norfolk, was listening to the meetings. His projects have left huge impacts worldwide. In advance of a needed large-scale redevelopment project of obsolete public housing, facilitators asked residents what they would like to see in their future community. Their responses were unpretentious. The loudest calls were for better safety, police presence, better lighting, no litter, and more accessibility to retail services such as a bank and grocery store. As best as I could tell, all many hoped for was an improved version of what they already had—small, mass-produced, government-style barracks, relics of the late 1950s. My colleague Bre McCoy said one woman was concerned with blinds. She didn't want the cheap vertical blinds. She wanted quality blinds.

Most did not seem to comprehend the whole area would be demolished and rebuilt. They had a world-renowned designer, yet the highest many dreamed was higher wattage streetlamps and decent blinds. It was a sobering reality that some have quit dreaming.

Dreams elevate behavior. Good vision renews neighborhood pride, unifies, attracts commitment, is semi-believable, and can gain traction. The problem is that good vision is rare, and bad vision leaves residents discouraged, disappointed, mistrustful, and less committed. So many communities are resistant, jaded, and angry from leaders over-promising and under-delivering.

William Peterman presented four case studies of grassroots neighborhood organizations as director of the Voorhees Center for Neighborhood and Community Improvement at the University of Illinois at Chicago. Each organization had its vision of its neighborhood's future, but none were "totally successful" at achieving that vision. Three attained some level of success.[52] The vision is often not as crucial as the unified resolve of people striving together toward something better.

Cornel West wrote some of the most profound thoughts about hope ever put to paper. The lack of hope, the collapse of meaning, and the threat of nihilism are not only the greatest threats to Black America;

they are an enormous threat to every community.[53] Unfortunately, a mistake we make in government and community development is to think that some new program or vision inspires hope. New programs and new visions may be temporary stimulants, but they are usually over-hyped. The real engine behind hope is in people's resolve.

The resolute don't give up. They defy the odds. They raise healthy families in difficult areas. They have been robbed, threatened, and had property vandalized. Undaunted, they have planted their flag in the neighborhood and sometimes win by sheer stubbornness. In Hazelwood, it was people like the Perris family, Juanita Godfrey, Rev. Tim Smith, Delores Livsey, the Dipietros, Fran Bertonacci, The Craigs, Lucile Kennedy, and so many others. People like them inspire others in the neighborhood and give residents a sense that someone has their back.

Few know about it today, but underneath a green neighborhood sign in the Norview area of Norfolk is a plaque dedicated to Jackie "Shortie" Hilton. It is in a triangle-shaped median in the Five Points Intersection. Neighbors took on the median as an "urban meadow" and maintained roses and other flowers. It reads

In Memorium

On April 29, 1998, Community Activist

Jackie Lee "Shorty" Hilton

Died after a courageous battle with cancer.

Let us remember what one person can do to

better a community. Take up the work

he started and do your part to make Five Points

a safer and better place for us all.

Even though I'm within walking distance of the plaque, I found out about this "Shortie" in a case study I found from Harvard's Kennedy School of Government.[54] Bothered by criminal activity in his neighborhood, Shortie formed the East Norview Neighborhood Block Watch in 1988 with a few of his neighbors. Not long after, a ruptured disk and quintuple-bypass heart surgery left him permanently impaired. After recovery, he resumed neighborhood patrols, albeit slowly and in pain. Unable to keep up with the rest of his group, his impairment became an asset. Stopping to rest provided the opportunity to talk with residents, which generated more interest in the block watch or more conscientiousness among those involved in criminal activity. The community police officer at the time, Judy Hash, reported that his work had an odd effect on the drug dealers themselves. Not given to dealing in front of their parents' homes, they appreciated the block watch for its protection of their families.

To deter drug dealing from the local gas station, he pulled up next to the pay phones, opened his sunroof and windows, and blared country music. The gas station owner was so appreciative that he provided gas for driving that involved his patrols. When another local activist, Bev Sell, became involved, she brought additional resources from the business community through the Five Points Partnership. In a joint project with the Partnership and local schools, they dressed Shortie in a Santa outfit and helped give gifts to people in need at Christmas. With the various partnerships, crime eventually dropped, thanks to resolute leaders like Hilton. It is understandable why a plaque now bears his name.

Communities do not need more here today and gone tomorrow visionaries. They do not need more ego-centric saviors. They already have plenty of both. Instead, they need the resolute. The resolute have dreams for their neighborhood, but more importantly, they are entrenched in doing mundane but essential tasks with extraordinary steadfastness. They may not make headlines, but they hold a neighborhood together. It doesn't matter what the neighborhood was in the past, nor what it will be in the future; they are fiercely determined to make the present the best it can be. The words on the plaque are well worth remembering, "Let us remember what one person can do to better a community. Take up the work he started and do your part."

Practical - A Path to Practicality

Key Idea: Practical people navigate the tension between virgin ideals and promiscuous behavior.

Like many, I love to hate big business. My wife and I enjoy supporting local coffee shops. The problem is that few local coffee shops can compete with Starbucks' consistency, convenient hours, and mobile app. I like the sound of supporting Main Street over those big, bad Wall Street investors—except where my retirement accounts are concerned. When it's my retirement on the line, I want double-digit returns from Wall Street. The number of manufacturing jobs sent overseas bothers me, but don't dare take away my iPhone, which is made in China. Most of us are a mess of contradictions. One of the more frustrating sources of un-neighborly behavior is those passionate about their ideals but with little tolerance for practical necessity. Duct-tape practicality helps us navigate the tension between our virgin ideals and our promiscuous behavior.

Practical people are creative. A Chicago church only had enough money to replace their organ or buy a new, state-of-the-art keyboard. They knew some might be disgruntled if they didn't replace the organ, so they devised a brilliant, practical solution. They bought the keyboard but built a custom wood cabinet resembling an organ to slide it. No one minded as long as the pianist used the organ sound on certain songs.

In a more severe instance, Teddy Roosevelt attempted to appoint a commission to arbitrate a coal strike before the winter of 1902. Corporate leaders refused any attempt to place a labor representative on the commission, but they said they would accept a sociologist's placement. Roosevelt nominated the same labor representative as before, the head of the Brotherhood of Railway Conductors. He changed his title to "eminent sociologist," and successfully appointed him to the commission with no objection. This is the value of the practical.

The Danger of Virgin Ideals

In the comparison contest, life is compared to someone else or some perfect ideal. Anyone not aspiring to the exact ideal becomes an enemy. Evidence of dangerous, impractical ideals and accompanying egos is readily apparent locally and nationally.

Consider an obsolete business corridor from the 1950s. One group's ideal was restoring a pedestrian-friendly, small retail corridor. This group won strict zoning to keep big businesses and storefront churches out. If the policy's intended outcome was to keep tenants out, it was one of the most successful policies ever. Few businesses came; fewer lasted. Right before the real estate crash in 2007, a competing group called for large-scale city acquisition, demolition, and redevelopment into a high-rise hotel and mid-rise condos. Passionate advocates on both sides dug in. Rivals exchanged harsh words and actions. The local government spent almost $80,000 in 2010 on a market study to break the stalemate. The consultants concluded that the local market would not support either extreme. Most practical people living in the neighborhood could have said that for free.[55] Meanwhile, as the idealists battled it out, the corridor grew worse.

Sadly, it feels like a microcosm of the national political scene. Neither party accepts ownership for their faulty policies. Nor does it matter what good ideas anyone proposes; the other party will oppose them. As egos battle it out, parts of the country remain lingering and ignored. The business side can act like jock-ish frat brothers weak on compassion who would sell their mother for a quick profit. They high-five any deal as a success regardless of community consequences. Conversely, the social service and social justice world is strong on compassion but has its share of pouty idealists living in la-la land regarding economic realities. The most enjoyable people to work with are those in the middle. They are compassionate but have a healthy bias toward reality.

Neighborhood Economics

Hazelwood made me interested in economics. At one time, the defunct steel company in Hazelwood had been a $6 billion employer. Forces impacted Hazelwood from the global steel market, over which the neighborhood, city, and state had no control. The steel industry's collapse evoked sadness, frustration, anger, and despair. Despite the emotion, it was clear there was no billion-dollar replacement. Pittsburgh could demo old houses, fund public art, build a few new homes, install new playgrounds, and open a new library branch, but none of those investments addressed, nor were equivalent in scale, to the underlying problem. There was no miracle bailout.

Some claim the post-World War II economic growth spurt ended in October 1973.[56] The loss of manufacturing jobs was visible in my hometown, Gary, Indiana, Chicago, and Hazelwood. To use highly technical economic terms, the end of that growth spurt came to suck for many people. A review of old Statistical Abstracts of the United States shows that Blacks' incomes were closing the gap with White counterparts from 1939 until around 1976. They have since stalled. Unfortunately, the best economic minds in the Western world have not found a solution to return to pre-1973 growth.

Another situation expanded my economic context. While picking up garbage in a vacant lot, I met a neighbor I'll call Barney, an early twenty-something, and his brother Fred. Fred came out with no shirt revealing his large beer belly, no shoes, droopy shorts with no underwear, his butt crack sticking out, and uncombed hair. Next, he confronted me about being on the vacant lot but warmed up when I said I was picking up garbage. He introduced his brother Barney. Through a series of conversations, I got to know Barney. I had not seen Barney before because he had just been released from prison.

Their late dad was an alcoholic. Their mom was a friendly neighbor who worked a low-wage job. Her skill level was not such that she had much hope of being a big earner. Barney hung out with the wrong people while a teen and sold drugs. He also impregnated a teen girl. His misdeeds landed him in jail. After being released, he had a felony conviction, no job, no insurance, child support and restitution to pay, and nowhere to go except the same neighborhood and the same family that got him in trouble in the first place. He worked demolition until he was injured and had no insurance. He collected scrap metal on the side. I paid $20 for some metal chairs he found on garbage pick-up night. Meanwhile, I learned that his brother Fred and his wife were both addicts, explaining why they had moved back in with Fred and Barney's mother. Barney then disappeared. I learned from his mother that he had received help and moved to another city.

Fred and Barney taught me three important lessons. First, their issues were genuine, even if they were outside my experience. Second, as harsh as it may sound, the most beneficial, practical decision Barney could have made was to get away from his family and the neighborhood that got him in trouble in the first place. Third, Barney urgently needed a job, better job skills, health insurance, and a place to live. Barney's situation helped explain the recidivism rate among prisoners. Thus, my interest in economics wasn't just academic but personal.

Prioritizing Facts Over Dreams

My no-nonsense mom would have liked Jim Collins and the Stockdale Paradox: "Retain faith that you will prevail in the end regardless of the difficulties and at the same time, confront the most brutal facts of your current reality, whatever they might be."[57] Mom was a trauma nurse whose career depended on compassionate but concise straight-talk without fluff. She once took one look at a voluminous newsletter we graduate students had enthusiastically created and said, "I'm never going to read all that, and neither is anyone else." She was painfully correct.

For Collins and Winston Churchill, facts are better than dreams.[58] Collins had the research to call out charismatic visionaries devoid of truth and humility. I keep Warren Buffet's 2018 letter to Berkshire Hathaway shareholders pinned to my bulletin board at work. It included the following statement:

> Once a C.E.O. hungers for a deal, he or she will never lack of forecasts that justify the purchase. Subordinates will be cheering, envisioning enlarged domains and the compensation levels that typically increase with corporate size. Investment bankers, smelling huge fees, will be applauding as well (don't ask the barber whether you need a haircut). If the historical performance of the target falls short of validating its acquisition, large "synergies" will be forecast. Spreadsheets never disappoint.[59]

Mr. Buffett's comments could just as easily apply to government and communities.

Overpromising is an incredible problem in community development the worldwide. Abhijit Banerjee and Esther Duflo, a husband-wife team and Nobel-winning economists, studied the effect micro-finance had in developing countries on lifting the poorest out of poverty. Their study confirmed the positive impact of micro-finance, but they warned that its impact is often oversold by agencies using exceptional anecdotal stories of dramatic transformation. Because anecdotal stories inflate funders' expectations, they are frequently disappointed when the aggregate numbers are not as dramatic.[60]

Adapting to Competitive Reality

Here is an essential distinction between neighborliness and economics: economics is competitive.[61] Harvard professor Michael Porter published an article in a 1995 *Harvard Business Review*.[62] He argued that many inner-city leaders base economic development programs on a social model intended to improve social outcomes rather than the competition's financial reality. Incentive programs in weak markets with too many social, zoning, or other regulatory mandates drive businesses in the opposite direction. They lose any competitive advantage gained by incentives. There are a few notable anecdotal successes, but most community-based enterprises operated by nonbusiness people were failures in Porter's study. He argued that the community and government should create a positive business environment that builds on inner-city assets like transportation routes and labor pools. A 20-year follow-up article by Porter in 2016 confirmed the same message and even more so with increased competition from globalism.[63] One of Porter's suggestions was that business has to be led by businesspeople.[64]

Think, for instance, about a food desert problem. When Dimperios Market closed in Hazelwood, a group protested its closure as the last neighborhood grocery store. It did not take a financial genius to analyze why it closed. Giant Eagle, a local chain, opened a new, giant, luxury grocery store across the river in Homestead. Next, Walmart opened its first superstore within a fifteen-minute drive. Anyone with access to a car did their regular shopping at the bigger stores. Compared to them, Dimperios was in drastic need of modernization. The floors were worn. Some of the equipment looked like it was from the 1960s. The owners reported shoplifting as a severe problem. Although it had wonderful chicken salad, the competition outflanked Dimperios. It couldn't compete in price, selection, or quality. Its only competitive advantage was its location for walkers and the emotional attachment to the neighborhood. No amount of editorials about food deserts, protests by activists, lectures at conferences, or other great intentions could change the fact that the store was not competitive. It was not sustainable as a business.

While I saw the devastating effects of the declining steel industry in Hazelwood, I simultaneously witnessed the positive impact of intervention strategies that helped people adapt to the new competitive realities rather than fight them. Through the help of a training program and an already existing love for computers, my friend Ed Provident made a mid-life career change from industrial management to computers. His three teenagers were accepted into City Charter High School, given laptops, and graduated with Microsoft certifications and business internships. They have all since graduated from college. Not everyone had the giftedness, opportunity, drive, or discipline to transition to the new economy, but I witnessed the power of solid intervention strategies to adapt, not fight competitive reality.

Getting Real about Trade-Offs

Another gap between our ideals and behavior is honesty about trade-offs. The second page of an economics textbook reads: "People make trade-offs because they can't have everything."[65] This is where humans regularly face their contradictions. City governments regularly say they care about the environment but will bulldoze acres of trees if it means more tax revenue. Trees don't pay taxes. Likewise, many community gardens start with a bang of enthusiasm and end in an overgrown headache. Enough volunteers are unwilling to trade off the time and labor necessary to maintain them.

Often, communities have not agreed on the trade-offs necessary to increase investment. The kind of businesses that residents say they want usually involve increasing housing density and attracting higher incomes. The fear then becomes gentrification. It is only possible to break the status quo by making trade-offs.

In addition, economists like to talk about the short-term and long-term. Today's solutions often become tomorrow's problems. Large-scale public housing solved the problem of the "slums" when the government constructed them. Now, concentrated poverty in large public housing projects is the problem. For decades, building out waterfront property to the water line and filling in wetlands with construction debris was an economical solution to hide debris and create more developable land. With the destruction of wetlands, flooding and rising sea levels are now the big problems. Cities and states become insolvent because they play short-term budget games to hide long-term financial woes. Honesty about practical trade-offs is invaluable.

Patience for the Long-Term

Most think of the U.S. space program during the 1960s leading up to the moon landing as a national defense program. Few think of it as a social program. By 1969, N.A.S.A. had an annual budget of $10 billion, which funded education, research, and equipment. Among others, Daniel Markovits attributes the growth of the super-skilled in part to the government investment in a handful of privileged (mostly White men) scientists, mathematicians, and engineers. When Congress cut N.A.S.A.'s budget after the moon landing, and as Vietnam's costs grew, many previously government-aided researchers transferred their skills to private industry.[66]

The point here is not for neighborhoods or cities to start space programs but to consider the long-term investments needed to build generational wealth. Wealth building requires the patience to invest long-term in research and education, only in more equitable ways than in the 1960s.

Unfortunately, this is not how we are conditioned to think. We generally prefer instant satisfaction. Confusion and conflict occur when the stated goal is generational wealth, but public investments are short-term, election-cycle, quality-of-life projects. Stated goals and activities are mismatched.

Praise for Ugly Businesses

The infatuation with curb appeal, appearance, and retail is part of this conflict. Nearly every neighborhood marks its rise in status with the arrival of a Starbucks or a Chick-Fil-A. Until our office helped conduct a small business survey, I never realized how many small and medium-sized but less attractive manufacturing businesses are tucked away in neighborhoods and industrial parks. Norfolk is dotted with specialty machine shops catering to the maritime industry. Many non-retail companies supply the immense logistical needs of the U.S. Navy. Two manufacturing shops had identical concerns. They had $30-an-hour jobs available but didn't have the skilled labor pool to fill them. Because they aren't as visible, ugly businesses' practical value often goes unnoticed and under-appreciated.

My Proudest Failure - The Value of Practical Advice

Two businessmen broke my heart once with their "facts are better than dreams" candor, but they saved me from making big mistakes. After four shootings on my block and doing the funeral for an 18-year-old neighbor, my dream was to start a non-profit coffee house on a run-down business corridor on Second Avenue in Hazelwood. I consumed all the information I could, acquired market research, and wrote a business plan. I researched available low-rent properties (almost all of them) and was ready to sign a lease and start raising money for a build-out. People in the neighborhood thought it was a great idea.

Before spending any money, I submitted the plan to two acquaintances for review. Rich Kocinski had an M.B.A. and was a general manager at a medical manufacturer. The other, Dave Cole, was an old family friend I had admired since I was a teenager. He was an executive with a doctorate at a $3 billion defense company. They provided separate, independent reviews but reached the same conclusion: the social goals mismatched the profit goal. A coffee house hangout in a low-income neighborhood with a pool table to attract youth from the same low-income neighborhood would not be a place that would attract spending customers sufficient to turn a profit. They urged me to choose between a social priority or a profit priority. It was unlikely that I would accomplish both in the business plan I proposed.

At the time, it was crushing, but I took their advice. I chose the social priority. Using the church basement, we became a special event coffee house. The first paycheck I ever wrote was to the younger sister of the murdered neighbor. We fulfilled an incredible social mission, had more fun than any other job I've ever had, and helped several youth cohorts but never turned a profit. It is my proudest failure.

Communities benefit from practical thinkers. Sales pitches and pretty pictures aren't always as good as they first appear. The practical challenge us to weigh short-term and long-term trade-offs carefully. They confront us with unpleasant facts. They give us the information to make better, more sensible, neighborly decisions. Everyone needs neighborly people like my mom, Dave Cole, and Rich Kocinski, who are practical, seek the facts, give and take tough love, and steer around egos. Practicality helps us navigate the tension between our virgin ideals and our promiscuous behavior.

Fun - Waking Up the Neighborhood

Key idea: Neighborhoods better at managing conflict have a deceptively simple characteristic: they have fun together.

The military awards medals and ribbons for service and campaigns. Some neighborhood residents should get ribbons for surviving neighborhood meetings. Some leave battle scars. Some are snooze-fests. Others are more entertaining than T.V. Neighbors could later compare ribbons. "This ribbon is for the park redesign meeting of '04." "This is the from the zoning fight of '08." The anger was so intense in one Virginia Beach civic league meeting that a member used Robert's Rules of Order uniquely. He threw a copy at the head table and hit the president in the ribs. Someone called the police, and it ended up in court.[67]

Conflict and the struggle with commitment are inherent in any human relationship. Conflict can be found in churches, PTAs, universities, government, and neighborhoods. Neighborhoods better at managing conflict have a deceptively simple characteristic: they have fun together.

Neighborhood leaders often voice frustration at the need for more involvement of nonmembers. The stated value is to increase involvement. The behavior is usually to resist any change that would do so. Here is a scenario for a civic league in decline or one that never had much community interest in the first place. A few in the civic league loyally attend but avoid the responsibility of leadership. Leadership defaults to residents who don't want it or people who like the status but whose insecurity and lack of interpersonal skills drive more away. Visitors sense a dysfunctional social situation and avoid the civic league. Others attend for the drama. Research supports that public behavior in some instances is so bad that some go for the entertainment value.[68] Healthy individuals with jobs and families do not have time for dysfunctional meetings.

For years, many neighborhood groups had the same motto: "We're here to be a voice for people's problems." Unfortunately, the emphasis on problems and not relationship building has left groups with only two or three people. Other neighborhoods, particularly H.O.A.s and Condo associations, are obsessed with appearance and rule enforcement, not relationships. Invisible leaders send nasty H.O.A. letters or dispatch code inspectors to enforce sometimes trivial rules.

Numerous studies point to the importance of social bonds. For example, a 1989 study researched the nearly universal problem of neighborhood associations' participation: Why do only a few residents in a neighborhood participate? They called it the "free rider" problem, where few people do the work, but everyone enjoys the benefits. Researchers surveyed participants in a random sample of three neighborhoods and established an index. Participation ranged as follows:

No knowledge of neighborhood association 50%

Knowledge of the association but no involvement 8%

Read association newsletter 13%

Belong to the association and pay dues 11%

Attend meetings of the association 9%

Served on a committee or as an officer 10%

They defined and analyzed eight strategies to increase involvement. Some come out of economic self-interest. A few come to be part of political action. Of the eight strategies, relationship building was the strongest and the easiest for neighborhood leaders to control. The authors concluded

> ...the best advice we can offer to community organizers and neighborhood leaders at this time is to do everything possible to strengthen the cohesion of a neighborhood. Sponsor all kinds of events that will bring neighbors together, promote interaction among them, and give them a strong sense of identification with the local neighborhood. In short, make the neighborhood a viable social entity for its members.[69]

This conclusion is still appropriate nearly 30 years after the article was published. Neighbors meeting other neighbors is the single most common denominator in healthy neighborhoods. A report by New York City after Hurricane Sandy emphasized the importance of relationships to resilience. Neighborhoods were more resilient, where residents had multiple strands of social relationships and higher capacity.[70] The bottom line is that relationships are more important than meetings.

What Peter Kageyama said about cities is true of neighborhoods; residents need to connect with their communities emotionally. They need reasons to love their neighborhood. In place-making, Partnership for Public Spaces experts call for "The Power of Ten." An attractive place should have ten reasons for people to come there. It could be "a place to sit, playgrounds to enjoy, art to touch, music to hear, food to eat, history to experience, and people to meet."[71]

There is an element of fun. There is more to do than go to meetings. Jane Jacobs named dullness as the great enemy of neighborhoods.

Most healthy neighborhood groups already know this. One contemporary perspective was best stated in 2015 by Ed Culpepper, then president of the Lafayette Winona Civic League. In his civic league meeting, he noted that norms have changed. Meeting attendance is no longer a measure of healthy neighborhood relations. There are multiple social networks in the neighborhood. Most neighbors do not attend an evening meeting, so attendance shouldn't be the measure of participation. What the civic league could do is be a connector between the different social networks.

Fortunately, many neighborhoods like Lafayette Winona are less concerned about protecting the vocal minority and more about waking the middle majority through social activities and projects. Here is a partial list of neighborhood activities.

- Movie night and cookout. Norview Heights received permission to use a private vacant lot for summer movie nights, complete with popcorn.

- Progressive Dinners. Some neighborhoods make progressive dinners through neighborhood homes.

- Sunshine committees. Norview Civic League has a committee that sends cards to neighbors. I remember receiving birthday cards from a kind woman in Hazelwood.

- Welcome packets. Saratoga East Lynn and Fairmount Park neighborhoods give welcome packets to new residents.

• Field Trips. Lafayette Winona makes a field trip every year. Garnzie West let me tag along to the Botanical Gardens with the Coronado Inglenook Civic League.

• Bumper Stickers. Elizabeth Park provides neighborhood bumper stickers to residents. So does Ocean View. I have seen OV stickers all across the state. OVers are proud of their neighborhood.

• Neighborhood Reunions. Berkeley, Lamberts Point, and Ingleside hold large annual neighborhood events/reunions.

• Art Festivals and Block Parties. Stockley Gardens is known for its big art festival.

• Fire and Police Demonstrations. Colonel Paul Olsen (U.S. Army, retired) says a fantastic free event is to ask the fire department to bring over a truck or the police to bring a police vehicle and do demonstrations.

• Trick-or-treating. Some neighborhoods don't like Trick-or-treating. Some wealthy neighborhoods discourage it because it attracts children from other neighborhoods. Other neighborhoods embrace it. One affluent neighborhood, despite some objectors, delights in it.

• Drive-Thru Art Gallery. Karen Rudd, Norfolk's Public Art Coordinator, paid local artists for one-time rights to their art, printed the art on approximately four-foot square vinyl sheets, and posted them along one business corridor. They launched the art with a street party. Karen did it on a large scale, but others could do it on a smaller scale. They have also printed art on political size signs and placed them temporarily around the city.

- Pocket Parks and Pop-Up Art. Antonio and Jeannie Davis took a corner in their Lindenwood neighborhood and created message signs out of styrofoam, like "Love," "Joy," and "Happy". They then complimented it with plantings and landscaping.

Healthy neighborhoods find fun ways to engage people at different levels and go to where people already are.

During the Covid-19 pandemic, we witnessed an inspiring level of creativity. We saw hearts and Teddy bears in windows. We saw sidewalk art, birthday parades, signs thanking front-line workers, driveway concerts, delivery-driver thank-you stations on front porches, and Easter bunnies waving from the street. I suspect much of this creativity did not originate in typical neighborhood meetings but spontaneous gestures of love.

Many neighborhood groups ask, "How do we get people (especially young people) to attend our meetings?" A better question might be, "What are we doing to support youth and parents in the neighborhood?"

These "feel good" activities also serve an economic purpose. Research from the Federal Reserve has shown that investment in middle neighborhoods makes the most economic sense. Ironically, most federal funding is limited to the most impoverished neighborhoods [72]. Retaining and engaging good property owners is better than waiting for neighborhoods to reach a crisis point. When things are good in a neighborhood, neighbors sometimes neglect relationship building. It isn't until a crisis that leaders notice that disengaged people have already begun fleeing the neighborhood. Consider wise words from long-time neighborhood expert David Boehlke:

> If asked about what made their neighborhood attractive when they first moved in, many long-time residents speak about how neighborly the place was. They knew everyone on the block, and people paid attention to one another. The sidewalk of the shut-in was shoveled. The missing dog was quickly found. The locked-out child was given a place to stay until his parents came home. People saw themselves as buying both a house and a neighborhood. Even though these memories are sometimes seen through rose-colored glasses, it is true that most middle neighborhoods were originally desired because of their stability and neighborliness.[73]

Neighborhoods should be fun. Just ask a teenager. Health researchers conducted a study of teenagers that compared official neighborhood census boundaries with teenager-defined boundaries. They tracked teenagers' movements with GPS and an accelerator to study where they spent their time and physical activity. Although there was some correlation with the official boundaries, the teen-defined neighborhood boundaries matched where they hung out, were active, and spent time.[74] The study is amusing because adults will fuss over neighborhood boundaries. Neighborhood boundaries are tied to real estate values and crime statistics. City GIS technicians are continually making adjustments to reflect resident demands. Yet the simple truth reflected by teenagers and forgotten by adults is that neighborhoods are ultimately defined by where you feel at home, where your friends are, and where you have fun.

Community Pride - Good and Bad Community Activism

Key idea: Good community activists inspire confidence within and without the community.

In an age of inequality, the title of activist has become a badge of honor. This chapter aims to distinguish the gap between community activists who can make noise about a problem and activists who can lead change into an improved normal and restore community pride. Two crucial features are peculiar to community leadership and positive outcomes. They have the long-term patience to 1) inspire confidence among the people inside the community and 2) inspire confidence to those outside the community, particularly potential investors and good neighbors. They attract good investment; they don't drive it away.

Community pride declines for any number of reasons. The appearance of decline is a symptom of economic and social causes. Here are a few.

- The local economy declines.

- As housing ages, new, modern housing with more amenities or desirable locations becomes available in other neighborhoods. Newer occupants in the older neighborhood do not have the same financial capacity for home maintenance.[75]

- The more transient a community becomes, the less stabilizing social bonds develop.

- Increasing numbers of renters are not evil but can bring more complexity and laxer accountability.

- Incompetent neighborhood leadership.

- Conflict—when residents aren't fighting outsiders, they fight each other.

- Historic racism and real-estate profiteering.

Communities enter a downward spiral of discouragement, less neighborliness, and declining pride. Neighborhood leaders in severely challenged neighborhoods face specific challenges to restoring pride.

Difficult Personalities

Building internal confidence can be thorny with the range of personalities in a given neighborhood. Several personalities keep community meetings entertaining. They are the people that make you groan inwardly when they are given the floor to speak.

Bitter Bob. Bitter Bob is someone whose ability to bring down a meeting knows no bounds. They are frequently wanna-be leaders that no one wants to follow. No one can do anything right. They have something negative to say about everything. Often, their bitterness stems from personal issues that have nothing to do with the neighborhood, but neighbors are the lucky recipients of their venom.

Dictator Demetrius views the group as his little army to command.

Lonely Lucy. Lonely Lucy is a person who comes to meetings primarily for social interaction in an otherwise lonely life. Lucy will start talking about the minuscule details of her life that have nothing to do with anything on the agenda.

Historical Hank. Historical Hank usually begins sentences with "Now years ago, I remember when ...," which is okay if they don't tell the same story every other meeting.

Time Delay Theresa. Time Delay Theresa will repeatedly ask questions about something the speaker already answered five minutes earlier. Either there is a gap in the time-space continuum, or they were't paying attention.

Political Percy. The word awkward is not in Political Percy's vocabulary. He always has a political agenda and can be counted on to inject it at the worst possible, most delicate situation in a neighborhood meeting.

One Issue Izzy. In larger meetings, at least one person is concerned with one issue and one issue only at every meeting. It is the sole issue through which they see the entire world, and they consider it an insult if not everyone is as passionate about this same issue.

Make It About Me Miles. Miles has a remarkable ability to make every issue about himself. No topic is too big or small that he doesn't feel the need to share his opinion and relate a personal story demonstrating his importance. He thinks of himself as a combination of Rambo, MacGyver, and Martin Luther King.

Tardy Tamaran. Tardy Tamaran will be late for her funeral. She is never quiet. She heads to the snack table, where she starts a conversation with someone who doesn't want the attention when neighbors start looking back in her direction. She can't just slip in and doesn't realize her whisper is the decibel level of a foghorn.

The challenge of organizing neighbors and congealing such an eclectic public group usually falls on volunteer leaders. They are responsible for guiding a collection of self-interested individuals into a community focused on shared interests and earning the confidence of other neighbors and outsiders.

Group Decision Making

The Harwood Institute for Public Innovation's Five Stages of Community Life helps set realistic expectations. Communities emerging from intense internal conflict require small steps to build community and less big vision. They need good facilitators who can calm an anxious group, listen, and move neighbors in a constructive direction. They don't make false promises they can't keep. Instead, they facilitate conversation and involve community members into small steps forward. They guide orderly group decision-making. When the decision-making process is perceived as fair, scholars call it procedural justice. Good facilitation improves group behavior, outcomes, and cohesion.[76]

The Funding Catch-22

Challenged communities face a catch-22. Grant and government funding relies on building evidence of how unstable a community is by producing a litany of societal ills. However, grant funding can be too faddish to be sustainable and is a relatively small financial pool. Economist Dambisa Moyo wrote a thought-provoking book warning about the over-dependence on aid in Africa that is worth noting in U.S. communities.[77] The much larger funding pool is private investment. Private investors want to know the opposite. They want assurance the community is a stable, safe investment.

Changing the Narrative

A prevalent form of neighborhood leadership is the neighborhood complainer. Neighborhood complainers take every opportunity to complain loudly about their neighborhood, especially if politicians or the media are around. If not used as a last resort, the complainer approach usually has the opposite of the intended effect. Neighborhood complainers scream to investors: "Don't come to our neighborhood. I will make your life miserable if you don't give me exactly what I want."

After a spike in crime on one street, a landlord complained to the paper, "It is the most dangerous street in the city." The response from the city government was swift and heavy. The street became the most patrolled street anywhere. Several years later, a landlord regretted the newspaper comment. Why? Because they essentially branded themselves as "the worst street in the city," which made it much more difficult to attract good tenants. Did they get government attention? Definitely! Did they turn off good investors and tenants? Unfortunately, yes. Neighborhood complainers may have support within a neighborhood from a handful who share the same frustrations. However, outside the neighborhood, they often drive a wedge between themselves and the resources they need to attract.

The Perks and Pitfalls of the Protestor/Activist Model

The community protestor or activist model can be positive or destructive. More than sufficient evidence exists in Chicago, Pittsburgh, and Norfolk for me to know corruption and injustice are always present. Gently waved red flags often don't capture decision-makers' attention. Sometimes, the only way to draw upper-level attention to a neglected area is to make public noise.

Norfolk is a better place today because of activists who challenged systematic problems. Norfolk was home to Evelyn T. Butts whose Supreme Court case successfully challenged the poll tax.

The best kind of protest leaders are reluctant protestors. They are thoughtful, measure risk, know the importance of timing, and have the pulse of the public, not just their constituents. They have calculated an end goal of shifting public sentiment toward their side. They logically attach their activism to realistic, actionable items.

The worst kind of activists are those who protest to protest. They take destructive risks with no logical connection to realistic, actionable items. They either don't have the pulse of the general public or don't care because they primarily want to preserve power among a fringe base. They drive investors and good neighbors in the opposite direction. Another pitfall of the protest model of community leadership is that they often burn many bridges. In protesting any number of ills, real and occasionally fictitious, they alienate themselves into a smaller and smaller circle.

Sociologist Elijah Anderson documents the unspoken battle in severely challenged communities between the code of decency and the code of the street. The former embodies neighborliness; the latter embodies rudeness and self-absorption. Anderson observed that the code of the street is an adaptation to profound alienation and a lack of faith in mainstream institutions, particularly among youth. [78] The best activists break the sense of alienation and establish connections to mainstream institutions. Sadly, the worst activists reinforce alienation and mistrust in any institution other than themselves. Some profit by it.

Another crucial variable is the leader's adaptability after they have made their point. Some community leaders are great at telling others what to do but not great at influencing change themselves. Behaviors within a community may need addressed. Successful outcomes partially depend on the activist's ability to be a positive model.

Community leaders who can only make noise and not create substantive change have a minimal, if not destructive, value.

A Positive Activist Example

Beatrice Garvin-Thompson is a queen bee in Norfolk neighborhoods and a positive activist who has earned the confidence of those inside and outside her neighborhood. Ms. Bea is the president of the Olde Huntersville Empowerment Coalition. She actively coalesces various parties to work together and has restored pride in their neighborhood for years. She periodically attends city council meetings to ensure that the City of Norfolk remembers that Olde Huntersville has its own voice. At one point in her past, Ms. Bea was part of a community development corporation (CDC) that built houses in the neighborhood to match the existing architectural style. She is always dressed as a business professional or in flowing African gowns. She is a retired teacher who is now chasing her bucket list, which included driving a bus.

Olde Huntersville is the crown jewel of Norfolk's historic Black neighborhoods. In pre-civil rights Norfolk, it was home to Norfolk's leading Black citizens and culture. It was self-sufficient until the City annexed it in 1911. It bustled with Black-owned businesses, including The Attucks Theatre, a hotel, it's own newspaper, and stores up and down Church Street. Out of Huntersville came Norfolk's first African American library, elementary school, high school, and college (now Norfolk State University). Adjacent to Olde Huntersville is the West Point Cemetery, which contains the remains of African American soldiers who served in the Union Army during the Civil War and a memorial to Sergeant William Carney.

As opportunities for African Americans expanded in the civil rights era, many middle-class African Americans began moving out. Over time, filtering (where properties receive less investment as newer housing with more amenities emerge elsewhere) occurred, which created a vacuum that predatory landlords filled. The percentage of transitional renters skyrocketed until the scales tipped, and they became the majority. Neighborhood pride declined, and many properties became shambles of their former beauty. Slum lords invest as little money as possible into properties, only enough to keep them out of jail. They don't require background checks for incoming tenants and rarely visit properties, if at all. If they have a lease, they don't enforce rules as long as the rent keeps coming. At best, they turn a blind eye to crime and safety violations; at worst, they participate.

Her neighborhood has every right to complain about the neighborhood. Decades earlier, weak and discriminatory zoning allowed anything to go into Huntersville with few buffers between residential and industrial. Weak zoning allowed the proliferation of rental properties. For years, local government used census data and low-income levels in the Huntersville census tract to bolster applications for federal grants. Still, the money went to public housing or other projects, not Huntersville.

Ms. Bea doesn't shy away from talking about those things from the past, but they are the background of the Huntersville she wants to project to the world, not the foreground. The foreground is about a Huntersville rich in history, full of good people, a desirable place to make a life, and a hopeful future.

When the Virginia Statewide Neighborhood Conference came to Norfolk in 2015, the Black history tour was the most popular. As a tour guide for part of the trip, Ms. Bea enthralled the participants with the richness of Olde Huntersville's history and architecture. She exudes confidence, pride, and love in her neighborhood. She has a contagious smile and the personality of warm cinnamon tea. She is soft-spoken but authoritative when she speaks.

Part of what makes her a terrific leader is that she took the time to learn how the City works. Mrs. Garvin-Thompson learned how zoning works and tracked what is moving through the City Planning Commission. She and other community members worked to change the zoning to reduce future rental properties. When a new property owner tried to sneak by the zoning and convert a property into more rental units, Ms. Bea and others noticed the addition of electric meters. They reported it to the City, which took action.

They are one of Norfolk's only neighborhoods to draft their own plan and have it recognized by the city council. They spent a year building relationships and partnerships. They identified assets in the neighborhood and used meetings to give recognition to those assets. They used some meetings for practical skill-building, such as learning CPR. They did resource fairs and flower sales. They created a logo and website. They drafted neighborhood standards on door hangers and distributed them throughout the neighborhood. The neighborhood standards communicate their vision and identify preferred neighborly behavior. They started a working committee that drafted their strategic plan with a Norfolk State University professor and my supervisor, Oneiceia Howard. Other neighborhoods now want to copy the Huntersville model, but few are willing to do the work that preceded it.

Olde Huntersville's efforts have paid off. Architects prepared a pattern book that the City adopted to protect the neighborhood's historic appearance. A developer took advantage of the decreased permitting costs from using the pattern book and made a $10,000 donation to the Olde Huntersville Empowerment Coalition. They are using the funds to extend more resources into the neighborhood.

Another aspect of Ms. Bea's teacher personality is her way with people. She is good at working over a tough crowd. We asked her and another neighborhood leader from the Ingleside neighborhood, Nikki Southall (who later joined our team), to facilitate a meeting in a neighborhood experiencing significant internal strife. The meeting started with opposing members sitting on opposite sides of the room from each other. I had never heard residents speak positively about their neighborhood. By thirty minutes into the meeting, Bea and Nikki had them laughing and telling us and each other what they liked about the neighborhood and why they moved there in the first place. The transformation was almost magical. Mrs. Bea called it "Sankofa." She got them to open up about a neighborhood they could love again.

In 1961, Jane Jacobs published a popular book (not *Harry Potter* famous, but well known in neighborhood development circles), the *Death and Life of Great American Cities*. In it, she challenged readers to think of neighborhoods as "mundane organs of self-government." [79] A neighborhood's success (at least internally) is shaped by its ability to self-manage, make the neighborhood interesting, build resilient networks of connections, and take collective action. A neighborhood's direction was also set by the tone of key residents—whether warm and welcoming or angry and bitter.

Neighborhood leaders like Bea and Nikki did just that. They are good at 1) giving the neighborhood an esteemed reputation with outsiders and 2) inspiring confidence to insiders. They can attract a following within the neighborhood and build a positive reputation to potential investors and future good neighbors. They draw people toward shared aspirations, facilitate productive discussion, and inspire confidence inside and outside the community. They stand up to the comparison game and enliven neighborliness by drawing out a community's unique assets.

Section 2: Government - the Call to Love but Manage

Service - Making Government Work

Key Idea: Public employees work in the gap between stated values and actual behavior.

Colon Powell's autobiography is a helpful primer for working in government. During a tour in Vietnam, one of Powell's assignments was to feed information to headquarters from the field. Powell provided data to an intelligence officer behind a green door marked "No Entry." The mysterious man behind the door was doing statistical analysis to predict when mortar attacks were most likely to happen. After compiling all the raw data, the intelligence officer announced that he could predict with great certainty when mortar fire would occur: at night. Powell's response: "Well, knock me over with a rice ball. Weeks of statistical analysis had taught this guy what any ARVN private could have told him in five seconds. It is more dangerous out there when it is dark."[80] Powell wrote that these were the same geniuses who came up with Agent Orange and the "people sniffer" that could detect urine concentrations from an airplane. They used the people sniffer to target bombing. Unfortunately, the people sniffer couldn't differentiate between the enemy, innocent peasants, or water buffalo.[81] A peasant's brief stop to relieve oneself could be their final act. They call it collateral damage. At the same time, he applauds the American private for the ingenuity to get things done.

Government employees work daily in the gap between stated values as a country and actual behavior. With thousands of existing papers about policy and political philosophy, the following section is less about policymakers or philosophers and more about the public servants called to implement policies, whether good or bad. It highlights their positive impact when acting as good neighbors and their role in compensating for bad policies.

Practical experience concurs with research that residents are "largely ignorant of the basic facts about how their local services were provided."[82] Few enter government work to be cogs in a very slow-moving machine. They, including teachers, join to be gladiators for the public good. Yet, even before Covid, over a fifth of new teachers in Virginia left their school in the first year, and over 50% left teaching in Virginia after 11 years.[83] Bad management, unrealistic expectations, and the ever-changing winds of political leadership can make gladiators feel like mill mules walking endlessly in circles, grinding away at bureaucratic inertia.

Naomi Eisenstadt made an astute observation. She noted that policymakers are brilliant but bore easily.[84] They analyze a problem, draft a policy, move on to the next challenge, and leave the long, messy implementation work to others. The program gradually loses its top-priority focus and is delegated to people already responsible for yesterday's big programs. Programs rarely die but fade out of favor or are defunded to abysmal amounts.

The public servants delivering services have the colossal task of turning unrealistic expectations into something that works, albeit imperfectly. I saw that kind of worker in Pittsburgh. When the upper levels of city government crashed in scandals, economic collapse, and political infighting, the lower levels of government workers continued to make city government work for the residents. When I moved to Pittsburgh in 2000, the police were under a federal consent decree. By 2003, Pittsburgh was on the verge of bankruptcy and had to appeal for state help. The City made steep budget cuts, including layoffs to 737 workers, 100 of whom were police. Not coincidentally, crime subsequently went up.

Despite such severe cuts and political turmoil, city workers still did their jobs. Representatives came to our meetings. At one such meeting, then Fire Chief Michael Huss stopped in his dress uniform to change a flat tire for Lois Tevis after the meeting. The area Public Works supervisor named Greg attended neighborhood meetings faithfully and was present to help on Saturday cleanups. While volunteering for a neighborhood 5K race once, he offered me a ride in the rain to the staging area. When trying to track down the church's charter from 1868, I was passed around from office to office in state and city government. Finally, a worker in the Prothonotary's office went to another office, pulled the file, and mailed me a copy at no charge. Others helped us navigate government paperwork or removed obstacles for us. Despite the turmoil and politics at the upper echelons, those government employees made government work for the people. When I started working for the City of Norfolk, I wanted to be like those employees in Pittsburgh.

Government employees who treat neighborhoods as their own have an incredible impact on neighborhood health—employees like Debbie Green. Debbie Green gave me one of the most rewarding days in government. She's responsible for Right-of-Way Permits. I contacted Debbie about a senior with a parking issue. A neighborhood leader had asked for zero-tolerance enforcement through his neighborhood. Inspectors complied. Then the neighborhood leader was bothered that an older woman had received a notice for parking on the grass. She didn't park on the street because there wasn't much space when opening the door into traffic. Parking around the corner was too far. Her neighbor permitted her to park in his yard, but parking on the grass was a violation.

Code inspectors referred me to the Right-of-Way Division for information about driveways. Could we create a gravel driveway? This is when I first met Debbie Green. Debbie frowned on the gravel idea because gravel ends in the street and the stormwater system. She said a crude driveway could be made of pavers. Volunteers from the neighborhood could help install it.

That is a mark of a good government employee, someone who makes every effort to offer solutions, not just give a "No" response or pass the problem on to someone else. What made her a superstar, though, was that she volunteered to help with the project on a weekend and contribute $50. I rode to work on a cloud I was so happy after getting Debbie's email on my BlackBerry. She is the kind of government worker with whom I wanted to work and wanted to be.

On a tour of the Utilities Department, our office encountered a gentleman with an incredibly important job that most people never think about. I regret not writing down his name. Neither he nor others in his role have ever been in the news for their work. No photo ops with politicians. No groundbreakings or ribbon cuttings. What is his job? He is a supervisor who keeps the City's sewer pump stations operating. If he doesn't do his job, the public will understand his importance very quickly. He is on call 24 hours a day with a dedicated phone. If electronic sensors in pump stations sense a problem, he receives a message regardless of where he is or what he is doing. He is also in charge of cleaning them out. This is more difficult since marketing gurus invented "flushable" wipes. Someone must suit up, wear a ventilator, climb down in the pit, and clean it out. I didn't even know the role existed. I was further surprised that the person doing it was so passionate about his job. Even though he gets no recognition, he was enthusiastic about his role and properly understood his importance. He was another public employee who dramatically shaped the quality of life for neighborhoods, but no one ever saw.

Public Service Motivation

In 1990, James Perry and Lois Wise released a study, *The Motivational Basis of Public Service* (PSM for short), measuring the motives, employee attitudes, and job satisfaction behind public service.[85] Since then, it has been studied from nearly every conceivable angle: the 24-item scale, a shortened scale, international application, relation to gender, race, age, and more. Perry measured six dimensions: attraction to public policymaking, commitment to the public interest, civic duty, social justice, self-sacrifice, and compassion.[86] They documented objectively what most government employees, from ditch diggers to cabinet secretaries, already know. They found that public employees have a range of motivations. Some are motivated by self-interest or the basic need to have a job to survive. Many, like Debbie Green, are motivated by love and compassion for people. Perry and Wise found that employees with good managers and leadership have better attitudes and job satisfaction. Not surprisingly, they also found that recruiting highly qualified young professionals becomes more complicated when public employees serve as the 'whipping boy' for politicians and the public.[87]

What motivates transportation engineer John Stevenson if not outward compassion and civic responsibility? Tom Vanderbilt wrote *Traffic: Why We Drive the Way We Do (and What it Says About Us)*, which I listened to, coincidentally, in the car driving to Memphis. About what Vanderbilt wrote, John Stevenson lives. John's image fits the typical bureaucratic stereotype. Before becoming Director in 2022, his small office in the nearly sixty-year-old City Hall was piled with stacks of studies, maps, and aerial photos printed from the plotter squeezed into the narrow hallway outside his door. He is trim and always dressed in a long-sleeve shirt and tie with government shades of gray, black, and Navy blue, but not in designer suits. He can speak engineer-ese and has a dry sense of humor accompanying his intellect.

Engineers working for Norfolk make less than their for-profit counterparts and some counterparts in nearby cities. He has a hopeless job of trying to slow speeders and reckless drivers. He spends many evenings listening to upset citizens complain about speeders. A simple Stop sign request can take two or more months to obtain all the correct approvals. In the meantime, John gets to answer all the nasty emails and phone calls about the time it takes. If 75% of residents on the street sign a petition requesting speed humps, John will still have to respond professionally to the one citizen fighting tooth and nail against them, who threatens to "call the Mayor," and claims, "I pay your salary."

John and his transportation division make improvements, but traffic calming measures will never stop all the imbecilic behavior. This discourages government workers who work hard yet know they are barely stemming the tide of poor behavior. On the other hand, government employees call this job security.

John's job offers another glimpse into the work of public servants, protection against our foolishness. John has a position where it is difficult ever to succeed. A profanity-laced post on NextDoor.com[1] complained about speeders on their street and the danger to their children. Thirty-six other people commented by the time I read it,

---

1. http://NextDoor.com

naming eight different streets where they wanted more enforcement. On my way home one day, I watched a car fly in and out of lanes on Princess Anne Road only to pull into the fried chicken restaurant. Evidently, he had a fried chicken emergency that was worth putting other people at risk. It was the same stretch of road where a child was killed.

It is usually the idiotic government worker caught sleeping on the job, making sexual advances, flipping someone off, or not showing up to work for 12 years but still getting paid that makes the news. Few people see the mostly patient, professional government workers dealing with all that comes with working with the general public. This includes people who have mental problems or intentionally abuse the very systems set up to help people. Day in and day out, government workers love people but manage the crazy human behavior that threatens society. Some cities have partnerships with mediation centers to reduce caseloads on inspectors stuck chasing invalid complaints between neighbors from hell. While not to the same extent as the military, police, fire-rescue, or other safety officials, good bureaucrats are hidden protectors of the democratic process.

Hidden Protectors of Democracy

Like most things, government workers' most significant strength is also their weakness. We are a nation that follows the rule of law. To protect neighborhoods from intrusion, enforcement officials need a law to cite. Unfortunately, laws designed to protect against nuisances make it difficult for little guys. When a home daycare wants to expand its capacity, they have to go through the zoning process to ensure that it doesn't annoy neighbors with traffic, noise, or parking problems. It isn't because planners hate daycare providers.

Inspectors who enforce rules sometimes know they are ridiculous. In October every year, Larchmont United Methodist Church sells pumpkins from its yard for mission projects. To absolutely no harm, they place pumpkins in the public's right of way between the curb and the sidewalk. All it took was one neighbor to complain, and some lucky city employee had to go on pumpkin patrol and tell the church to remove their excess squashes from the verge. Fortunately, the City Council created an ordinance, dubbed the pumpkin ordinance, allowing them to continue as long as they carried insurance to protect against lawsuits over the infringing pumpkins. [88] How would you like to have been the inspector who enforced the no pumpkin rule? Because one person complained, it takes a city council ordinance to create a special permit for a church to put out pumpkins.

Some nonsensical rules were established years ago or were politically motivated. Sadly, officials are obligated to enforce rules whether they agree with them or not. Secondly, many rules are because of some severe problems in the past. Inspectors have some discretion, but they must enforce the law if pressed. Property maintenance inspectors have a meaningful day when they take a slumlord to court and see justice. They have a meaningful day when they can contract to mow a property and bill the chronically lazy or cheap absentee owner who refuses to mow. It is not a meaningful day when some grouchy neighbor reports a missing shingle or chipped paint on a home that belongs to a single mother working two jobs, raising three kids, and being a caretaker for her parents. Fortunately, we have very compassionate code inspectors who work with social workers and community organizations to find help.

One challenge of government work is that no one can measure what doesn't happen. In this respect, the police deserve special mention. Community engagement is so ingrained in the Norfolk Police

Department (NPD) that I didn't realize it isn't universal. Each neighborhood in Norfolk has a Community Resource Officer (CRO) assigned to it whose role is to be part of the community. In addition, I collected information to give out in my service area. I counted over 20 different ongoing or one-time programs. Programs included Badges for Baseball, Trunk or Treat, soccer camp, youth cycling, boxing camp, basketball tournament, youth academies, bike rodeos, chess, call-in radio show, CAKE (Cops and Kids Eating) mentoring programs, Citizen's Police Academy, Clergy Community Connection, Five-O and Fades barbershop visits, neighborhood events, and the list goes on. One of my favorites is the Cops and Curls when NPD partners with a sorority and escorts 50 girls ages 6 to 12 in their best clothes to dance at the local Marriott hotel. I've known several CROs who hold or contribute to neighborhood projects out of their pocket. Some have started separate non-profits. No one will ever know about the crimes or the riots against police that didn't happen because community engagement is so ingrained.

In a webinar on public safety and race, Darryl McAllister, a retired Chief of Police from Union City, California, shared his story. He knew he wanted to be a police officer since he was eight. He and a friend had been playing in his yard when a police officer pulled up. The officer was Black, like McAllister, which was unusual then. The officer observed how well they played together and said, "I'm proud of you." The officer then reached in his pocket, pulled out some change, and told them to buy something at the corner store. That tiny interaction shaped McAllister's 37-year police career.

When I think of other examples of lasting achievements that are hard to measure, I think of a late environmental engineer named Lee Perkins. Over his 20-year career, his office restored the dune system, mostly naturally, along the seven-mile stretch of Norfolk's beaches on the Chesapeake Bay. Some beachfront property owners, whose views were obstructed by the dune restoration, were not his biggest fans. He is also one of the many retirees who most people will not recognize his name five years after retirement. There aren't any shrines or memorials in his name, no awards, no standing ovations, no stars on the sidewalk, no grand unveiling of a restored beach, just slow but steadfast dedication. Yet decades from now, his work will have stood the test of time, assuming no one reverses the policy. Nature's natural storm barriers are restored. Property and lives will be more protected than they would have otherwise without Lee Perkins being faithful to his duty. When storms come and there is no damage, few, if any, even think about it. Sadly, thousands of public servants will fade into history without anyone ever knowing their contribution.

Some equipment should be standard issue to government employees: gray-tinted glasses for navigating the nuances of government ethics, bus-resistant underwear for all the times they're thrown under one, an app for your phone for understanding doublespeak, and nausea medicine for all the flattery that goes on to get anything done. The following two chapters cover the delicate role between neighborhoods and government, but I want to begin with recognition of the thousands of upstanding public workers. Most have a professionalism that surpasses their natural human-emotional responses, especially the impulse to tell a few people where they can shove it. They see behind the veil of our political system what is occasionally beautiful, mostly average, and sometimes ruthlessly frightening. Few in the public will ever see the hidden role that public servants play in protecting democracy. There is undoubtedly substantial injustice in the country. It would be far greater were it not for employees of great character who dare to bring into public light and, if nothing else, at least slow down some of the greedy, conniving, and secretive special interests that would otherwise steamroll through our republic. They exemplify both resolves: they make the world a fairer place, and they remain neighborly in one that isn't.

Contrition - A Government Guide to Screwing Up

Key Idea: Reseeding community ownership requires contrition.

A certain Mr. Happypants raised questions in my mind about the relationship between government and neighborhoods. He had a caustic sense of entitlement that I came to experience in a handful of others. Where did it come from? I sensed that it was from a loss of autonomy caused by a history of government action. Re-seeding a neighborly sense of ownership requires a healthy sense of contrition from government employees.

In 2011, an analyst in charge of the Healthy Norfolk program held a focus group at the Norview Community Center. I went in support since it was in my service area. There were only three questions. One question was, "What is Norfolk doing positively to promote health?" "Health" for the focus group could be physical, social, psychological, or financial.

The group struggled to name one positive that the City of Norfolk did to promote good health. This was strange since they were sitting in a $7 million community center that was only two years old. It has a gymnasium, a fitness room with over 20 pieces of exercise equipment, a dance studio, an art studio, a multipurpose room with a commercial kitchen, two computer labs, a teen room, a game room, and offices. A multi-use trail loops around the community center and the adjacent schools. All of this surrounded them in the room where they were sitting, and still, they could only think of complaints.

The group's ringleader, whom I'll call Mr. Happypants, was obsessed with the fitness room. He considered himself a volunteer personal trainer for overweight women. He came in the morning and left in the early evening, spewing complaints to the staff the entire day. I quit exercising there because his or his companions' mouths ran the whole time. He wanted more equipment. The room wasn't clean enough. A machine was broken. The equipment wasn't top-of-the-line. His agenda was to swap the dance studio with the fitness room. He wanted management to kick out the little girls and seniors in the dance studio to have a bigger fitness room. He wanted city government to provide a Planet Fitness level fitness club free to the public.

As a new government employee, my reaction was, "What the heck was that?" Since I'm from a small town, it was hard to understand why they and others complained so much. I didn't have a community center growing up. Dad had a used weight bench with mismatched weights from yard sales in our unfinished basement with exposed dirt. We had to walk partially bent over unless standing in between floor joists. Our weight room had one advantage over Norview, however. Dad had an apocalyptic supply of canned green beans and peas in case of emergencies.

Like the steady drip of Chinese water torture, Mr. Happypants complained daily to the center supervisor and staff. Then he complained to the chain of command in the recreation department. When that didn't work, he complained in a city council session. Recreation management did everything to placate his requests without changing rooms. They squeezed more equipment into the space, making being so close to the next person awkward.

The Expectations Struggle

A contrast may be helpful. The Ringgold Ruritan building is a small, two-floor schoolhouse that was used as a community center in a tiny rural village outside Smithsburg, Maryland. In contrast to Norview, the Ringgold Ruritan had a multi-generational sense of ownership for their all-volunteer building. They did the work, raised funds, and paid the expenses directly. When it needed painted, they painted it. When the electric bill was due, the treasurer wrote a check from the Ruritan's account and paid the bill.

In Norview, there is a disconnect between usage and the responsibility of ownership. The various taxes that fund local government are diffused over 30 different departments and dozens of external organizations. The average resident does not know it takes $430,000 annually to operate the Norview Center. The Department of Parks and Recreation manages the center's programming. The Department of General Services maintains the facility. A janitorial company cleans it. The central energy plant controls the thermostat from downtown. When youth vandalize the center, urinate on the bathroom floor, or shove paper towels down the toilet, under-paid staff remove them—not the youth themselves or their parents.

In Ringgold, youth and their parents were involved in maintaining the property. This made them less likely to vandalize it. Though about $7 million times nicer, the city-run center doesn't have the same sense of ownership because citizens are disconnected from the work and responsibility. This small-scale gap between usage and ownership responsibility is typical of the broader gap in expectations between the public and government.

Negative Impacts of Government Policies

The interaction with Mr. Happypants caused me to research local history and policy. I wanted to understand where this raw bitterness and attitude of entitlement came from. I've encountered the same attitude of entitlement many times over in nice, low-crime neighborhoods. Why do some neighborhoods have a greater positive pride and ownership than others? Why are some more neighborly?

Unfortunately, much of it can be traced to government's history. As a product of the American education system, I was well-versed in taking standardized tests. I was not so well versed in our own U.S. Civil War. By the time I moved to Virginia, the total of what I knew about the Civil War could have fit within a long paragraph. Worse, if my knowledge of the Civil War fit into a paragraph, my understanding of the Reconstruction period was nonexistent. It has only been through the Librivox app that I've come into contact with this profoundly influential period of our history that gets little attention.[89]

When North Carolina and Virginia proposed requiring picture ID's for voting, I couldn't understand all the fuss. It seemed nonsensical that if I had to provide a picture ID to check into a hotel or board a flight, I would need an ID to confirm my identity for voting. I understand why it is such a sensitive issue only after reading Charles W. Chestnutt and Wilford H. Smith about the disenfranchisement of African Americans during Reconstruction in the South.[90] I further read parts of the 1902 Virginia Constitution that disenfranchised Black Americans but waived the restrictions on Confederate veterans. The voting rolls in the predominantly Black Jackson Ward of Richmond dropped from 3000 to 33 in 1903 as the new Virginia constitution took effect.[91]

Personal bitterness in Mr. Happypants plays a role, but historical factors also explain the deflated sense of ownership and pride residents like Mr. Happypants feel toward their neighborhood. Many have lost a sense of ownership because government has a history of taking over communities and promising them that government knows best.

Transportation

Following precedents across the country, Norfolk went on a road-building spree in the 1950s to widen roads downtown, such as Brambleton Avenue and Tidewater Drive. These widened roads served the dual role of separating Black neighborhoods from the downtown core. Norfolk documents from 1957 brag gleefully at how the new thoroughfares "are the pride of engineers and the joy of motorists."[92] By "motorist" they meant the people in White neighborhoods who benefited from the new thoroughfares, not the people living in public housing cut off by them.

The exodus to lower-cost suburbs accelerated after the 1944 GI Bill provided guaranteed home loans for returning World War II veterans. The Federal Aid Highway Act of 1956 created highways for the growing suburbs to bypass city neighborhoods on their commute to work downtown but had disastrous effects on traditional urban neighborhoods. They condemned historic homes, businesses, and other structures in their path and left noise, concrete, pollution, and congestion in their place. They severed connections from different parts of the same neighborhoods. Thousands of residents from ethnic neighborhoods in Chicago, like Greektown and Little Italy, were severed from their neighborhood by the Eisenhower Expressway and the University of Illinois Chicago campus in the early 1960s.

Changing Housing Policies

Lawrence Vale identified three fundamental questions regarding poverty that have been around since the Puritans first landed:

- Who among the poor qualifies for public assistance?

- How do we help them?

- Where do we house them?[93]

We wrestle with the same three questions today. As of writing, no one has invented a moral worthiness detection wand capable of determining if someone is worthy of assistance or if they will abuse the system.

The history of housing policy demonstrates the constantly shifting, inconsistent attempts to answer those three questions. In the 1930s, public housing focused on slum clearance. Government took over entire neighborhoods. They condemned slums and intended to re-seed the neighborhood with higher-income residents. When the U.S. entered World War II, projects initiated in the thirties became war housing. The emphasis shifted to solving the workers' housing shortage. When the war ended, the focus shifted again to housing veterans. As veterans moved to the suburbs, the strategy changed again.

Entrance requirements were initially stringent but were relaxed. Public housing became used as housing of last resort. After the novelty wore off, funding and the rent projected by policymakers no longer covered expenses. Governments failed to fund ongoing maintenance. By the mid-fifties, public housing had already earned a bad reputation. Finally, early housing policy didn't allow men in the home under the assumption that men should be working and thus not need public housing. This policy effectively separated thousands of children from their fathers.

The Rivers brothers' story in the book *There Are No Children Here* put faces on mismanagement's damage. It tells the story of two brothers growing up in the Henry Horner homes of Chicago with broken elevators, plumbing that didn't work, rats, grime, and crime.

Racism and Segregation

Racism and segregation were built into most of these policies. Richard Rothstein's popular book, *Color of Law*, summarizes the extensive long-term effects of government-supported racial segregation and discrimination. African Americans were discriminated against in education, so they received lower skills and fewer chances to build wealth. Unions and employers discriminated against them by restricting them to the lowest level jobs, denying promotions and supervisory positions, and paying them less than White peers. Discrimination and segregation in housing forced them to live further away from job sites. While federal policy helped White veterans receive mortgages after World War II, policy funneled Black veterans into public housing. This meant longer commutes, higher expenses, increased absenteeism, and the absence of equity in a home. Zoning often pushed Black neighborhoods into industrial zones with higher pollution, higher asthma cases, and more long-term health problems. Finally, the tolerance of violence against African Americans by federal, state, and local governments left residual fear, mistrust, and hopelessness.

Norfolk passed a formal segregation ordinance in 1914 outlawing African Americans from White neighborhoods. In the 1920s, City leaders and real estate executives designated Corprew Avenue as the dividing line between White and Black people. They went so far as to create a formula for property taxes by race that allocated less or no money for streets, streetlights, curbs, sidewalks, or parks in Black neighborhoods.[94] Black neighborhoods fell into disrepair over time, lacking equal public infrastructure investment and unequal economic opportunities, and became known as the slum problem. As part of the national craze to rid cities of slums, Norfolk's housing authority condemned hundreds of acres of Black neighborhoods.

Ironically, Norfolk won the All-America City award from the National Municipal League (NML) in 1959 for its slum clearance. Executives from *Look Magazine* and the NML came to Norfolk to celebrate at a big dinner at the old municipal auditorium (now storage for the Harrison Opera House). Sadly, dinner planners didn't invite a single Black person to an award supposedly about their neighborhoods. As whites celebrated inside the arena, Black people, including Joseph Jordan (an attorney and disabled World War II veteran), were left outside in the cold protesting.[95]

Before their famous namesake development in Levittown, New York, William J. Levitt and the Levitt Brothers company had a government contract to build the Oakdale Farms neighborhood in Norfolk between 1941 and 1942. The subdivision map lists the deed restrictions excluding anyone but the Caucasian race except for the occupancy of domestic servants.

Drive through Norfolk's Coronado/Inglenook neighborhood today, and you would never guess the turmoil it endured in 1954. Today, neatly trimmed yards, edged sidewalks, flowers, and well-maintained Norfolk cottages give no hint of the mob rule in the post-World War II boom. African Americans outgrew their designated segregated Black neighborhoods and began expanding. In the segregated south, they were not welcome, particularly in the Coronado neighborhood. As Black people moved into the neighborhood, they came under attack by whites who hoped to intimidate them into selling back to whites. Shrewd real estate speculators moved Black people into White neighborhoods to create panic among whites. They would then buy low from panicked Whites and sell high to Black families.

Old news stories tell how Bennie Parker and his fiancée Almary Payne were unpacking dishes in their new home on Widgeon Road when someone placed a dynamite charge near their house, and it exploded. After they escaped, White youth and adults roamed through their house, smashing remaining dishes and taking valuables.[96] This was the worst in a series of three bombings. White neighbors shot one resident while on his porch. They threw rocks through windows. They broke into one vacant house, turned on the water, and flooded it.

Initially, the government was of little help. Coronado was still a part of Norfolk County (until January 1955, when the City of Norfolk annexed it), so the city refused to send help. Black leaders appealed to the governor, who likewise declined to intervene. The County only sent one sheriff's deputy, who showed little interest. When they eventually caught the bomber, he only paid a $25 fine. Emboldened by government apathy, whites started caravans anytime they saw African Americans viewing houses in the neighborhood. They pulled up at a house in a caravan and intimidated potential homeowners. On one occasion, they blocked the street of a moving van. As a result, the new homeowners had to move in the middle of the night.

Neighborhood Planning

Another influence was weak, unjust zoning. Today, the historical evidence remains of low-income and primarily minority neighborhoods that received the leftovers that stronger neighborhoods didn't want. Industrial buildings are wedged right up against residential areas. Ugly, poorly designed, poorly constructed, dense rental housing is crammed against historic single-family homes with no regard for the surrounding neighborhood.

Despite opposition, in most cases government did what it wanted. Until 2007, government agencies in Virginia were still gobbling up neighborhood property using the threat of eminent domain. It set the precedent that if government, powerful real estate, construction, and banking lobbies will take over and do what they wish with your neighborhood, why take personal responsibility? In the 1960s, Jane Jacobs called for neighborhood districts that were strong enough to fight government.[97] The prevailing model of neighborhood leadership became someone who could fight City Hall.

Overpromising and Under-delivered Capital Spending

Former Harvard professor James Q. Wilson observed in 1985: "In almost every instance, leaders proposing a new policy erred in the direction of understating rather than overstating future costs."[98] He further noted that policymakers often prefer to attempt what they wish is possible over doing what is possible.

Earlier in the new millennium, during the real estate boom as Norfolk reaped collections from real estate taxes, its capital budget (mostly debt spending) jumped by 240% from 2004 to 2007. In 2004, the city embarked on four new, big-budget, neighborhood revitalization plans that were part of a big-spending plan. Consultants drew beautiful pictures that called for large-scale property acquisition, redevelopment, and the latest amenities. Then the real estate market crashed and the Virginia legislature restricted the use of eminent domain for private development. This significantly curtailed the City's big plans.

Indirect negative consequences were an unhealthy focus on fixing problems, an unrealistic emphasis on big money more than community, a lack of neighborhood ownership among other neighborhoods not receiving funds, an over-reliance on government, and an adversarial relationship between neighborhoods and government. It is usually frontline employees working in this gap between expectations and reality.

Citizens vs. Customers

Fortunately, Mr. Happypants is an extreme example. He only represents a few people who use Norview Community Center, but he demonstrates another gap between citizens and customers. Customer service collides untidily with the concept of citizenship (not as citizenship relates to the national debate over immigration, but to residents having a responsibility to their local community and government).

When residents only view themselves as "customers" of government, democracy suffers. President Kennedy expressed the concept of public responsibility in the famous quote, "Ask not what your country can do for you, but what you can do for your country." The nations founders embedded public responsibility in our early history. "Public Works" were originally done by the public, not paid professionals. Benjamin Franklin founded The Leather Apron Club in Philadelphia in 1727.[99] This group undertook civic projects for the public good, including street sweeping, firefighting, libraries, hospitals, schools, and the postal system.

John McKnight, Professor Emeritus at Northwestern University, laments this transfer of ownership of the public good and services from neighborhoods to government. In one example, he cites a study by Jamie Vollmer identifying 95 new functions assigned to public schools since 1900.[100] Problems and responsibilities once held by families and communities have now become the expectation of the public schools, reducing a sense of community ownership.

Mr. Happypants illustrates a problem that carries into a sense of neighborhood ownership. Habitat for Humanity involves the future homeowner in building their house, known as sweat equity. When people don't have any skin in the game or haven't earned any sweat equity, there is a disconnectedness and, at worst, a toxic sense of entitlement. Sadly, in too many cases, government, under both political parties, is responsible for taking away that sense of ownership. The responsibility of restoring a sense of ownership often falls on frontline workers but it begins with contrition. A little contrition over government's history can go a long way in rebuilding trust.

Ownership - Creative Tension

Key Idea: Wise government employees maintain a creative tension with communities.

In a rural Indonesian village, a well-intentioned government agency decided to improve an irrigation system for farmers using a simple log to split water between two channels. Engineers designed a plan, and contractors built a new concrete structure. They didn't realize, until too late, that their improvement upset an invisible, complex social contract that had negotiated fair water usage. While improving water efficiency, it upended a social and economic balance. Farmers eventually reverted to using another log.

Nobel Laureate Elinor Ostrom told that story as a warning about unintended social consequences.[101] Government and non-profits are attracted to brick-and-mortar projects. They provide something tangible to see, take pictures of, and do ribbon cuttings. However, engineering a neighborly sense of ownership is much more complex than engineering a site plan.

Booker T. Washington encouraged teachers to recruit the community when building schoolhouses. If community members couldn't donate cash, they could donate supplies. If they couldn't donate supplies, they could donate time hauling wood, hosting fundraisers, or assisting with construction. When starting Tuskegee Institute, one woman donated six eggs because that was all she could afford. Her donation was still appreciated. He asked every community member to contribute. In this way, "They will have all the more interest in the schoolhouse because they have had a hand in its erection."[102] Washington knew the importance of community ownership to neighborliness.

Regardless of political party, policymakers base every program on assumptions about the future and human nature.[103] Time reveals which assumptions were reasonable and which weren't. For example, home-ownership programs assume the owner of a property aided by the program will accrue future gains in wealth sufficient to offset future maintenance costs. When this assumption proves true, as it has for hundreds of thousands, the recipient receives safe, affordable housing plus increased equity. When the assumption proves untrue, the housing crisis will repeat at some future point. Another assumption is that residents can be self-governing within the complex legal frameworks of community associations. When that assumption is wrong, the housing intervention today becomes a legal mess tomorrow for someone else. When assumptions prove incorrect, it is rarely the policymakers who made the policy on the frontlines dealing with the gap between assumptions and reality. It is usually police, teachers, social workers, code inspectors, etc. How they relate to neighborhoods is critical.

Dr. William Peterman shared a case study of Leclaire Courts, a public housing community on the west side of Chicago, where residents lobbied for resident management. When the Chicago Housing Authority's (CHA) relationship was adversarial, residents took on more neighborhood ownership. With assistance from the Voorhees Center for Neighborhood and Community Improvement, they recruited an outside advisory board of specialists to provide technical assistance. They became responsible for managing their community. As Leclaire earned national attention and reforms took hold within the CHA, the relationship became cozy again. Leclaire residents increasingly relied more and more on CHA and less on their own efforts. They eventually dispensed with the outside advisors, and resident management gradually disintegrated.

One of Dr. Peterman's concluding criteria for successful neighborhood development is a "creative tension" between neighborhoods and government agencies. Relationships between the two "must be neither too friendly nor confrontational."[104] This has proven to be sound advice. In maintaining creative tension, it is helpful to register a community's temperament. Many neighborhoods are perfectly content. Others are more temperamental.

Temperamental Communities

Grief. Mostly, I went about 20 years without losing anyone significant in my family. Then, during 18 months beginning in 2012, I lost my mom, my living grandparents, my great aunt, my only maternal aunt, and a church grandmother. Life was unpleasantly upended and wasn't the same afterward. Vacations weren't the same. Holidays weren't the same. Birthdays weren't the same. Places that once brought comfort and security now felt empty. For the first time, I understood deep grief. I also turned 40, which didn't help. I was older than some of our interns' parents. Some of the younger, newer hires were advancing up the career ladder faster, and I felt left behind.

Grief opened my eyes to what I often saw in neighborhood meetings and partially explained why I had met so many crabby residents. It explained why so many older residents resist change: they are grieving. Like my neighbor, they grieve not having the health to know all the neighbors. With declining health and mobility, they can't be as involved as they once were. Moreover, the neighbors they knew had died or moved to nursing homes. They are grieving changes in neighborly behavior. They grieve a lack of pride. They grieve youth in the neighborhood they no longer know and with whom they no longer have the strength to control. The feeling of grief and being left behind by change has greatly aided my ability to relate to neighborhoods.

Anger. As the previous chapter would suggest, neighborhoods have legitimate reasons to be angry. As a government employee, I feel well-versed in being on the receiving end of that anger. I've met a few bitter bullies and Captain Morons who want to be heroes but pick the wrong battles or stir the pot for selfish gain. Most of the community anger, however, that I've experienced is legitimate or simply misinformed. Misinformed anger is a matter of building trust and giving accurate information. Legitimate anger is a matter of reflecting their anger and looking for ways to make corrections.

As is true with individuals, groups can transfer anger to the wrong people. Neighborhoods that are victims of a complex web of past bad policies or leaders (who are no longer around) don't know where or how to direct their anger, so they vent on anyone who comes close, usually frontline workers. Anger, though, is not always a bad thing. Anger can be an easier emotion to work with than apathy. When people are fired up about something meaningful, the opportunity is there to direct that anger into meaningful action. When people are angry, they show up to meetings. It is difficult to accomplish anything when people are apathetic and have given up.

How to Kill Grassroots Movements

If PowerPoint presentations could change neighborhoods, Norfolk would have perfect neighborhoods. Norfolk set about to restore a sense of ownership in neighborhoods with a new initiative called Neighbors Building Neighborhoods, or NBN for short (Norfolk borrowed the name from Rochester). Our first attempt was an example of what not to do to neighborhoods.

It originated with a grassroots neighborhood movement in Norfolk's Park Place area. Years of mistrust over traditional redevelopment methods failed to stimulate revitalization beyond select blocks, so the neighborhood and the city tried something different. They invited consultant Charles Buki and his team (CZB, Inc.). They did a year-long Vision and Engagement Project (VEP) with the community and asked city government to step back.

They set up neighborhood committees and held meetings in homes and coffee shops—outside government facilities. Likewise, neighborhood leaders organized social events. Neighborhood projects built the community's social fabric and engaged residents in a vision. Neighborhood leaders worked tirelessly to place residents in the driver's seat of neighborhood health.

One of the signature pieces of their VEP was a property evaluation. At Buki's suggestion, residents formed a team that set evaluation criteria and then went property by property to evaluate some 2000 properties. One of the residents' conclusions was that a lack of pride, ownership, and property standards depressed their neighborhood's desirability. Engaging residents in a vision for higher standards became essential. Buki's final report made a critical statement,

> "And in the past year [community members] have begun the especially grueling task of coming to terms with the complex reality that any real turnaround will ultimately hinge more on how committed the community is than on how much money the City can provide."[105]

This was a significant change in thinking. Of course, Buki could have told them that from the beginning, but residents needed to reach that conclusion on their own.

Norfolk management adopted this approach and entrusted our office to replicate it. Unfortunately, we did one of the worst things to a grassroots community movement: we government-ized it. Staff spent dozens of hours downtown sitting in conference rooms, coming up with a long list of sky-high, big, hairy, audacious, predetermined outcomes and measures to hold ourselves accountable.[106]

Next, leadership met behind closed doors, contacted council members, and selected four pilot neighborhoods from each ward that were amenable to the elected representatives. After they made the selection, we arranged meetings and loaded up our projectors, laptops, and screens to announce to the four neighborhoods that they had been selected for a new program. How did neighborhoods ever survive without our scintillating government presentations? We wooed the chosen neighborhoods into joining our new initiative and enticed them into a tango of neighborhood engagement with our masterfully crafted PowerPoint presentations and government matrices.

Next, we spent months crafting more PowerPoint presentations with neighborhood data. We had all the best Excel 2007 offered: pie charts, line charts, gradient colors. We had IT-generated maps. What neighborhood wouldn't be stimulated by such a sensuous mix of census figures and real estate data?

Confident from our terrific presentations, we announced to the four neighborhoods that we wanted to replicate the Park Place model. We encouraged them to set up the same committees and do the same property evaluation. If it worked in Park Place, then by George, it would work everywhere. Then we ran into problems. First, neither Norview, the pilot neighborhood I was assigned, nor most of the other three were interested in the property evaluation. In Norview, neither a casual drive nor the voluminous, color-coordinated data we presented suggested that residential property maintenance was a severe issue. Norview was more interested in the redevelopment of the business corridor. Since they and other pilot neighborhoods weren't interested in property evaluation, we were assigned as staff to do it ourselves, which ultimately defeated the purpose of what they did in Park Place.

Let me recap some of our early mistakes.

Predetermined Outcomes. When we went to the neighborhoods, we already had predetermined outcomes and measures before meeting with the neighborhoods. Without residents' buy-in, staff tried to prop up the program.

Unrealistic Outcomes. The new program was responsible for shifting 27 different measures. In addition to reducing crime and code violations, our program was supposed to increase housing values to the exclusion of all other variables that could influence the market. Sure, no problem.

Political Selection, not Community Motivation. Rather than ask neighborhoods who would be interested, leaders chose neighborhoods based on ward boundaries. Healthy Neighborhoods in Baltimore, by contrast, used a competitive process to select neighborhoods, assuring neighborhoods have some level of motivation from the beginning.

Cookie Cutter Approach. We ignored what was important to individual neighborhoods while imposing the Park Place model. We asked Norview what they wanted. They said in near unison, "Do something about Five Points." We responded, "Great, we need you to do a residential property survey anyway."

Staff Driven, not Neighborhood or Relationship Driven. We related as professional staff to run a program rather than as partners supporting their work and dreams.

PowerPoint Overkill. Ten years later, I still avoid screen presentations as much as possible. Relationship building should take precedence over impressing them.

From a Program to a Philosophy

As concerns about NBN reached the City Manager, Marcus Jones, at the time, he sent us back to the drawing board by contracting Buki and his team to train staff. One of Buki's key mantras was that the community should manage the neighborhood's day-to-day life and lead to positive investments. As a result, Mr. Jones changed NBN from a program to a philosophy: "Neighbors Building Neighborhoods is a community ownership and investment philosophy aimed at creating neighborhoods of choice through the City of Norfolk."

Mr. Jones was a fan of the Peter Kageyama book *For the Love of Cities*, so our team read it and adapted it to neighborhood work. The quest was to replace disconnectedness or toxic entitlement with collective responsibility in daily interactions and city government. It placed a high value on small interactions, which Robert Putnam's research supports: "smaller is better from a social capital point of view."[107] This returns us to Dr. Peterman's call for creative tension. Communities must be held accountable for their share of responsibility. This is neither easy nor fun, but it is the only way to be healthy. Some of those small things that I've seen work among frontline employees are below.

Keeping a Creative Tension

1. *Be professional without standing on a professional pedestal.*

Officer Erica Bennett was a School Resource Officer for the Norfolk Police Department. She was one of four officers invited to speak at a luncheon and had the crowd moved with her story. When she first started as a school resource officer, she was miserable. She said that the uniform had changed her. The uniform gave her an authoritarian police posture. When she wore the uniform, she took on a drill sergeant's persona whose primary purpose was to break the students' wills and bring them into submission to authority. A few of the problem kids resisted, making her job miserable. Before giving up, however, she remembered that she used to be one of those kids. She began to question where she would be if people hadn't invested in her along the way. Instead of seeing herself first as a police officer, she began to see herself as a human who could invest in those young problem kids as a police officer. She began to see the 800 students at her school as her investments. It completely changed her attitude, approach, and the teenagers' response. She made it a point to learn names and greet students as they entered the building. It is crucial to be a professional but to get off a professional pedestal. Annoyed residents can sense arrogance a mile away.

2. *Acknowledge the Unacknowledged.*

During our annual conference, Dr. Greg Ellison placed a three-foot measuring tape from Ikea on some 80 chairs in the front of a lecture hall at Norfolk State University. The comforting and rhythmic sounds of jazz played as people entered the hall. Some walked their way inside. Some danced. Greeters welcomed everyone: "Welcome. Are you ready for change?". He skipped the usual blah blah blah of introductions and started his presentation silently by going around the room and making eye contact with all 80 people. He then expressed his gratitude for being able to meet everyone. He asked for a volunteer. The youngest member's hand shot up, a young man in elementary school. Dr. Ellison recruited him as his helper and then asked for another volunteer to read in their most dramatic, deep voice from within themselves. It was from William James

> No more fiendish punishment could be devised, were such a thing physically possible, than that one should be urged loose in society to remain absolutely unnoticed by all the members thereof. If no one turned around when we entered, answered when we spoke, or minded what we did, but if every person we met 'cut us dead' and acted as if we were non-existent things a kind of rage and impotent despair would before long well up in us from which the cruelest bodily torture would be relief. Cut dead But Still Alive.

Dr. Ellison concluded by giving the measuring tapes to everyone with his father's challenge, "You may not be able to change the world but change the three feet around you. Acknowledge the people around you." The theme for his Fearless Dialogues group is SEE the Invisible, HEAR the Silenced, and Work for CHANGE.

Temperamental neighborhoods are full of unacknowledged people. Few higher privileges exist in public service than to acknowledge the unacknowledged. There are many issues that government employees may not be able to do a thing. Still, they can always acknowledge people and their value. Some of the negative behaviors we see in neighborhoods are from residents not feeling respected. One of the high callings of those in neighborhood work is to give people respect who may not even have a high degree of respect for themselves. It is transformative.

3. *Show residents the positives in themselves and their neighborhood.*

"The challenge," said David Boehlke, "is to think about neighborhoods in a new way, not as problems to be solved, but as assets to celebrate and grow." When I started with Norfolk, we were instructed to drive through neighborhoods finding problems before council members did. I didn't realize how conditioned I became to look for problems until I asked permission to switch it up. I took my bike out on non-busy mornings and left positive notes on residents' doors for neighbors demonstrating pride. People are used to only hearing from the city when there is a problem, so I thought it would be fun. I planned on spending two to three hours. Instead, I ran out within 45 minutes. I had been so conditioned to look for problems that I wasn't paying attention to everyone who maintained their property. It was so encouraging.

Residents, too, can be conditioned only to see the negative. Every meeting I attended in one neighborhood was nearly identical for six years—the same complaints, misinformation, and personal attacks. One of their complaints was a lack of participation. Who would guess that people don't return to meetings and listen to the same five people complain year after year? Our summer interns took a different approach. They created a short video using their mobile phones. They asked a few people in the neighborhood what they liked about their neighborhood. It was such a positive experience. Others, outside the meeting, enjoyed their neighbors. We discovered that Mr. Sydney and his wife raised two daughters with master's degrees. These were the kind of stories that no one ever got the chance to share, much less celebrate in their meetings. The interns edited the comments to a two-minute snippet, and we showed the video at a meeting. It was great. At least temporarily, it changed the atmosphere from seeing themselves as helpless victims to people capable of producing success stories.

About my sixth year working for the city, our office had a new intern named Raven Bland. She was smart, a published poet, energetic, passionate, caring, and funny. To my embarrassment, she was from the same neighborhood mentioned above. We didn't know she existed because we had never bothered to look. Maintaining positive tension sometimes means challenging neighborhoods to look at themselves differently.

4. *Practice mutual accountability.*

Government can be slow—like any organization that involves so many egos and is responsible for the entire population within its jurisdiction with competing agendas. Government officials make promises that they later can't keep. Being cautious of time, place, and audience, employees who own it are far better at building trust. Employees will make mistakes. It is best to own them. When a local non-profit in 2009 conducted a representative sample survey of 1,997 people in the Hampton Roads region, local government employees held higher trust levels than the local T.V. news, newspaper, and elected representatives.[108] The public expects employees to tell the truth.

This is sometimes where marketing and communications are confused. Marketing and communication are not the same. As a government employee, I consider it my responsibility to do my job with integrity and competence; I have never viewed managing the City's brand as a priority. Honesty is the best brand, whether it fits the carefully constructed messaging statements or not. The money spent on marketing consultants, website redesign, brand architecture, marketing videos, and trademarked logos give an organization a sharp appearance. Ultimately, they aren't worth jack crap if residents don't trust the people behind them. Without transparent leadership, marketing can be to communication what porn is to intimacy. Integrity is worth more in the long run.

Residents need transparent communication with their government. In one example, the official message years back was that budget cuts didn't affect services. Most line workers in city government knew differently. It was refreshing when later city leaders publicly stated that Norfolk was behind on infrastructure and services. Trust comes from truthfulness, integrity, and reliability, not marketing gimmicks, technology, or carefully scripted messaging points.

A neighborhood begged for planters and won them under a signed agreement that neighbors would maintain them. The planters didn't last long before residents grew tired of weeding them. Imbalanced accountability is destructive. Residents destroy city facilities, parks, and public spaces because, after all, doesn't the city pay people to take care of them? Trust is indispensable if government workers are to hold neighborhoods mutually accountable.

5. Share resources for small wins.

One of the bookmarks on my office web browser is news coverage of the Bat-kid in San Fransisco. The City of San Fransisco came together to make child cancer survivor Miles Scott's wish of being Batman's sidekick for a day come true. The love of superheroes in our culture taps into a childhood dream and a primal urge to be a protector, fight for something worthwhile, make a difference, and be admired. In communities, I encounter frustrated residents who want to be a superhero to their families and communities. They want to fight for their child's school. They want to fight for safety. They want to fight to preserve the personality of their neighborhood. Sharing resources helps residents be the heroes they want to be, one small win at a time.

6. *Use Bridge Builders.*

Bridge builders are of irreplaceable value. Knowing a relational gap exists, finding neighborhood influencers who can bridge the gap is helpful. When I began an urban career, it was painfully obvious that I would struggle to relate to street youth. I'm White, from a peaceful neighborhood in the country, dislike sports, and like bluegrass music. I am an introverted bookworm, and I was dressed (at the time) in jeans and a disproportionate number of plaid, flannel shirts. I had virtually nothing in common with those growing up on the streets of Chicago or Pittsburgh. The only way I could overcome my relational retardation was to build relationships with bridge builders who could connect with the people I couldn't.

Bridge builders are the people with whom more transparent, profound conversations are possible. The public usually prefers diplomatic brevity in meetings. However, diplomatic brevity doesn't replace behind-the-scenes explanations that go into greater detail about issues. Understanding relationships with bridge builders and negotiating behind the scenes prevents many conflicts from boiling over.

7. *Keep showing up in love.*

Harlem Children's Zone is a wonderful success story of a neighborhood transformation that created a cradle-to-college pipeline with wrap-around services to help children succeed. Purpose Built Communities, based in Atlanta, is another remarkable turnaround story of an impoverished public-housing project turned into a thriving community.

One similarity is that they both consume enormous resources. Harlem Children's Zone's budget is up to $100 million annually. Warren Buffet supports Purpose Built Communities. Most community police officers, teachers, social workers, code inspectors, and neighborhood development specialists do not have a $100 million budget to pour into single neighborhoods. Many find themselves paying for supplies out of their own under $50,000 per year salary.

Sparing some miraculous intervention by a philanthropist, many neighborhoods who need it have little hope of becoming a Purpose Built Community. Many don't have the leadership and networks to be a Harlem Children's Zone. Many aren't on the radar to compete for H.U.D. funding. The workers responsible for these neighborhoods usually have dozens of other communities. Dr. Peterman's book was a source of encouragement because it shared case studies that more closely resembled reality.

In his speech to a joint session of Congress, Vaclav Havel described democracy as a horizon that can be approached but never attained. [109] This is not for lack of trying. The country has made many improvements since Jacob Reis' 1890 coverage of New York's slums, but the same problems of slumlords, building maintenance, and unhealthy social conditions are still around.[110] New papers will be written, new policies will be proposed, and new laws will be passed every year. They will all rely on a given set of assumptions. In every community, frontline workers fill the gap between those assumptions and reality. Every place has its version of Mr. Happypants. There are fewer than there would be because of good employees who maintain a creative tension. They are friendly, but they don't parent neighborhoods. On the contrary, they are intentional about keeping ownership with communities.

Section 3: Getting Along in the Country and the City

Empathy - Building Understanding over Beer and BBQ

Key Idea: The nation is big enough for government intervention and self-reliance.

Approximately 258 miles northwest of Norview Community Center, where Mr. Happypants spread his love and cheer, is the Ringgold Ruritan building. The Ringgold Ruritan building is an old, two-floor schoolhouse from 1921 where my grandfather went to school and later served as a community center. Ringgold is a rural village outside Hagerstown, Maryland. The contrast between the two centers may offer a helpful perspective for building empathy toward the two cultures surrounding them. They also prove that our nation is big enough for government intervention and self-reliance.

The Ringgold building doesn't have central air conditioning. It's wooden floors creak and show the wear of grit, gravel, high heels, work boots, table legs, and chairs abasing its surface for 100 years. It smells of dust that has settled into cracks and crevices that a broom doesn't reach. When the county schools finished with it in 1954, the Ringgold Ruritan Club took it over as a community center.

Despite its rickety appearance, it is full of terrific memories. It was the site of baby showers, wedding showers, anniversaries, and funeral meals for years. They held oyster dinners, a strawberry festival, and auctions on Labor Day and Memorial Day. My parents got to know each other at one oyster supper in the late sixties. My great-grandparents had their 50th-anniversary party there. We went there for the meal after Aunt Louise's funeral.

The all-volunteer club maintained it. They painted it when it needed painting, cleaned it when it was dirty, paid for repairs, and raised money for a few upgrades now and then, like a wheelchair ramp or a playground in the eighties. It was a model of neighborly cooperation.

My favorite memory was the annual Ruritan corn day while spending summers on my grandfather's dairy farm. My grandfather and uncle grew Silver Queen sweet corn and donated 1200 ears to the Ruritan Club. Our family started at about 7:00 a.m., picking corn using five-gallon buckets and dumping them into a pickup truck. My work boots and pant legs got wet from the dew-drenched fields. Around 8:00 a.m., we drove a full pickup to the schoolhouse and met other families from the community: the Fryes, Fosters, Bayers, Newcomers, and others. There were people of all ages, including my younger cousins. There we husked, cooked, cooled, and cut the corn for freezing.

In Ringgold, community life predated modern media technology with countless entertainment options behind screens in temperature-controlled houses. Food was a common relational currency of community. In Ringgold, Grandma and Pappy shared sweet corn or homemade ice cream. Uncle Bill Fager shared raspberries from his raspberry bushes. Others shared apples they picked up at Lewis's or Ivy Hill orchards around the bend. If you drove to the strawberry patch, you picked some to share. Grandma and others usually baked or cooked extra to give away. Someone in the community usually had a need.

Sadly, rural life in Ringgold is slowly fading into history. The old-timers have passed. Urban sprawl from Baltimore and D.C. continues to creep nearer. The hazy glow of a grocery store, Lowes, Walmart, Applebee's, and a new string of national chains in nearby Rouzerville, Pennsylvania, replaced the pitch-black, starry sky that I knew and loved. New residents from the city and suburbs build houses on former farmland and then complain about the manure smell.

In my office are binders, handbooks, manuals, and booklets on how to be good neighbors, solve neighborhood problems, or do neighborhood projects. Some are as long as 80 pages. Curiously, the neighbors in Ringgold, with only high school educations, didn't need a manual or a government PowerPoint presentation. It was just who they were and how they lived.

Returning 258 miles southeast, the much larger and newer Norview Community Center results from the persevering advocacy of neighbors like Margaret and Larry Hoots, Walter Dickerson, and Bev Sell. Though small and frail in physical stature with an 80-plus-year-old frame, Mrs. Hoots' personality was as strong as ever. I made the mistake of calling Mrs. Hoots a "former" Marine. She quickly corrected me in her gentle but firm way: there are no "former" Marines. Once a Marine, always a Marine. She liked to fist-bump people at the community center and share a country saying from her native, rural North Carolina.

The Hoots and the others were instrumental in holding the city to its promise to rebuild a community center after another closed to build a Walmart. As mentioned earlier, Norview Community Center cost $7 million to build in 2009. It has a gymnasium, a fitness room with over 20 pieces of exercise equipment, a dance studio, an art studio with a kiln, a mini library, a multipurpose room with a commercial kitchen, two computer labs, a teen room, a game room, and offices. It is adjacent to an elementary school that uses the gym daily. If I had any, I would trust my kids with the dedicated workers who staff the center. One worker, Tongia, rightly described the center as a second home for many children. She knew kids and parents by name. Many working-class families with single-parent households or dual earners can't afford pricey before or aftercare. Center staff are often on the front lines to offer encouragement when families are struggling. Marsha Bowe greeted everyone at the front desk with a smile. She saw it as a way to help parents. Sharita was proudest of making kids smile. Janelle Henry was the proudest of challenging kids to excel through sports and moved on to supervise another center.

Structural Differences

The two community centers are microcosms of my divided life and a divided nation. The center in a low-density community is small, offers few programs, has a high degree of ownership, and is entirely self-sufficient from government. The center in a higher-density neighborhood is much larger, offers professionally run programs, and is almost wholly dependent on government. One is majority (or perhaps exclusively) White people. The other is majority Black people. They represent two different ways of viewing government. Self-sufficiency and independence from government are a higher priority among those who used the Ringgold Ruritan. Government services are a higher priority among most who use Norview Community Center.

As vastly different as they are, both community centers represent the best attributes of American community life. I love them both. Neighborly character is found in both, and neither is better than the other. Community happens in both, and both centers are places to meet terrific people who invest in others' lives.

They also have more in common than is first visible. People at Norview Community Center like barbecue. So do people in Ringgold. My cousin Andrew welded a portable barbecue pit. Many people in Norfolk like beer. If you haven't listened to country music, drinking is popular in the country, too. If ordinary people from both localities sat down over barbecue and listened to each others' lives, they would probably like each other. People would talk about food, football, kids, military service, world events, pop culture, movies, favorite vacation spots, cars, or home improvement projects. When people start with relationships and commonalities, they relate directly to each other as individuals and fellow human beings. They begin to understand each other and build empathy.

Being from the country but having a city career, one of my heartaches is the bitter divisions between the two. I feel a deep grief when those direct relationships are missing or too shallow for deeper understanding. A polarizing dynamic happens as people relate to each other through groups, experts, media personalities, and professional representatives. The dynamic changes from relating to each other as individual human beings to adversarial us-versus-them groups.

The friction between rural and urban is nothing new. In 1795, Thomas Jefferson wrote that the Federalists, the chief opponents to his views, appeared to have more political power, because they congregated in cities, had concentrated wealth, and commanded the day's newspapers.[111] Instead, his party represented more agricultural interests and was more dispersed over a wider area. Booker T. Washington considered cities to be full of temptations.

Living in cities for over 25 years has brought about considerable adjustments in my perspective and lifestyle. We hung our underwear on the clothesline in the country. I'm sure my neighbors in Norfolk are not interested in seeing my underwear. Increasing density brings more rules, greater dependency on government services, and more traffic.

The following chapters are my imperfect attempt to bridge my upbringing, family, and friends in the country with my 25-year career, friends, and colleagues in cities. If relations weren't strained enough, Donald Trump came along. The mere mention of his name in a conversation brings out emotions in my family and friends. Which emotions depends on which friends I'm with.

The two most significant challenges in writing this section have been 1) to write in such a way as to be understood by two vastly different audiences while keeping friends in both areas and 2) to emphasize finding the good in people. The only way I know to do so is to write as a fellow struggler, not an expert.

Experience is King

Of paramount importance is the power of experience. Experience is king. Images are queen. Rhetoric, white papers, and seminars are distant cousins. It reminds me of the Taco Bell problem. Growing up in Cumberland, Hispanic cuisine was Taco Bell, Chi Chis, and boxed taco kits from the grocery store. I thought all that Latinos ate were tacos and burritos. Later, during summer breaks in college, I stayed with a young couple, Tom and Lou Michael. Lou was of Cuban descent from Miami and introduced me to Mojo Criollo chicken, black beans with rice, and flan. The Almengor family, from Central America, introduced me to fried plantains. When I did a rotation in Chicago with a Hispanic church, the Rivers family's tacos were much better than Taco Bell or the boxed dinners, and their homemade tamales were terrific. Growing up in Cumberland, however, Taco Bell and Chi Chis were all we knew. The same is valid for understanding others. If the only impression of others is from the T.V. or movies, it is probably not realistic.

Experience shapes everything. Consider police and gun issues. When I think about growing up, it is hard to think about adverse interactions with law enforcement because I don't remember *any* interactions besides directing traffic around accidents or parking at the fair. There was very little crime, certainly nothing violent.

In the early 2000s, while I was living in Pittsburgh, Dad was attacked inside the church building in small-town Cumberland by a juvenile escapee from a forestry camp. The youth jumped him from behind with shoestrings around Dad's neck and a shiv, but the youth was from Baltimore, not local.

Aside from the occasional vandalized mailbox on the farm, I don't remember any crime. Besides, there was no expectation that the police would arrive in time if there were an incident. This explains why almost everyone I knew had guns. In the country, a noisy, pump-action shotgun is considered more of a deterrent than a block watch sticker. Gun safety was a rite of passage. Newer generations have gun safes, but my grandparents had unloaded guns all over the house. I once saw them behind the bathroom door. The West Virginia county next to us closed schools when deer season opened. Our family doesn't have a negative view of the police because we had no experience. Likewise, our family has a positive view of guns because we didn't know anyone murdered.

That changed when I moved into the city. I had to start a file folder for crime reports. Part of my assigned duties as a work-study student in Chicago was cleaning urine off the stoop and picking up drug needles in the side yard of the offices. I had tools stolen and once stopped to call the police for a woman screaming for help from her boyfriend in the car.

In Pittsburgh, a woman hit and scratched me in the face. I discovered she was living with a relative recently arrested for murder. They also had a fish tank with curiously large goldfish, which I found out had been stolen from a public park. We replaced four vandalized windows over ten years, had gravel cleaned out of the church van's gas tank, and cleaned up eggs and other projectiles around Halloween or other holidays. Gunshots and shootings were so frequent I gave up calling during the summer. I had a Palm Pilot device stolen during church services, and a T.V. went missing from the wall downstairs. I got back from visiting family after Easter, and someone, presumably drunk, had driven through the fence, spun out in the yard, hit the tree, and drove off, doing $650 damage. Another time, an illegal four-wheeler ATV ran a Stop sign by my house and hit my car. I later watched from my kitchen window as one of the drug dealers pulled out a gun and started shooting. The DEA eventually came in full tactical gear and automatic rifles and evicted them, after which it was more peaceful. I was making lunch one day and saw three young women with the same make and model as my neighbor's car pull up next to her's. When I looked out again, they were stealing a tire off my neighbor's car to fix a flat on their's.

Over several months, we received at least a dozen harassing, profanity-laced phone calls with racial epithets from someone with a mental illness. It progressed to sending us nasty letters, a used sanitary napkin, and dollar bills with writing that included "God is a stupid mother f———-", "Jesus was in the KKK," and a lot more language about body parts, blow jobs, my wife, and the n-word. The police eventually visited him, and he apologized. On another occasion, one December, a man pounded at my front door and started yelling in my face after I opened it. Someone had told him I had stolen his daughter's puppy. Although those are the highlights, suffice it to say my own crime experience grew dramatically after moving to the city.

Crime and crime victims became more personal in other ways. I started meeting people who had lost relatives murdered by guns. When I lived in Chicago, it was widely known that there was corruption within the police department; I knew colleagues who experienced it firsthand. When I moved to Pittsburgh, the Pittsburgh Police were under a consent decree from a Federal judge for misbehavior. In both locations, most officers were ethical, trustworthy, brave, and kindhearted, but an average citizen cannot know who is who. Even as a White man interacting with police, I don't know whether it is Sheriff Andy Griffith or Officer Tony Testosterone, the trigger-happy Rambo wanna-be. I've seen both. I've also met police officers who have the customer service skills of rocks. If you live somewhere where crime is higher, you naturally have more police interactions, both good and bad. Experience is king in shaping all these viewpoints.

Relationships vs. Representatives

At one point in my career with the City of Norfolk, my experience included having a chain of command above me that was all African American. To the extent that I knew the higher officials, they were all intelligent, humble leaders. They were people of integrity, who took good care of me, I admire, and positively shaped me. James Rogers is probably the government employee I most want to be like.

For a few years, our team only had one other White member. I related to the Black members of the team as colleagues and friends, not "the Black community." None of them ever claimed to speak as representatives of the Black or Hispanic community, and it is comedic to think that a dork like me would represent the White community. My affection for them and so many residents we work with runs deeper than skin or culture. They care about me, protect me from criticism, guide me, and do me the courtesy of laughing at my dry sense of humor. Unquestionably, some weaponize race and victimhood for unhealthy gain, but they are far from the norm in my world.

These relationships are a tremendous blessing. If it were not for them, I would be completely confused by the national experts and media. I can't keep up with the latest trends and ever-changing terms. The above relationships provide me (and hopefully I to them) a better understanding of middle America, and we both struggle with being misrepresented by extreme views in the media.

The problem is that friends and family in rural areas that are overwhelmingly White do not have those relationships. They relate to "the Black community", urban America, and political liberals through media figures like Al Sharpton, gangsta rap, Rachel Dolezal, and the riots that they see on T.V. Conversely, I hear conversations among city folk who relate to White, conservative, rural residents through Donald Trump, David Duke, Barney Fife, and Confederate flags.

Neighborly relations are further complicated because it is nearly impossible to have a meaningful conversation about issues in public. Media personalities, politicians, pundits, and podcasters dominate the public space. Like oxygen to fire, brand identities are fueled by finding targets to keep supporters angry, fired up, and directing money in their direction. Passion is used as an exemption for rudeness. All the labels come out. If you make yourself vulnerable in public, predators will attack. I feel safer skipping through the woods in brown, furry clothes and a big, fluffy, white cotton ball tied to my rear during West Virginia's deer season than having those conversations in public or at conferences.

Humanizing Government Intervention

Being from the country, my standard motto is that less government is better. Seeing firsthand government's inefficiency, lack of focus for very long, slow speed, and neglecting the important to chase the squeaky wheel, I still lean in that direction in theory. On this matter, though, I've had to face my hypocrisy. I benefit from a 30-year amortized mortgage. I hold bank accounts insured by the FDIC. The Federal Reserve partially protects me from inflation and fraudulent banks. I drive on expressways and have access to emergency services with a call to 911. Pre-Covid-19, I rode an elevator at least 20 times a week in a mid-rise office tower without fear because of building inspectors. I eat inspected meat without worrying that it is roadkill. All these are government interventions.

My experience with others in the city has also changed me more than white papers and conferences. When residents of a suburban-style neighborhood objected to a 2018 proposed low-income housing tax credit rental project coming to their neighborhood, some talked during a public hearing about "getting their guns out when those people move into the neighborhood." It felt more like 1958 than 2018.

It pains me to hear very un-neighborly comments about urban liberals or Black people made by rural residents. I wish they could meet people I've met. For example, I wish people in the country could meet Mrs. Shirley Butts, a dear senior in my neighborhood. Mrs. Butts is not likely to make anyone defensive. She is older, slightly bent over, and has a soft, round, aged face. Her power is not in physical stature or rhetorical prowess. It is in the strength of her story and the grace of her words, movements, and actions. She doesn't sling around hot political buzzwords, but her story speaks forcefully. I met her at a civic league meeting.

Mrs. Butts grew up as a little girl in segregated Norfolk. On trips downtown to pay bills for her mother, she couldn't use the restrooms, water fountains, or buy a drink in the White businesses. She would have to hold her bladder, which sometimes made it a painful trip. She attended segregated, less-funded schools, some known for not having good heat in the winter. When she began college, she wasn't allowed to attend the Norfolk extension of William and Mary, now Old Dominion University. Rules changed, and she later graduated from Old Dominion in 2001 in her sixties with a Bachelor of Science in Business Administration after taking one class per semester for fifteen years while she worked full time.

She holds no ill will toward White people and not an ounce of bitterness. In her same seniors' group at the Sherwood Forest Recreation Center, I met others like her who rode in the back of the bus or transferred to the back of the train in D.C. when coming from New York to Richmond. I met others who were the first to integrate local hospitals and offices. If it weren't for government intervention, Mrs. Butts would still be required to use separate drinking fountains, bathrooms, and be barred from graduating at Old Dominion.

An 18-year-old woman I'll call Monique personalized the public housing challenge. A woman from our church in Pittsburgh asked for help moving her goddaughter, Monique. Monique didn't know her father. Her mother had a drug problem, so social services placed Monique and her sister in foster care. Like many others, Monique thought she found love and security with boys who paid attention to her. Instead, she became a teen mother twice by the time she turned 18. She aged out of the foster care system and had nowhere else to go. They placed her in St. Clair Village, a project that opened in

1953 and initially housed 1,083 families.[112] It was barracks-style housing with two-story walk-ups.

The first thing that caught my attention was a mural dedicated to all the residents killed by violence in the neighborhood. The second thing that stood out was how isolated it was. The housing authority sited it on top of a hill. I have no idea what it looked like in 1953, but there was no serious retail anywhere close in the mid-2000s. Imagine an 18-year-old mother of a toddler and an infant without a car, catching at least one bus, possibly more, to a grocery store and then making the return trip with bags of groceries.

The buildings were concrete blocks, well-constructed and sturdy, but not very inviting. They were to architects what canned ham is to chefs. Monique had no furnishings except that which people had given her, all second-hand. She had no curtains, so she used sheets. Whoever donated her microwave didn't bother to clean it out first. It had years of yellowish popcorn grease and exploded tomato sauce in it. The only equally disgusting microwave was the employee microwave on the third floor of Norfolk's City Hall.

Many people speak disparagingly of all people in public housing as if they are all lazy gangsters. Those who think so lack understanding of all the residents and how they end up there. It is far easier to stand outside and criticize if you don't have to figure out what to do about the thousands of cases like Monique. There are far more criticisms than solutions for seniors, the mentally challenged, and young mothers like Monique, who have nowhere else to go. A visit to public housing will shed any myths about them being luxurious. Monique is one of thousands of examples of when the government is involved because no one else is acting on a scale comparable to the problem.

Humanizing Rural Self-Reliance

Now, to the country. Just as public housing is looked down upon, so is rural culture, as fewer people understand it. James Gimpel and Kimberly Karnes summarize it well: "The unflattering views that urban sophisticates have come to harbor toward rural Americans and vice versa, have dredged a wide moat. City dwellers evidently believe that rural Americans are dumb, boorish, and bigoted."[113] To be fair, some are. Most are not.

There is room in a nation as big as ours for rural independence. It equally saddens me when urban dwellers, journalists, and scholars use the great American comparison contest to make sweeping, un-neighborly generalizations about rural dwellers and ignore rural independence as a strength. Places like Ringgold reinforce Robert Putnam's claim that social capital trends higher in small towns and that residents are "more altruistic, honest, and trusting than other Americans".[114] They are more likely to obtain food by growing fresh fruits and vegetables or trading with others.[115] When a local history magazine in Washington County, Maryland, interviewed old-time Ringgold residents, they concluded:

> As we interviewed these folks, who all grew up through the Depression of the late 1920s and the 1930s, it is clear that to them happiness was not predicated on wealth, but on love of family and neighbors, content with what they had. Whether they realized it or not, they mastered the concept that 'more is never enough'.[116]

Research shows rural residents are more self-reliant, are frequently self-employed in their businesses, and see themselves as independent entrepreneurs.[117] Low-income residents in rural areas are more likely to rely on a barter economy.[118] They have wells for water and septic tanks for sewage. They often take their garbage to the dump themselves.

Studies from the U.S., Switzerland, and New Zealand show that farmers value autonomy as part of their identity.[119] I grieve when I read articles attributing rural resistance to large social programs exclusively to ignorance or racism. Some of racism's combatants calcify soft prejudice into a hardened bias when they misidentify rural values, misjudge motives, insult rural dwellers, and label them. Experts who make such broad generalizations have little understanding of how deeply rural dwellers value self-sufficiency and independence, even if sometimes to their detriment.

Rural independence runs deep. Justice Clarence Thomas, a descendant of West African slaves and raised in segregated Georgia, shares the influence his grandfather's self-reliance had on him. His grandfather, who raised Thomas, had a house in Savannah but bought a small farm in the country. He grew food during the summer, which he shared with others. Justice Thomas attributes part of his conservative streak to his rural upbringing.

Small towns nationwide celebrate self-sufficiency through festivals that raise money for their volunteer fire departments. Bridgeville, Delaware, celebrates Apple Scrapple with T.S. Smith's orchards and Rapa Scrapple. In Sharptown, Maryland, the annual 24-day festival is so popular that the volunteer fire department invested in carnival rides. Their specialty is oyster fritters. Preston County, West Virginia, combines the annual Buckwheat Festival with the county fair. It dates back over 80 years to the Great Depression when the lowly buckwheat helped sustain the community. The dining hall packs with people dining on buckwheat cakes and sausage as local teen volunteers serve. Behind the dining hall are exhibit halls showing off area youth's hard work. Rural residents raise animals, can fruit, bake blue ribbon cakes, grow prized crops, and sew quilts. Much more than just carnivals, these local festivals showcase their rural independence and self-sustaining skills.

My cousin Jeni's four blond-haired daughters are rural youth participating in those fairs. Jeni has a warm, bubbly personality whose energy could only be contained on a wide-open farm. Feeling her enthusiasm for farming, nature, and animals only takes a brief conversation. The family creamery run by my aunt, uncle and cousin is across the road. My cousin Andrew's house, where our grandparents lived, sits across a creek and dates to the late 1780s. He lives with his wife, Jacqueline, and his son. Another cousin, Katie, married into another farming family across the county. They opened a cheesery and farm store. Another cousin, Kimberly, joined the Navy, married a co-worker, and settled in Pennsylvania. Farming shattered the glass ceiling for women decades ago.

Taking friends in the city to their farm would be a fun adventure. I would love to watch colleagues from the city in sandals and bottles of hand sanitizer slop and bed calves with the farm girls. Slopping calves is so named because buckets of sloshing milk are messy. Bedding entails placing fresh straw in the pens to keep the calves dry, clean, and warm. The smell on the farm might catch some by surprise, but, in all fairness, it is no worse than the men's bathroom in our offices. Often, the farm smells better.

Our Herbst ancestors immigrated from Germany after 1860. They settled on the mountainside in Wolfsville, Maryland, before coming off the mountain in 1918. My grandfather borrowed against a life insurance policy to buy his first 50 acres, eight cows, two workhorses, other small animals, and some machinery. By the time he retired, he farmed 500 acres.

Jeni's girls will be at least the sixth generation on this continent whose chores include feeding and bedding calves every morning and every evening, 365 days a year. The girls show cows and goats at the annual Washington County Fair. They play sports and take music lessons like kids across the country. Until a recent upgrade to robots, Jeni began most of her adult life milking cows at 3:30 a.m. and again twelve hours later, finishing up after 6:00 p.m. She handles all the animals. The adult cows have ear tags that bear a number and their name. Like a teacher in a classroom, Jeni calls cows by name. For them, the cows, goats, ponies, dogs, chickens, and other animals are like having 200 pets. The girls' dad, Justin, is a fireman and handles the crops.

The farm continues to win awards for its conservation efforts. As farming techniques evolved, the farm evolved with it. The girls' grandparents, Dave and Betsy Herbst (my aunt and uncle) took out a loan in 2011 and opened a creamery with a small country store, petting zoo, and corn maze to support the growing family. They continue to contribute to their community and are very involved in agricultural education and hosting tours nearly year-round.

Farming Economics

When I hear city folk talk about life in the country being easier, I wonder what life they refer to. It has its rewards, but it is a hard life. Farming is capital-asset intensive (land, buildings, equipment), but capital assets don't pay monthly bills. Like most other businesses, agriculture has shifted to favor big corporations who can work on an economy of scale. Driving down consumer prices is good for the consumers reading this book but aids in the decline of smaller, local farms. Farms like Misty Meadows are landlocked by urban sprawl and have few expansion opportunities. Some of their farmer neighbors have moved further west to Ohio and beyond to support their families. Technology has improved efficiency, but the market is far more competitive. When evaluating profit margins, the U.S.D.A. places 70.1% of all U.S. farms in the high-risk zone. Small family farms show greater financial risk. Large farms show less financial risk. [120] Of nearly 2 million family farms, 946,257 report farming as their principal occupation.

The industrialization of agriculture is transforming rural America. University of Missouri researchers document how farmers feel ever more constrained by big food distributors and retailers. Companies increasingly dictate every aspect of farming. This lessens farmer autonomy, creates financial constraints for the farmer, reduces skill levels, decreases biodiversity, adds to environmental problems, and changes farmers' perceptions of themselves. They become cogs in a machine rather than independent entrepreneurs, which, in turn, impacts their ethics.[121]

My cousins inherited land, a herd, old equipment, and opportunities others may not have had, but it has not been free nor easy. When my grandparents purchased the main farm in 1959, it only had to feed five people. Income from this farm now must support 11 family members. The entire time my dad was growing up, his family only took one vacation because they had to work the farm.

With farm life comes indebtedness. Equipment costs on a farm add up quickly. Here is a quick internet search for the cost of common equipment. A used combine starts at around $300,000. Combines take fuel. A smaller John Deere combine has a 250-gallon fuel tank. At $5.06 a gallon for diesel fuel, that's $1264 for every fill-up. A small used tractor may start at around $50,000. Add to these planters, mowers, tedders, rakes, balers, a manure spreader, milking equipment, a veterinarian, and costs climb quickly. A serious concern for my cousins is how to stay solvent financially: managing debt, managing risk, staying ahead of breakdowns, droughts, and floods, putting money away for college, and making a life for their kids.

In their case, there is some limited benefit to urban sprawl. My cousins benefit from better schools, access to technology, and the healthcare accompanying growth. However, most social indicators are worse in rural areas. Political power is diffused, and rural problems don't attract as much attention. Some mark the Kennedy election when the national economy and political power shifted from rural to urban.[122] There is more poverty in rural areas than in urban areas. Healthcare options are severely limited, and overall health indicators are worse in rural America. Rural counties can't offer the diverse specialized programs that urban areas provide. States can offer online courses but only where broadband is accessible.

Conflicting Emotions

I have very conflicting emotions in this tug-of-war between government intervention and self-reliance. The federal government takes one month's salary via income taxes every year I work. State and local governments take another month's salary through income and property taxes. I feel good about taxes when I interact with military members, look at the majestic Navy ships in Norfolk's waterways, drive on expressways, or see the potholes on my street repaired. In cases like Monique's, I'm happy about the resources government makes available. Stories like Ms. Butts stir my compassion. And, although I've worked hard, I can never claim to have pulled myself up by bootstraps alone.

On the other hand, I feel a mild rage toward government when I observe all the wasted time and money spent accommodating egos or those who abuse every resource but demand more. I'm infuriated by the sense of entitlement I hear and all the people who litter, vandalize, and abuse public spaces because they know someone else is responsible for cleaning up. Some days I want to say, "Screw'em all!"

My emotions are further complicated when children are involved. How does government avoid waste and yet help children whose parents are idiots? In the end, there is no perfect solution. Government requires constant adjustment. The fight in this book isn't against any policy but against the greed, materialism, and self-centeredness that drive both the need for government programs and their abuse. What I offer now are two ways to generate more empathy.

Protect a compassionate heart.

The first request is to protect a compassionate heart from resentment and jealousy. The Mrs. Butts and the Moniques protect my heart by reminding me that struggles are real for many beyond the few who I would pay to move to another city.

Jealousy is never far away. On the days when I sit at each of the 13 red lights on my way to work or am exhausted having done nothing but sit in meetings all day, I find myself jealous of farm-life perks like no traffic, independence, nature, solitude, driving tractors, physical activity, and having my own creamery. Oddly enough, I've never been jealous of the seven-day-a-week work, fluctuating income, equipment breakdowns, weather dependency, financial stress, and the hours accompanying the farm or creamery.

Jealousy and resentment blind us to others' struggles. It takes intentional willfulness to protect a compassionate heart. Economics is competitive. Neighborliness is not. Economists, sociologists, politicians, and others break everyone down into percentages and ratios of who has access to scarce resources. People become viewed as balance sheets—add up advantages and subtract disadvantages. Human empathy and compassion don't face that limitation. I'm not required to limit my compassion to 65% for person A and 35% for person B. Acknowledging one person's struggles doesn't have to diminish someone else's.

Turn off the Screens

The second ask is to turn off the screens. *Farmland* is a 2014 documentary about six young farm families across the U.S. sponsored by the U.S. Farmers and Ranchers Alliance. Based on the farmers I know, the film gave a meaningful, realistic, behind-the-scenes glimpse into farm life's risk, criticism, unpredictability, hard work, and ups and downs. At the same time, the film also demonstrates a part of the problem. Of the 946,257 family farms where farming is the primary occupation, the producers did not use one family of color. Many of us from the city instantly recognize the lack of diversity because not seeing it seems odd. In an otherwise helpful film, it missed connecting with the non-White population.

A communion meditation at a rural church is another example. The speaker implored the audience to watch Fox News and drink prune juice to stay regular. I still don't know what Fox News and bowel movements had to do with communion, but herein lies a huge part of the problem. Before opening one's mouth (or keyboard) to make more incendiary comments, more people need to turn off their screens, whether X (which everyone still thinks of as Twitter), Facebook, Fox News, CNN, or MSNBC, and meet each other. It is always easier to criticize people that you've never met. It is difficult to understand why we allow ourselves as Americans to see each other purely through political lenses. It is equally difficult to comprehend why people will spend hours on social media manically arguing issues without changing anyone's heart except for the narcissistic delusion that the world can't survive without our opinions.

Compliments are a better start than criticisms if empathy is an authentic value. Looking for strengths is more important than pointing out weaknesses. People who are the most critical of others are usually the most sensitive. If good people on both sides met each other and looked at each other through strengths, they would be far less susceptible to the misleading, nut-picking, sensationalized stories by those who have a self-interest in keeping the nation divided. Although I prefer a milkshake over alcohol, I'm convinced meeting people over beer and BBQ would be far more productive at building neighborly empathy than more tweets or op-ed pieces.

Healing Truth - Hearing through the Noise

Key Idea: Sometimes quiet voices and quiet places speak healing truth.

The state of divisiveness today makes me feel like I'm in a room with 50 TVs and radios blaring 50 different channels, all yelling different things. It is challenging to make sense of it all, reconcile competing voices, and separate what is worthy of attention from what will pass. Amongst all the yelling, sometimes quiet voices and quiet places speak healing truth.

The contest for truth is nothing new. Teddy Roosevelt recorded the bewildering number of contradicting claims given to the public in his fight for social justice. A conflict emerged over appointing a new Superintendent of Insurance in New York, an industry that Roosevelt wanted to reform over a hundred years before the A.I.G. bailout. Insurance companies published resolutions and open letters demanding the existing superintendent remain. Secretly, some men who signed those resolutions wrote to ask Roosevelt to remove him. Other opponents of reform covertly supported the most radical reformers, knowing that the more radical the radicals were, the more the general public would resist reform. Roosevelt identified pretend reformers who attempted to steer the public conversation toward divisive personal assaults and away from practical solutions. He criticized prominent newspapers controlled by private interests, which spread half-truths, misdirection, and outright lies.[123] Technology has accelerated our ability to communicate faster and broader since Roosevelt's day but has done nothing to make us more innately truthful.

When it comes to uncomfortable truths about race, I can say confidently what is least effective: wealthy academics, politicians, business leaders, entertainers, and athletes telling White families with working-class backgrounds that they are racists, ignorant, and need to confront their White privilege and fragility. There is a class barrier. It is like calling fat kids fat. Even when true, it isn't very productive. Jim Goad calls the class conflict "White trash vs. White cash."[124] One of Goad's complaints in his 255-page rant is, "It isn't the condo-owning East Village social theorist who die of black lung, it's the West Virginia miners."[125]

So why does uncomfortable truth from one person open my heart and from someone else shut me down? The quiet, healing voice of people who can get past assumptions, labels, sensationalism, and divisive showmanship is beneficial.

Ms. Alice Coles is one of those voices. Ms. Coles is from Virginia's Bayview community on Virginia's eastern shore, one of the few places where my rural background and urban life converge. Few people have heard of the predominantly African American community. Its mostly White neighbor on the West side of Route 13, Cape Charles, is more popular with its quaint bed and breakfasts, small-town boutiques, two PGA golf courses, luxury condos, and two marinas. There is also the popular Cherrystone campground nearby.

As late as 1994, homes in Bayview had no indoor plumbing—no kitchens or bathrooms. As Ms. Alice Coles put it, any room in the house could be a kitchen because there was no plumbing. Residents still carried buckets from a shared well and relied on outhouses. To iterate for clarity, this was the 1990s, not the 1890s. Most of the residents were said to be descendants of slaves. Along Bayview Circle sits Holmes Presbyterian Church, which dates to 1846. Ms. Coles asked me to pay attention to the door on the building's side, mere feet from the main entrance. It was the slave door.

Cape Charles grew as a ferry and hub. When the Bay Bridge and Tunnel opened in 1964, vehicular traffic replaced the ferry and the railroad. The area sank into decline. Outsiders largely ignored the area. That changed for lawmakers in 1994 when the state tried to locate a maximum-security prison in Bayview. Wealthier communities certainly didn't want it. Feeling ignored by state leaders until those leaders wished to place a prison in Bayview, fed-up residents organized the Bayview Citizens for Social Justice. They joined forces with nature advocacy groups to protect the eastern shore from the over-development that typified other beachfront localities, namely Virginia Beach and Norfolk. Notable architect and urban planner Maurice Cox became involved, provided the Bayview Citizens for Social Justice technical guidance, and helped navigate government bureaucracy. Their protest attracted much-needed attention. CBS News and later the *New York Times* picked up their story.

Following the Civil War period, workers from Bayview historically provided labor for nearby farms and seafood processing plants until those industries declined with increased mechanization on farms and pollution in the Chesapeake Bay. Their labor was no longer needed. Outsiders saw Bayview only as valuable enough to place a prison. With collective action and assistance from outside advisors, Bayview Citizens for Social Justice won the prison battle and obtained national, state, and local grants. They bought the proposed prison site, built a sewer system, rental units, single-family homes, a community center, a greenhouse, and farmed the remaining land.

They requested that the housing design include front porches and the houses face each other so that pre-existing social interactions between neighbors could continue.

Ms. Alice Coles was the most visible leader. She successfully built a coalition of technical advisers to assist Bayview. When I met with her in Bayview in April 2018, her experience and wisdom dealing with communities stood out. The still strong contrast between Cape Charles and Bayview also struck me. While the state planned a prison for Bayview, a private developer was already finalizing legal approvals to turn 2000 acres adjacent to Cape Charles into luxury housing and a resort for the wealthy. Cape Charles now has both Jack Nicklaus and Arnold Palmer golf courses from the early 2000s, along with luxury real estate to go with them.

Bayview is still struggling. When I met with Ms. Coles, they still farmed the field by hand and lacked modern equipment. "God is our irrigation system," she said. Some buildings built with assistance now have mismatched roof shingles, faded paint, and other signs of maintenance needs. Many renters who originally formed the community are gone and replaced with outsiders. Several ventures failed, like a sweet potato chip company. According to Coles, the culprit wasn't a lack of work ethic but a lack of business skills. They have farmers ready to work, carpenters who can build anything, and mechanics who can run any engine. Still, they don't have marketing skills, supply chain management, and web-based business development.

Andrew Carnegie described labor, business ability, and capital as the three-legs of business success. In simple, easy-to-understand terms, Ms. Coles indicated that Bayview had labor but lacked business ability and capital. What she said made perfect sense. Although I am not involved with Bayview, it explains why capital access programs, small business and minority contracting opportunities, scholarships, and entrepreneur training programs that Norfolk uses are so important.

Places like Bayview awaken a sense of neighborly compassion and realness in me more than national celebrities. I enjoyed spending an hour with Ms. Coles. She didn't use the big words and "isms" that experts and journalists love. She wasn't combative about inequality; she didn't have to be. It was right there in front of my eyes. The West side of Route 13 had two golf courses and luxury boutiques; the East side still had a few shacks and a church building with a slave door.

Civil Rights - a Cancelled T.V. Show?

A group of us sat in silent shock while discussing generational diversity during a class in Norfolk. The oldest in the group, a stately Black gentleman named Mr. Riggins, told how a White landowner shot his grandfather on the steps of a courthouse in South Carolina after the White man lost a case about property rights. Authorities never prosecuted the White landowner.

One hypothetical running through my mind is, "What if whites had stayed the civil rights course in the 1870s instead of giving up?" How would the nation look different today? John R. Lynch recounted the heartbreaking demise of civil rights following the Civil War and the diminution of hope by African Americans.[126] Some 360,000 soldiers, 40,000 of whom were Black, died fighting for the Union and an end to slavery. Their deaths and the victory of their surviving brothers-in-arms brought the Thirteenth through Fifteen Constitutional Amendments abolishing slavery, providing equal protection under the law, and the right to vote regardless of race, color, or previous condition of servitude.

In the 1870s, the first Black Americans held seats in the U.S. House of Representatives and the U.S. Senate, all Republicans, all from former slave-holding southern states. The 1870 census shows that Black Americans outnumbered whites in the southern states of Louisiana, Mississippi, and South Carolina. After being emancipated, Mississippian John R. Lynch rose through the political ranks and became speaker of the Mississippi House before being elected to Congress. By the time he entered the House during the 43rd Congress in 1873, there were seven Black Congressmen, and the number rose to eight in the 44th Congress of 1875, all Republicans. At one point, Lynch was even temporary chair of the Republican Convention.

Unfortunately, that was the zenith. As local control in the South was ceded back over to the states and the northern armies withdrew their protection, Whites began to return Black people to slave-like conditions through intimidation and legal maneuvering. Democrats held meetings with armed militiamen to threaten residents. The Ku Klux Klan threatened, maimed, and lynched Black people and those voting for Republicans. Southern states passed peonage laws that allowed Black people and others to be arrested for minor misdemeanors and auctioned out to private landholders to serve their sentence—essentially slavery 2.0.

Congress passed the Civil Rights Act of 1875, but the wind for civil rights had gone out of the sails. The executive branch didn't enforce it. By 1901, no African Americans held seats in the House or Senate. Industry helped win the war for the North, but it greatly expanded big corporations' reach, legal protections, and power. With the abuse of workers, attention shifted to labor and women's movements. It is like civil rights was once a popular T.V. show that eventually lost attention spans and faded into cancellation. The question remains:

Where would race relations be today if White people had not worn out and given up back then?

Quiet moments have changed my experience of history. Harriet Tubman's birthplace was in Dorchester County, Maryland, and the store in Bucktown, where she was permanently injured, is twenty minutes from where my dad now lives. Further North is where Frederick Douglass had been a slave. I stopped in Salisbury, Maryland, near the location of the 1931 lynching of Matthew Williams. I stepped silently through slave quarters at an old plantation outside Charleston, South Carolina, and at Appomattox Court House, Virginia. I visited the slave market in Savannah. I did a speed tour of the African American museum after class while in D.C. for training. Although the Lorraine Motel in Memphis was closed for maintenance when I was there, I was able to see from the street where King was assassinated. I toured the Equal Justice Initiative Memorial in Montgomery, Alabama, and stood at the bus stop where Rosa Parks boarded the bus.

I happened to begin Isabel Wilkerson's *The Warmth of Other Suns* while on vacation with my in-laws to Myrtle Beach. She told the history of African Americans' great migration from the rural South to the urban North. While in Myrtle Beach, I drove to the Freewoods Farm, a living museum demonstrating small, typical African American farms between 1865 and 1900. Workers farm by hand and with mules or horse labor. The farm was deserted when I arrived, so I was utterly alone with my thoughts and that awful South Carolina humidity. I tried placing myself in the shoes of the millions of slaves and sharecroppers who worked the land by hand under threat of starvation, beatings, or imprisonment. The soul-sucking humidity and the quiet solitude brought more clarity about the past than all the chatter elsewhere.

Our country's blemished past comes across in other ways. I once asked my neighbor Mrs. Ramirez's family about their history. I knew they were of Mexican heritage and asked if Mrs. Ramirez was a first or second-generation immigrant. They said neither. Their family never immigrated. Their hometown, Rio Grande City, was on the Rio Grande River. They were Mexican until the United States invaded Mexico in the Mexican-American War and claimed the territory. As Mrs. Ramirez's son, Danny, put it, the border moved; they didn't. Yet another embarrassing part of our history became personal. In all of these instances, there is no defense for what happened.

Other experiences revealed how much we can live in widespread denial. Southampton County, Virginia, was originally the home of Dred Scott and, before Scott, Nat Turner's slave rebellion. As I drove by cotton fields, it was a deceptively beautiful day complimented with a rainbow, giving no hint of the slaves who most likely cleared those fields initially. While visiting Courtland, Virginia (formerly named Jerusalem), where Turner was hung, I didn't see a historical marker. I saw a confederate monument rededicated in 1992 commemorating the men who fought the "Northern Invaders" in the "War of Northern Aggression." That deception could be so widespread and run for so long troubles me. It makes me wonder what popular cultural fads today are BS-smeared bologna.

Listening for Common Denominators

The commonalities between my background and Michelle Obama's are short and generic. We were born on the same planet and the same continent. We have both eaten at McDonald's. For a short time, we lived in the same city. The list of differences is much longer. I'm a White male who grew up in a rural, Republican area. She is a Black female who grew up in deep-blue Chicago. My family attended church every time the doors were open. Church was not a regular part of her childhood. I attended a small, largely unknown Lincoln Christian University. She attended Princeton and Harvard. You may have heard of them.

Despite the gulf of differences, there was something oddly bridging when reading Michelle Obama's book *Becoming*. I felt myself finding common denominators from listening to her struggles. I didn't know her father had M.S. I instantly felt a spark of empathy from watching friends and family with the disease. When she talked about Barak being attacked in his run for Congress by some of their own people, mainly out of jealousy, it resonated with me. Regardless of political party affiliation, I detest devilish critics who malign others' motives, assign guilt by association, or present false choices anytime they disagree. I could feel her frustration when she talked about turning off news networks because they sensationalized news and pretended to know others' motives. I share the same frustration.

Despite all the differences, Michelle Obama seemed relatable. This gives me a glimmer of hope that we can bridge more differences and be more respectful where we can't. This sharing of humanness has a profound bearing on how we understand each other.

Michelle Obama writes about wanting to be known for who she really is and not letting others define her inaccurately.[127] Elsewhere, she said, "I couldn't help but feel haunted by the ways I'd been criticized, by the people who'd made assumptions about me based on the color of my skin."[128] This is a powerful point of connection. I want the same thing: to be evaluated for who I am, not assumptions about my whiteness or rural background.

What Labels Apply?

Part of the comparison problem is wading through the labels. What labels apply to me? Am I trailer trash, country boy, or city slicker? There is a gap between who I want to be and who I am. The comparison trap never goes away. How or if we view our imperfections influences how we view neighborhoods and those different from us.

My maternal grandfather's parents came from Rileyville and Seven Fountains, Virginia, little unincorporated towns in the Blue Ridge Mountains near the Shenandoah Valley. Pappy Ivan would have been around when the federal government displaced neighbors to create Shenandoah National Park. His mother died of Rabbit Fever in 1932. He only finished two years of high school before becoming a carpenter across the Potomac River in Williamsport, Maryland, during the Great Depression. There, he met my grandmother, married, and had my aunt.

When he entered the Navy in 1943, he already had scars and birdshot still in his chest from a gunshot wound before entering the military. He had reached for a gun in a boat earlier in his life, and it went off. At the close of the war, he returned to carpentry. My mom came along when Pap Ivan was nearly 40.

He, my grandmother, and my mom moved around frequently as construction jobs dictated. They either rented or spent much of their adult life living in trailers, as best as I can tell.

I never knew my maternal grandmother. They lived in a trailer in the Antietam Trailer Court outside Hagerstown, Maryland, in 1972 when Hurricane Agnes flooded the area. The flood itself didn't kill her, but the heart attack afterward did. Pappy Ivan bought another trailer and moved it onto Pappy Herbst's farm next to the trailer where I spent several years. Does that make me part trailer trash?

In the movie, *The Long, Long Trailer,* Lucille Ball and Dezi Arnaz play a newlywed couple buying a trailer for their first home and traveling on their honeymoon. In one scene, Dezi Arnaz attempts to back the trailer into a relative's driveway, taking out the hedges, flowers, and, eventually, the porch. I can picture my grandparents doing likewise with their trailer—only with more profanity and hand gestures than in the 1954 film.

I didn't know anyone from Pap Ivan's extended family. As oral history goes, one of his brothers was a bootlegger and was kicked out of Virginia. He changed his last name and moved to Delaware. Pappy Ivan retired from construction and was offered a "great investment deal" with his family back in Virginia. He lost his retirement savings in a lousy business deal, moved back north, and became a school janitor to pay bills.

I knew Pap Ivan as a calm, well-dressed, respectable grandfather and Navy veteran with a nice-smelling cologne in a pheasant-shaped, dark glass bottle from Avon. Only later did I learn that he had been a heavy drinker earlier in his life. At some point in the past, my grandmother met him at the door with a gun and told him not to come home until he sobered up.

Before mom went back to work after my sister started school and the church where dad was minister grew, our finances were tight. As a child, I loved visiting my grandparents on the farm 90 minutes away. Until a few years ago, I didn't know that we made the trip so frequently because we needed food from my grandparents. I had some clue about our financial position because we always shopped for clothes at Hills or Zayre's department stores (Walmart's predecessors in Cumberland) and not the mall where other kids shopped. I resented that my parents never bought me name-brand jeans or shoes. I'm not sure that my dad has ever bought a new push mower. We had a push mower he purchased at an auction. Turning it off required shorting it out by using the metal blade of a rubber-handled screwdriver to connect the spark plug to the mower's body. I discovered the hard way how vital the rubber handle was. I also had a clue about our financial position when we carried a woodblock around in our hand-me-down Ford Granada's back seat. It served as a chuck for the wheels until Dad could fix the emergency brake. I looked with envy at others who had new Apple Macintosh computers while I had a Commodore 64 and its external floppy drive the size of a toaster. One of my first splurges as an adult was softer, thicker toilet paper. We always had the thin, translucent kind that doubled as high-grit sandpaper.

My teen years were tough. Middle school ranked students by reading level. I didn't make the top section. I tried the choir and didn't like it. In high school, I didn't have much to claim either. I had no interest in sports, art, music, or any athletic auxiliary groups. I asked about the mock trial team, but it was already full. I tried an essay contest and didn't win. The National Honor Society asked me to apply my junior year but then rejected me. What few distinctions I had were being named with Melanie Hutter as the two quietest students in our senior class and winning a history award at graduation.

Several jocks snapped their towels at me in freshman gym class. In those days, you got extra credit for taking showers, and I needed all the extra credit I could get in gym class. One of the jocks was one of the few African American males in my school. Although I may bear some resentment toward jocks, I have never inferred from that one case that he was representative of his entire race. Two other White students gave me wedgies in the hallway, and a freshman would sneak up and light his cigarette lighter under my butt in the lunch line my senior year. It was clear people could be cruel irrespective of their skin color.

High school was a preview of the adult world; bad behavior is just more sophisticated. Only family members have given me wedgies since high school, but drivers, mechanics, repair people, banks, insurance companies, and others screw people over and get away with it all the time. Life is not fair at any stage.

My favorite part of my teen years was working on my grandfather's farm during the summers. It was hard, sweaty, dirty work (sometimes 12-hour days during harvest), but I loved it. I could be covered in hay dust or manure up to my elbows and knees. I did not enjoy the occasional getting up at 3:30 a.m. to help with milking, but most other outdoor work brought great satisfaction. I still miss it every summer. Laziness and whining were mortal sins on the farm. It was back-breaking labor, but there was instant satisfaction in seeing the fruits of that labor. I miss the feeling of being physically exhausted at the end of the day but looking out over the meadow from grandma's kitchen window and watching the sun set on green hayfields, golden wheat fields, the rows of budding tassels in the cornfields, a meandering creek, and cows grazing without a care in the world. It was much more exciting than looking out and seeing my faded privacy fence where I now live.

Degrees of Privilege

Here is the connection to neighborliness. White privilege and White fragility are true of me.[129] However, I find them subject in degree to context and class. When I heard of White privilege, it was challenging to understand or see what was privileged about being me. Others didn't know how disconnected I felt from any race, including my own. What was White privilege? Was it feeling like a nobody in high school? Was it in having other kids, White and Black, snap their towels at me or give me wedgies in the hallway? Was it having my arms covered in cow manure cutting bailer twine off the manure spreader while working long days on the farm? Was it feeling rejected after being asked to apply to the National Honor Society? Was it our family having generic clothes, video games, and hand-me-down cars? Was it carrying a block of wood around in the back seat as a hillbilly emergency brake, a lawnmower with no cut-off switch, or translucent toilet paper?

The same was true of my family. My mom and her mother waited tables and cleaned toilets at Howard Johnson for mom to get through nursing school. One grandfather lived in trailers most of his life and ended his career as a janitor. My other grandfather accumulated some wealth but had worn-out joints from decades of milking cows twice daily, seven days a week. So, what is privileged about me or my family?

I first became aware of privilege from seeing it in others. A professor at Duquesne University was doing a project in our Pittsburgh neighborhood. One of the students refused to drive her BMW into our neighborhood. Another professor said it is not unusual for college students to hire interior decorators for dorm rooms. In Norfolk, I once sat at the stoplight outside the private Norfolk Academy (tuition $27,200) during high school dismissal. First came busloads of primarily White students leaving the school. Then, mostly White teen drivers exited, many in luxury cars. For over six years, I was assigned to the Five Points area of Norfolk. When I did a property study of the deteriorating business corridor, all the owners were White. Most of them had inherited property or owned it since the 60s. None of them lived in the neighborhood.

The truth remains that historically as a White male, I am a long-term beneficiary of opportunities that my grandfathers had in the post-World War II years that were not the same opportunities that African Americans or women had during that same time. That I can trace my ancestors back to Germany is part of my hidden privilege. They weren't separated as children and sold as property. That I can look up ship logs on Ancestry.com of my ancestors and not see a dollar figure of their estimated value is part of my hidden privilege. That I had grandparents who gave me no-interest car loans or helped with the downpayment on my house is part of generational wealth. I can't escape it or argue my way out of it. I can only hope to use it in meaningful ways.

As long as I act and dress confidently, I can walk around any neighborhood without anyone calling the police. Except for military surplus stores, for some reason, I can usually shop without being followed around. When I tried to connect a Black teen and his lawn-mowing business with a White senior and her overgrown yard, I knew that I better contact the widow first.

Privilege, though, comes in degrees. I suspect more of Peggy McIntosh's "I" statements would be true in Wellesley, Massachusetts, where she teaches (94% White with a 2017 estimated median household income of $176,852) than in the census block group where I live (34% White with a median income of $41,243). In addition, White fragility is one of my many. A good therapist could go wild with my fragilities. There is my introvert fragility, over-eater fragility, lazy-eye fragility, and not-having-kids fragility, among others. When criticized, I'm sensitive, uncomfortable, and defensive about all those subjects. And, like Michelle Obama, I resent it when others make assumptions about me because of my skin color and talk about all whites as if we all play polo and shop at Nordstrom.

Finding Healing Truth in Quiet Voices

If one's motivation is to be genuinely more neighborly and understand others, filtering out noise becomes necessary. You might imagine a large soundboard for an auditorium with a dizzying array of dials, switches, and slides.

Controlling the Volume of the Experts

I first heard Col. Paul Olsen (U.S. Army, retired) quote Teddy Roosevelt's famous Man in the Arena Speech at one of our events. The most famous part of the quote is below.

> It is not the critic who counts; not the man who points out how the strong man stumbles, or where the doer of deeds could have done them better. The credit belongs to the man who is actually in the arena, whose face is marred by dust and sweat and blood; who strives valiantly; who errs, who comes short again and again, because there is no effort without error and shortcoming.[130]

The quote is even more significant in the context of the entire speech. Although it has become known as the "Man in the Arena" speech, the original title was "Citizenship in a Republic". Roosevelt gave it at the Sorbonne in Paris on April 23, 1910. It was a hard-hitting speech against elitism. He pays respect to the intellectual development and specialized training of his audience. Then he added "that more important still are the commonplace, everyday qualities and virtues." He attacks those who set lofty ideals, criticize and divide, and particularly those who divide along class lines. He argues that the conduct of and quality of ordinary citizens have a higher value than the philosophers: "the closest philosopher, the refined and cultured individual who from his library tells how men ought to be governed under ideal conditions, is of no use in actual governmental work." If his speech were true in 1910, what would it be today in an era of non-stop talk radio, 24-hour news commentary, and the age of "broadcast yourself."

I hope the bibliography is ample evidence that I value scholarship. What I am suggesting is that experts' volume must be controlled. Sometimes, their volume needs to be turned up. They are knowledgeable, have worked hard to get where they are, and deserve respect. Other times, they drown out regular people, and their volume needs to be turned down. Some experts remind me of the mechanic who offered me a $1200 deal to fix a $60 problem.

Experts generate volumes of specialized vocabulary and labels that sometimes help and sometimes hurt. It is one thing to discuss social issues in professional conferences. It is another thing to talk about social landmines with chicken farmers, steelworkers, or carpenters. Language accentuates an educational disparity that comes across as condescending. It communicates, "For us to have a conversation, I need to bring you up to my level." The conversation ends before it ever starts.

Words at the practical level are defined more by actions and experiences than by dictionary definitions. In the social sciences, much of the vocabulary is so abstract that experts don't agree on the definitions. If they disagree, I place the odds of 20 random people selected from the city and country having the exact definition as King Charles and me meeting in a Victoria's Secret store in Anchorage, Alaska.

A final reason to temper the volume of experts is the framing problem. Since high school, I've had a glossy book about our nation's Christian heritage on my shelf. It has full-page patriotic photographs on thick paper and quotes from influential politicians. It is not untruthful. It leaves out other history unfavorable to the picture they want to present. By its own admission, the introductory essay of the 1619 Project employs the same technique: framing. They both create a frame and fill it with the facts and images favorable to the picture they want to present. Both have truth, but any reader must be aware of the framing lens. Neither piece can stand alone.

The more impactful experiences in my life have been the quiet moments and places without a frame—living in Uptown and Hazelwood, talking with seniors at a community center, or talking with Ms. Coles. Hearing healing truth requires controlling the volume of the experts.

Sliding between the Broad and Narrow

Some microphones are designed for large choirs. Others are better for soloists. It is essential to adjust for the general and specific. The Hebrew book of Job is an ancient example of the need to zoom in between general and particular truths. It is the story of a heavenly wager between Satan and God. In a brutal test of faith, Job lost his family, his possessions, and his health. Job's supposed friends visited him, but they offered commentary instead of consolation. Of 42 chapters in the book, 35 (83%) are Job's "friends" arguing over why Job was in the condition he was. Their thoughts were deep, passionate, and poetic. Maybe their motives were well-intentioned. Despite their verbosity, none were correct. All were hurtful. Their analysis of cause and effect was rushed and flawed. God finally interrupted and said, "Would you just shut up" [my interpretation]. God scolded them to be more cautious about their assumptions and words.

The story tells me human nature hasn't changed much. The anxiousness to critique is far greater than the patience to understand. Much of what Job's friends said may have been true in a general sense but absolutely wrong in Job's specific case. Such is the danger of moving from the general to the particular when questioning motives and assigning blame. Rather than understand, Job's friends offered commentary. Job would have many similar friends today.

An explosive modern example of this collision between general truth and specific truth is Ferguson, Missouri, after the August 9, 2014, shooting of Michael Brown by Ferguson Police Officer Darren Wilson. It sparked unrest and riots in Ferguson and across the country. In the immediate wake of the shooting, emotions were high; facts were short. Commentators filled hundreds of hours speculating.

On March 4, 2015, the Department of Justice (DOJ) under Eric Holder during the Obama administration issued two reports after an exhaustive investigation. One report concluded from a prosecutorial analysis that Officer Wilson did not use unreasonable force under the law and did not willfully violate Mr. Brown's constitutional right to be free from unreasonable force. In addition, it concluded the famous slogan "Hands up, Don't Shoot" likely did not originate from Mr. Brown.

However, the other, more extensive report was a scathing litany of abuses within the Ferguson government. Sadly, it read much like the 1968 Kerner Report about riots nearly 45 years earlier. The Ferguson police department had effectively no community engagement, and there was minimal separation of powers between the court system and city government. City government used the court system to rack up revenue. Minor code violations turned into thousand-dollar fines, and they issued arrest warrants over minor fees. Citizens were left out in the rain waiting to pay fines during published business hours while employees sat inside, ignoring them. Clear instructions on how to pay fines were absent from the website. It may have, unfortunately, been Mr. Brown and Officer Wilson that ignited the spark, but the context for combustion was set by far more longstanding injustice and far longer than either Mr. Brown or Officer Wilson. Healing truth adjusts to general and specific truth.

Prideful Feedback Loops

A sound system's high-pitched, nails-on-a-chalkboard squeal occurs when a microphone's open end enters the field of sound waves from the speakers and creates a nasty feedback loop. There is a similar nasty result when we circulate the same noise without paying attention to our prideful contradictions. In the great comparison trap, we proclaim our ideals and hide our contradictions.

The U.S. has always been a nation of contradictions. It comes naturally with being human. It is easier to relate to those who are self-aware about it. Thomas Jefferson railed against the abuse of presidential power until he became president. Once presented with the office's responsibility, he secretly negotiated the most extensive land deal in U.S. history with Napoleon. It was one among other stretches of power that made him grimace when it was someone else. People who are not self-aware tend to preach perched from their soapbox, looking down at others.

Group pride can be beneficial and destructive. Pride in harmful behavior is mistaken for pride in oneself. Chewing tobacco, being macho, and eating voluminous amounts of fatty, sugary foods are associated with cultural pride but are ultimately self-destructive.

Marketers know the power of pride. Pride sells even when it is harmful. Pride, image, and stereotypes sell rap albums that personify bad behavior. Pride, image, and stereotypes sell country music albums that personify bad behavior. Pride sells bumper stickers, comedy shows, t-shirts, flags, and books. Pride is promoted without reflection on the health of its object.

Many negative behaviors in the city or country stem from pride in the wrong things. In her book, *Ghetto Nation,* Cora Daniels laments the broad acceptance in pop culture of low expectations for what she calls ghetto culture. She calls for a higher level of self-respect.

Maddie and Tae's "Girl in a Country Song" confronts the blatant stereotyping of country women as Daisy Duke. I'm a fan of the song because the women in my life did not fit the country stereotype of being barefoot, perpetually pregnant, or wearing Daisy Duke shorts. My mother and grandmother were skilled nurses who were caring, intelligent, and worked well under intense pressure. Carla Eckard, a longtime friend I grew up with and have always admired, has her Master's degree in engineering. She lives on a small farm and works in the defense industry with her husband, Dan, a fellow engineer. She can bake bread, bale hay, and build rockets. My grandmother, mother, and Carla don't fit the popular stereotype.

Separating Identity and Behavior into Different Channels

Filtering noise from healing truth further involves separating identity and behavior into different channels. Group identities break down as compounds into molecules, molecules into atoms, and atoms into subatomic particles. This creates the potential for an almost limitless number of us. vs. them conflicts. In the introduction, I mentioned a meeting with a fired-up but divided crowd over police tactics. The race was the same. The division was more along generational lines.

Separating behavior from identity is vital to physical health. On the farm, ice cream and desserts were expected a minimum of two meals a day, usually three. In addition to a free milk supply, local orchards, strawberry fields, and raspberry bushes surrounded the farm. "Superfoods" for us were homemade ice cream, grandma's strawberry jelly, pancakes, cheesecake, cookies, cobbler, apple crisp, and warm tapioca. "Superfoods" had nothing to do with kale and quinoa. When someone first served edamame well into my thirties, I thought it was some exotic, crunchy, tasteless Asian import. It turns out that I spent my summers around edamame fields. They are more commonly known as soybeans, which we fed the cows once they were dried. I will occasionally eat edamame for their health benefit, but cows enjoy them more. Eating a butter pecan ice cream cone takes me back to sitting with my grandparents on the swing or grandma taking me to Highs Dairy Store. I know that I must give up more sugar to be healthy, but there is a deep-rooted emotional connection.

The ability to make truth-based, healing judgments also applies to the Not in My Back Yard (NIMBY) challenge. A big part of working in communities has been helping articulate fears in positive ways, especially when it comes to NIMBYism. It is essential to isolate negative behaviors that residents fear from bias against entire groups of people. When negative behavior is isolated and articulated separately from whole groups, most of the negative behaviors are true across racial, cultural, and class boundaries. Strategies exist to isolate and mitigate negative behavior, not people.

Bad neighbors can make life miserable; I've had my share. No one likes to have the police knock at your door looking for your neighbor who robbed a convenience store. No one enjoys smelling dog crap wafting from the neighbor who never cleans up after their dog. No one enjoys putting hard work into their own house to have a neighbor who doesn't have a blade of grass left from the junk, inoperable vehicle, and toys all over the yard. There is nothing morally wrong with protecting yourself or your family from harmful behavior. The problem is when bad behavior is associated with entire groups of people.

Unfortunately, complex federal programs like the Low-Income Housing Tax Credit (LIHTC) or Section 8 Housing Choice

Vouchers (HCV) make them rife for misunderstanding and hijacking. They are compounded when government and housing advocates do a poor job of explaining them. They are both excellent programs that have built-in control mechanisms for bad behavior. The HCV program especially gets a bad rap because federal law requires privacy. Agencies can't disclose who HCV recipients are. This makes them highly vulnerable to rumors. In more cases than not, every bad tenant is falsely assumed to be an HCV recipient.

Martin Luther King, Jr. looked forward to the day when a person would be judged on the content of their character, not on the color of their skin. Character, though, isn't immediately visible or easily measurable like skin color, annual income, or religion. Unfortunately, we use appearance and group identities as quick proxies to make fast, often false judgments.

The Power of Community

Finally, and most importantly, community supporters are another commonality I have with Michelle Obama. Like most teenagers, I didn't realize how good I had it. My parents gave me all I needed: a loving, safe, secure home and the best that they had.

I was also surrounded by a loving community, even if I didn't recognize it or thought they were old and nerdy. As others have noted, the big difference between someone not having much money and living in poverty is their support system. Mine was ginormous. I was part of a loving church community with various role models to which no dollar value can be assigned. I'll never know what it is like to go away to college or graduate school without people back home sending cookies, care packages, cash, and cards of encouragement. I still have many of the cards. With all the yelling, screaming, labeling, and criticizing, their quiet encouragement grounds me. They taught me to take a long view on life, not the immediate hurt or insult. I learned neighborliness and learned to stand up to the comparison contest.

Finding Healing Truth

I still struggle with the gap between who I want to be and who I am. If I view myself as an evolved, enlightened specimen perched atop the meritocratic order unaware of any privilege, I am less likely to be patient with others' imperfections. If I consider myself a permanent victim trapped at a disadvantage by bad luck, genetics, or others, I will be equally unlikely to see past my victimhood to our shared humanity. How willing we are to face our imperfections and rise higher shapes our common destiny as members of an imperfect human community.

Amongst all the yelling in the U.S., sometimes quiet voices and quiet places speak healing truth. Quiet places and quiet voices like Bayview the need to address inequities put in plain view. People like Ms. Coles awaken a compassion in me far more than academics and wealthy entertainers. She can communicate healing truths. Bayview does not need do-gooder saviors to make false promises or create unhealthy dependencies. They do not need friends like Job, who pat themselves on the back for their incisive commentary while making it worse. They neither need nor want Columbus-like predatory investors. Communities like Bayview also aren't looking for a government handout. They are willing to work and have valuable skills but lack the capital and business acumen to compete with larger businesses. In my dream world, more capital, scholarships for minority farmers, online opportunities, and agricultural experts would be directed to places like Bayview so that when the U.S. Farmers and Ranch Association does another video, more people of color will be in it.

Honor - Resisting the Market, Political and Religious Phish

Key Idea: Honor is something to be given not taken—with or without power.

George Akerlof and Robert Shiller, both Nobel Prize-winning economists, wrote an enlightening book, *Phishing for Phools - The Economics of Manipulation and Deception,* about how market and political forces manipulate us into bad behavior. Deception sells prescription drugs more dangerous than the underlying conditions they help, loans we can't afford, food that kills us (long-term), addictions as glamorous lifestyles, and financial instruments that destroy life savings. Manipulation by politicians and lobbyists sells elections, laws that sound good but are never fully funded, enforcement agencies without teeth, and policies with buried loopholes for special constituencies. Appearances are everything.

Phisher-people blare their value system at high volume. If it sells and government can tax it, it must be right. Comparison contest masters sell us overpriced brand names. They try to convince us that we are shorted something in life and deserve more. Sometimes this is true. Many times, it is not. They feed pride's dark side that only finds contentment in being better than someone else—having a better job, driving a more expensive car, having better-looking kids, or living in a wealthier neighborhood than others. Jealousy is a powerful sales tool. Phisher-people grow rich by stirring discontent.

Outsiders using a social or an economic lens often view duct-tape communities like Uptown, Hazelwood, and Ringgold as behind the times. The assumption is that this is a bad thing. Contrary to that belief, happy people live there who don't need everything that market deception tells them they need to be satisfied. They are unique places to me precisely because important people in my life didn't buy into every phish from the ever-changing market-morality bandwagon. They are willing to take their unpopularity punishment on the front end rather than down the road when market values change.

One of their great values is honor. Few tools are more potent in the arsenal of neighborliness than honor. The people who raised me treated honor as something to be given, not taken. It was deeply rooted in a value system independent of market manipulation. A marriage counselor once explained the concept of honor in marriage by saying that marriage can't be 50/50 equality because couples will always be fighting over the ambiguity of where the 50/50 is. Honor in a healthy marriage is about giving more than 50/50. The same might be true of neighborliness. Honor has an elastic quality that stretches the gap between our 50/50. It is not denying our rights but rather planting flowers on the metes and bounds of our rights instead of barbed wire.

The Honorable Parts of My Culture

Four people who remarkably influenced my life grew up in large families in the mountains near Paw Paw, West Virginia. On the Maryland side of the Potomac River in Green Ridge, two brothers, Raymond and Roy McCabe, and ten siblings, grew up during the 1920s and 1930s. Since 1931, Green Ridge has been part of the national forest program between 500 and 2000 feet above sea level. Around 1900, however, it was the site of the country's largest apple orchard. On the West Virginia side in Great Cacapon, two sisters named Rita and Nola Hiett grew up simultaneously as Raymond and Roy. Raymond married Rita, and Roy married Nola. They told stories of living off the land and making food stretch during the Great Depression. They grew up hunting primarily for food, not just for sport. They canned and used apples from the orchards to make apple butter every year—a family tradition they continued long after it was necessary. During my childhood, Raymond and Rita would go mushroom hunting. They had the experience from growing up in the woods to find safe wild mushrooms.

Roy, or "Skinny," as they referred to him, served in the Navy during World War II. Raymond served in the Army's Company A, 97th Signal Corps, which fought during the Battle of the Bulge. Raymond regaled in telling stories about General Patton and MacArthur. Raymond was known to embellish a little, but I trust his stories were mostly accurate. Raymond had worked at the tannery in Paw Paw before the war. After the war, he started as a telephone lineman in Hagerstown, Maryland, and rose in the ranks of the Bell Telephone Company. Roy went into insurance and eventually owned his business in Keyser, West Virginia. He proudly wore his "Almost Heaven" West Virginia tie at every opportunity. Roy and Nola gave much of their retirement savings away, building a chapel and dormitories at the church camp where they had given so much of their time to youth. Roy and Nola were successful small-town businesspeople but were never too proud to clean toilets, run the vacuum, or clean the church building. I have fond memories of spending time with the McCabes and of them taking us to Western Sizzlin Steakhouse after church. The four of them, among others, helped contribute to my scholarship and were at my college graduation.

When I think of what it means to be a man from the country, I think of my dad, my grandfather, Roy, Raymond, and others like Verle Blankenship, Leo Lavin, and Bob Saville. They all grew up poor in financial resources in rural villages but rich in other resources. They had the unmistakable quality of honor. Dad, Verle, and Bob went to college; the rest did not. They could do well with high school educations because of yesteryear's economy and because they were self-learners. They didn't need entertained to learn. They were all as from the country as one could get. They all had pickup trucks at one point, but they were work trucks, not country-pimped status symbols. They didn't buy the depiction of country men as the Marlboro man. Identity wasn't tied to appearances.

I learned from them the importance of civic involvement. My grandfather was active in his church, Ruritan, Rotary, and the grange. He served on numerous boards: the zoning commission, Farm Bureau, the Soil Conservation District, local cooperatives, the Chamber of Commerce, the Washington County Economic Development Commission, the Maryland Department of Agriculture Board of Review, and the former Hagerstown Trust Company Bank.

When not involved with Cub Scouts, my brother and sister's football, cheerleading, basketball, or volleyball, Dad volunteered with the March of Dimes and helped deliver food baskets for the Shriners. He visited the sick, helped a family repair their porch, or dropped by seniors. As a kid, the Herbst family dined in at least one family of hoarders and one older woman with a broken one-burner stove and a refrigerator held closed with a rubber strap. We ate in a few homes with cooks whose hygiene and culinary skills were severely lacking, but mom and dad always treated them like a five-star restaurant. The rule was always to clean up your plate out of respect for the host. Honor was always given to people regardless of their station in life.

They rarely talked about race, but I learned later that Dad lost a few friendships who didn't like it when a Black man with a White wife started attending church. To me as a kid, Les Kemp looked like Mr. T. without the mohawk. He was muscular and athletic but a kindhearted, gentle giant. He had transferred to Cumberland from Pittsburgh to work at the PPG plant. As far as I could tell, Dad and the other men in my life treated them like any other friends. They played softball, hung out, and watched each other's kids. I remember their sons J.R. and Jeremey playing in our backyard when their sister Tara was born. They later moved back to the Pittsburgh area. I didn't yet know about structural racism, but I knew that interpersonal racism had no place in our lives.

Despite our rural location, my role models connected with people worldwide who taught me the importance of global citizenship. I met people like Paul and Adela Bajko, an older couple from Poland. The Nazis held Paul in labor camp during World War II. Adela's village was first occupied by the Germans and then by the Russians. The Russian soldiers pillaged the town and raped her neighbor's two teenage daughters. The two escaped the Russian zone, met through church friends, immigrated to the United States, reunited, and married. They then made return trips to Poland over the decades, working quietly to take resources behind the Iron Curtain to promote freedom.

A newlywed couple from India once stayed with us. They came to the United States for college and then returned to India to begin a relief organization in central India. They started children's homes, schools, hospitals, and mobile clinics. I met a couple from Mexico City working with kids in dire poverty. I knew medical doctors who began their careers in African villages and my dentist had served on a Native American reservation. In honorable, quiet ways, they made what contributions they could to balance the scales of justice for those who needed it the most. Honor wasn't putting yourself first or risking a minuscule part of your wealth; honor meant risking nearly everything. They contrasted with Rockefeller and Carnegie's model of philanthropy, who enriched themselves first before turning to others.

Honor also applied to how I learned to treat women. The men I watched were faithful to their wives and had long-lasting marriages—until death did they part. They didn't chew, smoke, or cuss (much), and I never saw any of them drunk. They were happy, joyful people without the images sold by pop culture to make us happy. Honoring women for the men I grew up around was more straightforward than it is today. Women were not something to be consumed or conquered. When we were growing up, Mom always intercepted my brother's *Sports Illustrated* swimsuit issue before it made it into our hands. Mom didn't want her boys drooling over women's flesh. She thought it was demeaning to women and did moral damage to us. I still feel awkward passing Victoria's Secret stores with larger-than-life window wraps of young, picture-perfect women in panties and bras. Some may believe the open sex symbols represent women's liberation from the past. Not my late mother. I still feel like she would slap me on the back of the head if she caught me staring. I might also note a conspicuous absence of window wraps of equally liberated 90-year-old women wearing the same clothes or lack thereof.

Mom's view of women and sex was at odds with movies, T.V., the music industry, and comedy shows where sex is in your face nearly every waking hour. What mom considered soft porn is now everyday T.V. Phisher-people know how well sex sells. It sells everything from hamburgers to dishwasher detergent. I can't eat my raisin bran and listen to the news or music in the morning without hearing a commercial about some guy's erection problems or a new razor for pubic hair.

Growing up, the men I watched didn't live up to their ideals, but they were better for trying. They weren't perfect, especially as they became older. They grew more resistant to change when they weren't driving it. They worked hard with their hands and weren't afraid to get dirty. They were wise and highly disciplined with money, not to have more for themselves but to give more away. Serve God, family, country, community, and serve yourself last. Depression-era poverty, World War II, the Cold War, and Vietnam tested their metal, but they came through better.

Their honor and influence had a domino effect on me. When Roy died, the funeral home was packed. I remember driving my grandparents to Roy's graveside at the Veterans cemetery and looking back in the rearview mirror at what seemed like a mile and a half of cars in his funeral procession thinking, "I want that when I die. I want to die knowing I lived a life that touched other people."

I didn't know it or appreciate it at the time, but I was learning from those country hicks the value of honor and the tools to navigate complex social situations. I remember memorizing a passage for church.

> *Love must be sincere. Hate what is evil; cling to what is good.*

> *Be devoted to one another in love. Honor one another above yourselves.*

> *Never be lacking in zeal, but keep your spiritual fervor, serving the Lord.*

> *Be joyful in hope, patient in affliction, faithful in prayer.*

Share with the Lord's people who are in need. Practice hospitality.

Bless those who persecute you; bless and do not curse.

Rejoice with those who rejoice; mourn with those who mourn.

Live in harmony with one another. Do not be proud, but be willing to associate with people of low position. Do not be conceited.

Do not repay anyone evil for evil. Be careful to do what is right in the eyes of everyone.

If it is possible, as far as it depends on you, live at peace with everyone. [131]

The words above—love, sincerity, devotion, honor, service, zeal, joy, faithful, blessing, right, hospitality, peace, and humility—are more important to me than community development jargon. The words above have worked in any neighborhood of which I've ever been a part, urban or rural, White or Black, wealthy or less wealthy. They supersede ideology and are more profound than political divides. They are instructive on how to disagree. They provide grounding, bring comfort, and give direction. They define neighborly behavior. The text explicitly states that honor is given to enemies, not just people you like or agree with.

The words above had power in themselves but had even more power because I watched them lived in a disciplined chase of consistency in life. The people around me exercised them in every detail of life, from not walking on others' grass to disciplined speech. They fixed these words to something ancient and enduring, not the latest commercial or Gallup poll. They knew they weren't society's elite, upper crust, or power brokers. They realized that they didn't need to be neighborly people. Education is often mistaken as a path to being a good person. Education opens many doors but is no guarantee of character. There are a great many well-educated jackasses.

Character Gaps

True honor is transparent about weaknesses and not beholden to appearances. In the comparison contest, most people focus only on their cultural ideals, not their failures. "Slaveholders pride themselves upon being honorable men," said Harriet Jacobs, a slave girl whose domineering master, a well-regarded doctor, sexually abused her in Edenton, North Carolina.[132] She spent seven years curled up in the tiny hiding space over her grandmother's shed before she could escape to the North. The "southern gentleman" honor system was a facade. It wasn't defined by authenticity to the scriptural words earlier. It was a public pretense of title, clothes, possessions, good public deeds, and other appearances. In today's terms, it was good public relations. Behind appearances, the honor system bore the stench of a rotting corpse.

When I moved to Chicago, the immense cultural diversity I encountered was electrifying but intensely confusing. There were nearly as many people in Chicago's Uptown neighborhood as in the whole county where I grew up. Moreover, Allegany County, Maryland, was 97% White during the 1990 census, so race relations weren't something I encountered often. Chicago and urban life changed that and exposed other character gaps.

Inner conflict emerged when I realized that my values were wrapped in a tidy, White, rural, politically conservative, evangelical Christian cultural package. As my context changed, the cultural package unraveled. I received contradicting labels and became aware that some viewed me as a traitor. I've been called a liberal and a fundamentalist, a socialist and a right winger, a peacemaker and a hater. "Labels," said Elton Trueblood, "instead of encouraging thought, have the effect of diminishing it in that once a person's classification is known, there seems to be no need of further inquiry." [133]

When people say, "We just need to go back to when America was a Christian country," I wonder when that was. During the golden age of church attendance in the 1950s? In Norfolk, the same year (1954) that "under God" was added to the pledge of allegiance, White residents were bombing and shooting at Black residents in the Coronado neighborhood. The same year (1956) that "In God We Trust" was added to coins, the governor of Virginia and U.S. Senator Harry Byrd planned to shut down public schools rather than integrate them after the 1954 Supreme Court decision in *Brown vs. Board of Education*. I can't reconcile that as an honorable Christian heritage. Unfortunately, the use of power has not always been as honorable as presented.

City life in Chicago brought other challenges to my stated values and my behavior. I read business ethics books from the library about how our technology, conveniences, and the mass consumption provided by Western companies are often at the expense of labor and environmental abuses in poor, distant parts of the planet where we have no comprehension of what life is like. Western companies have plundered poor countries in Africa, Asia, and South America to provide the luxuries that we demand. The gap between American ideals and behavior was much more significant than I realized.

The character gap was especially true with Christianity and politics. Christian politics of the mid-nineties made me feel betrayed, dirty, and used by people using faith as a cover for power plays. I felt phished as a fool. I decided it was time for me to step off the Christian, evangelical political train. I don't like complex, important issues reduced to divisive, emotional sound bites. I resent self-designated spokespersons telling me who "the Christian candidate" is. I resent my beliefs associated with slander, labeling, lies, dirty tactics, antagonistic speech, greed, hidden motives, unlawful activity, and the ruined ethics that often characterize faith and politics.

I was not alone in my disillusionment. Robert Putnam's research shows a solid and lasting counter-reaction among younger people to evangelical politics in the church, as evidenced by them leaving it.[134] Peter Hitchens, the Christian brother of famed atheist Christopher Hitchens, similarly attributes part of the decline of faith in Britain to confusion between patriotism and Christianity, between spiritual power and political power.[135] Even Billy Graham regretted being so closely involved with politics—a lesson seemingly lost today.

Cultural Confusion

If I've felt like a traitor for stepping off the conservative, evangelical, Republican train in rural America, I've correspondingly felt a 25-year stigma for not boarding the progressive, liberal, Democratic political train in urban America. There is unquestionably a false, misplaced nostalgia about pre-1960s America, but there is, arguably to be sure, equal cultural dishonesty that everything post-1960s has been progress.

Much of what my mentors knew and held dear has been deconstructed. Education, parenting, institutions like the Boy Scouts, and even math are now different. My influencers valued physical and emotional modesty. They didn't talk as much about themselves or share their every emotion as today. Feelings weren't as important as duty. My parents spanked us for lying or disrespecting authority, and they let us do risky things like work on the farm or ride our bikes all over south Cumberland without adult supervision. Under the new standards for parenting, my parents and generations before them are considered abusive. Self-expression now occupies a higher value than self-control. Ironically, my dad points out that in the pre-challenge-authority, pre-let-your-feelings-be-your-guide days, previous generations didn't need school-shooting drills or school metal detectors.

We now live in a politically correct but post-truth world.[136] My circle of influencers assumed a universal truth and purpose existed even if they disagreed on interpreting it. Truth was more objective, propositional, deductive, and non-contradictory. In a post-modern, post-truth society, truth is more inductive, personal, internal, and contradictory. Everyone now has their "my truth." Experience defines truth. In the great philosophical epic *Spider-man: Far From Home*, M.J. and Mysterio contemplate the fading of any objective truth and whether people will believe anything. Time will tell how unified we can be if we each manufacture the truth that best suits us.

For my dad, religion was more public. For me, faith is more of a private affair. This generational divide isn't just urban/rural. Many older civic leagues in Norfolk open with prayer and the pledge of allegiance, regardless of race. Younger generations now question if that is appropriate. In a twist of irony, a group of senior women, who in their teens were told to sit in the back of the bus, are now discouraged in their eighties from opening meetings in a public facility with prayer because we're a more inclusive society.

Stepping off the rural, conservative, evangelical, Republican train in my quest for neighborliness does not mean I have jumped on the progressive, liberal, Democrat express. Instead, it has left me confused and hungry for something more profound than political power.

Finding Neighborliness without Power

A wonderful source of encouragement comes from historical figures who lived honorable lives before having power. Booker T. Washington (the former slave and founder of Tuskegee University) used Sunday evening addresses to transmit values to his students. [137] Despite racial differences, those values were nearly identical to those transmitted to me over a century later.

In South Africa, Nelson Mandela refused to curse or lose his temper when in prison for his stand against apartheid. In the USSR, Aleksandr Solzhenitsyn endured the Soviet gulag and cried out for freedom, truth, and a return to spiritual life.

In 1958, Martin Luther King, Jr. referenced "the Christian virtues of love, mercy, and forgiveness" in his appeal for non-violent protests; "these virtues should stand at the center of our lives."[138] King valued liberalism's social action but backed away from theological liberalism as overly sentimental, overly optimistic, and overlooking man's sinful nature.

A turbulent decade later, after King's assassination in 1968, Dr. Elton Trueblood wrote a book concerned that virtues were being unraveled and separated from their source. Dr. Trueblood was a theologian, philosopher, and chaplain at universities, including Harvard and Stanford.

> Many terms can be applied to our age, but one of the most accurate affirmations is that ours has become an age of confusion, in which people simply do not know what to

think. Part of this is the result of bitter disappointment. Technology has not brought Utopia; the Great Society has not emerged; peace is elusive as ever; poverty still exists. In no area is the perplexity greater than in that of religious belief. Millions, including large sections of the nominal membership of churches, are without any firm conviction on which to base and rebuild their lives.[139]

The confusion and disappointment about which he wrote do not seem to have diminished since his writing in 1969. He was concerned that culture was increasingly becoming unmoored from any moral compass, which would only create more confusion and meaninglessness.

Underneath the urban-rural rift and culture wars are existential questions that are just as important whether asked by Stanford philosophers or farmers in overalls. It is a quest for meaning, certitude, and something solid to stand. I unintentionally read Nelson Mandela's autobiography simultaneously as Friedrich Nietzsche's, the famous "God is dead" philosopher. The two provide a strong contrast between an other-centered, principled life spent in service toward a higher purpose and one spent philosophically chasing liberation from any such constraints.

In writing this chapter, I wondered if I would be dismissed as a stodgy member of the "Old Farts Club." Robert Putnam and Shaylyn Romney Garrett's research bolstered my confidence. America has become an "extremely self-centered nation" that shifted from a "We" mentality to an individualistic "I" mentality sometime in the sixties with an imbalance between rights and community responsibilities.[140] It confirmed that values held by people like Booker T. Washington are tragically being lost. If unity through shamed conformity didn't work pre-1960, a diversity that devolves into me-first is so far not showing signs of doing much better. Time will tell if a house divided will stand. Unity in history has rarely been through love. It is usually in having a common enemy.

Being Your "Authentic Self"

An astute observer may wonder why there is no chapter specifically on trust, a question I contemplated for six years. The decision not to include a chapter on trust is based on my belief that trust is a byproduct of these other values, especially honor.

In an age of self-expression and personal branding, there is much talk among Millennials and Gen Z about being true to "your authentic self." University of Chicago philosopher Benjamin Callard questions whether there is an authentic self. He uses the illustration of attending a wedding where the bride and groom have requested that attendees wear formal wear.[141] If you hate dressing up, are you violating your authentic self when dressing up for the wedding, or should you go in the ripped jeans and flip-flops to which you are comfortable? Here is where honor comes to bear. If honoring other people is not a part of the authentic self to which you are striving, I would argue you are an authentic, self-centered jerk.

The people I had growing up in those backcountry towns demonstrated duct-tape values that transcend time and the White, rural culture in which they lived. They taught me to recognize what is and isn't honor.

Growing up, I had a dad who avoided titles and always parked in the farthest parking spot from the doors to the church building so others could park closer. He cooked, cleaned, and had us do likewise because he knew it would make Mom happy when she got home from work. One Sunday after church, Dad invited everyone to stay for a brief presentation. He showed some transparencies of our family's finances and taxes on the overhead projector. It was short, with no explanation why. Years later, I found out that someone had accused Dad of cheating on his taxes. He didn't put church members in a position where they had to choose sides. He didn't get sidetracked by making it personal or being defensive. Instead, he handled the conflict by giving people the transparent facts (literally for those who remember overhead projectors), and it silenced the criticism. To this day, I've never seen Dad lose his temper in public (at home, yes). In Cumberland, he helped a member build a horse stable. While in Missouri for school, he helped a farmer during harvest. When he moved to Delaware, he got up early and helped a chicken farmer wade angle deep in chicken poop to pick up dead chickens.

When I moved away from rural Maryland, I picked up my first issues of *Esquire* and *GQ* in a bookstore. They exposed me to a world I didn't know existed. I found out about $1000 designer suits and $350 dress shoes. Decades later, in the wake of corporate scandals, the real estate crisis, too big to fail bailouts, and the #MeToo movement, I'm convinced that many men behind those scandals know much more about $350 shoes than they do about honor.

My hope for more traditionally-minded rural dwellers is to listen more, talk more about meaning, and find a confident faith and moral influence without political power. The values of people I knew growing up are worth preserving with or without power. Those values can't be preserved by yelling, screaming, clawing, and bullying culture into submission. They can only be preserved by living them.

My hope for more postmodern urban dwellers is not to give lip service to diversity, look down on rural dwellers as unsophisticated brutes, or treat them like they need to be indoctrinated. Instead, it is to consider some of the deeper questions of meaning and identity that are raised.

Scholars have produced much thoughtful and insightful material. Still, I go back to the principles I learned from a farmer, an insurance agent, a telephone lineman, a principal, and my dad, the country preacher. Thanks to them, I will be phished as a fool far less by market morality and political manipulation. Honor is in service, not in position. Be cautious of using your pulpit to criticize. Don't talk down. Don't seek first to yell or shake the fist of your ideology but serve in love. Leave the good spots for others. To understand people, enter their world, and help them pick up dead chickens.

Section 4: The Soul of Neighborhoods
Faith - Beyond Wish Fulfillment

Key Idea: Religious faith is more than wish fulfillment.

Some consider religion a quiet retreat from the comparison contest and market competition. Sometimes it is; sometimes it isn't. Jesus' disciples fought over who was the greatest. The religious today have not yet mastered leaving competitiveness at the door. In the Christian world, it can be a contest to be bigger, holier, right-er, biblical-er, relevant-er, successful-er, edgier, or even humbler than someone else. Attendance figures, podcast downloads, offerings, and social media followers are watched and compared like Nielsen ratings. Still, there are glimpses of something more profound and higher about faith.

Many may consider the Willis (formerly Sears) Tower the most impressive place in Chicago. Others might say the Signature Room restaurant on the 95th floor of the John Hancock building. Others may say the museums, the Magnificent Mile, Soldier Field, Wrigley Field, or the Chicago Board Options Exchange. None may be as impressive to duct-tape communities as a simple gymnasium in the North Lawndale neighborhood at Lawndale Community Church. Many of the mainline attractions in Chicago are dedicated to the architects, artists, corporations, or patrons whose name they usually bear—the Sears Tower or Rockefeller Chapel. The gym at Lawndale Community Church and the Lawndale Community Health Center building testify to the character of a neighborhood's youth when given a meaningful but challenging cause.

Once the fifteen poorest census tract in the United States, a high school coach in Lawndale, Wayne Gordon, his students, and additional partners had a vision to turn a dilapidated Cadillac dealership into a health center and gym. Thirty high schoolers gave up their spring break in 1984 to tear off the old roof and begin work on the health center. One of the coach's former wrestlers stood guard at night. With the health center open, teens from the neighborhood returned for nine straight months to lower the floor in the section that became the gym. With a jackhammer, picks, shovels, and wheel barrels, they dug a hole 6 feet deep, 125 feet long, and 50 feet wide by hand. Only after a relative lent a Caterpillar were they able to finish the dig in three days. In January 1986, a friend poured the concrete slab and moved in a portable basket. By this point, the project had caught the attention of the Chicago Bears. The wives of the Chicago Bears held a fundraiser and presented a check for $42,000, which covered the cost of plumbing, wood floors, locker room furnishings, and glass backboards.[142]

There are few places more inspiring in all of Chicago than that gym. Motivating teens to do manual labor voluntarily is an accomplishment anytime and anywhere, making Lawndale's story all the more meaningful. When I started working with youth in Hazelwood, one of the saddest shocks was that so many had never been expected to do anything challenging. Their self-esteem suffered because they didn't feel the reward of working toward something challenging. Being from a tough home or neighborhood was too often used by adults as an excuse. Not in Lawndale.

The Impact of Faith

Lawndale and organizations like it may be why Robert Putnam considers faith communities "arguably the single most important repository of social capital in America."[143] Research collected by

Putnam correlates religious involvement with higher levels of community involvement, connectedness to others, visitation of friends, civic concern, and generosity, to name a few.[144] When his *Bowling Alone* came out in 2000, he gauged religious communities spend $15 to $20 billion a year on social services. Moreover, in Putnam's later landmark study on religion, the spiritual not only volunteer and give more to spiritual causes, they do more for secular causes than their non-religious counterparts.[145]

When I started working in the Norview area of Norfolk, I visited the three most prominent churches in the center of Five Points. This is a list of the ministries: food bank (all three churches), career development and job fairs, military ministry, partnership with the Urban League and Chamber of Commerce, job assistance and workforce development, homeless ministry, support of the elementary school (bookbags, holiday food baskets, Christmas sponsorship) (two churches), clothing ministry/thrift shop, prisoner re-integration ministry (two churches), recovery groups, community garden, utility bill assistance, Boy Scouts, and a polling location. That is just three of hundreds of religious organizations. Clearly, they have a far reach into neighborhoods. After his life-changing experience studying children on a corner of the south Bronx, Jonathan Kozol named a book after something he experienced: *Amazing Grace*.

> Saddened by the streets, I was repeatedly attracted into churches. I search them out, and although some of the pastors speak of politics and strategies of change, it is not their politics that I am really seeking, but their company. ... Many really do see Jesus in the faces of the poorest people whom they serve."[146]

Further evidence points to faith's importance. Researchers established a moderately strong association between attending religious services and decreased mortality.[147]

When I first heard of the World Happiness Report and World Happiness Day, I pictured a boardroom of clowns chaired by Ronald McDonald. Contrary to my first impression, it is a legitimate subsidiary of the United Nations that uses research by scholars and Gallup, Inc. It measures and compares world happiness and makes policy recommendations. One of the policy goals in the 2016 update was to arrive at a "Happiness Principle."[148] As religion worldwide declines, they are looking for ways to fill the void in happiness without faith. I suppose it is a backward compliment to faith's extensive role. In his epic book, *For the Love of Cities*, Peter Kageyama names meaning as a critical value in building an emotional connection to their neighborhoods and cities. He states, "I believe we are moving to a time when people will chase meaning the way they used to chase stock options and bonuses."[149] Faith is a significant avenue for finding that meaning.

Anchored in the Ancient

The faith community provides an interesting juxtaposition with government and academia. As the oldest grandson, I was the first to raid my grandparents' attic for historical treasures. Among the artifacts was a periodical from 1891 with the title *Public Opinion*. The ads were amusing. There were numerous ads for sanatoriums and two for property near the fledgling Stanford University. Another ad for Packer's Tar Soap made of an infusion of "Pure Pine Tar, Vegetable Oils and Glycerine" was said to be suitable for chapping, chafing, and dandruff.[150]

More importantly, it offered a look into life in 1891. One editorial reprinted from the *Atlanta Constitution* titled, "A Southern Opinion of Confederate Flags" defended the confederate flag.[151] In another column titled "Crime and Its Causes", Chicago Chief of Police addressed the causes of an increase in crime: "The chief causes of this increase Major McClaughry holds to be: Criminal parentage and association, neglect of children by their parents, idleness, intemperance, and gambling."[152] He called for prevention rather than punishment and dignified labor. Another editorial debated the influence of nurture vs. heredity on criminal behavior and countering it with social factors. An editorial from another periodical from 1866 complains about the state of schools. It called for more school funding and for parents to be more involved.[153] In the post-civil war period, they debated establishing a federal education bureau to equalize education and curriculum across the now unified states based on European models.[154]

Government and academic documents from a century ago sound eerily like today's. They frequently use the same flowery, visionary appeal to moral consciousness and call to action. When technology allowed photographs to be more widely used, carefully selected photos, frequently of children, became used to tug at heartstrings. The words "new" and "change" are ever popular: new models, new approaches, new thinking, new paradigms, etc. Take the following quotes from three different decades.

> "The lessons lie at the heart of ... [this] agenda, which seeks to transform high-poverty communities into high-opportunity communities—places that provide all the resources people need to thrive, including employment, job training, good schools, safe streets,

parks, healthy food retailers, transportation and affordable, high-quality housing."[155]

"A decent home and suitable living environment for every American family."[156]

"In order to break the poverty cycle, which has prevailed in most families within the ... area for scores of years, attention should be centered on the children in that cycle. The projects in this area do just that, but some are geared towards adults as well."[157]

[This program called for instructional improvement in schools, expanded school-community partnership, flexible organization of schools, facility improvements, economic development, housing, street improvements, healthy projects, justice and legal aid, recreation, and citizen participation.]

Literature from the Model Cities program in the late 1960s and early 1970s doesn't read much differently than today.

Political parties and academics differ on the amount. The general guesstimate is that the federal government has spent trillions of dollars on poverty since President Johnson declared war on poverty in 1964. Poverty is climbing, falling, and staying the same, depending on who is talking. An analysis by the Opportunity Insights group paints a neutral picture of 133 historical policy changes to welfare policies. Some programs, especially targeted toward low-income children's health and education, have admirable benefits relative to their cost.[158] Other programs, often targeting adults, have a lower benefit to cost value. Despite all the new programs, paradigms, models, innovation, conferences, books, and journal articles, poverty is still prevalent. If academics, businesses, and government pursue the new and fabulous, then religion anchors community to ancient wisdom.

Struggling with the Wonderful and Wacky World of Religion

Working with religious groups is as diverse as going to the zoo and often as entertaining. Many religious people are normal. Some are radicals. Some are dangerous. Some are looney. A healthy dose of skepticism is helpful because one never knows who one is dealing with. Here are some of the more entertaining headlines from my church embarrassments file: "Man Sues Church for $2.5M After being 'Felled by the Holy Spirit'" and "Pastor with 666 Tattoo Claims to be Divine."[159]

Looking for a way to break the news to kids that the Easter Bunny doesn't exist? Try this. A Pennsylvania church dressed a youth minister in a bunny costume, mock-whipped the costumed bunny, and smashed colored eggs to declare the true Easter message.[160] What communicates the love of Jesus better than beating up the Easter Bunny?

Have you received a lovely prayer rug from a church in Tulsa, Oklahoma? It came to my house addressed to "Dear friend" (from strangers I've never heard of). It wasn't so much a rug as an 11 x 17-inch piece of paper with the face of Jesus layered over the design of a Persian carpet. The summary instructions said to first stare into Jesus' eyes, which were closed. As you continue to look, his eyes will open. I have a lazy eye, so that may be why it didn't work for me. Next, one is to kneel on it with both knees. I'm unsure what happens if you only touch it with one knee. Maybe Jesus will wink in disapproval with only one eye. Finally, you are to return it the next day with your prayer card and donation so that someone else can benefit. The detailed instructions give additional options.

I once received a letter in a hand-addressed envelope from a Ms. Eaton in Chicago, IL. Ms. Eaton was concerned that God, Satan, demons, and aliens from other planets were here on Earth with us. Through the aid of disguises, another person can look just like you. She is, of course, the only one who knows these things. The letter concluded with, "Listen to Gerald Flurry ... He is a friend from another world. He is a space pilot."

In the wacky world of religion, I would describe myself as a bad evangelical. Much of faith is waiting, which is a problem for my impatience. I'm analytical and naturally curious, which puts me at odds with the always confident. I'm conservative in core theology, but life in the city has caused me to see things differently than popular suburban and rural evangelicalism.

Another struggle is that I'm quiet. Susan Cain and Brian Little are two of my heroes. Quiet thoughtfulness isn't always highly valued in a circle emphasizing living in constant community, outward confidence, and save-the-world busyness.

I'm bad at group prayer for the same reason I don't like round table discussions in meetings. I prefer executive summary communication, where there is a point, and people get to it quickly. I visited a prayer service at Norfolk's City Hall. They split into prayer groups of 12 to 15 people. The long-winded got revved up. As a loyal rule follower, I stayed in the group with my eyes closed until it ended. I was one of only three people left when I opened my eyes. The rest of the group had disintegrated while waiting on the impassioned verbose. After the prayer groups, they reconvened with a different speaker who started yelling and complaining about government. Since I work for government, I took it as my cue to leave. I could still hear him five floors up inside.

Another hurdle is that I can't sustain the feelings, nor do I understand the hyper-romantic "relationship/intimacy with Jesus" that is popular. I have moments of intense emotion, but my daily life doesn't make me swoon over Jesus or skip around and burp daisies. God-talk sometimes feels like a competition to one-up each other who is bosomier with Jesus. In the 1980s, there was a boys' stuffed doll named My Buddy that you could take with you, hug, and do whatever you wanted. Sometimes I think that Jesus has been turned into the My Buddy doll.

A Los Angeles gang beat down Van Zan Frater in the 1980s. He lay bleeding on the asphalt with a gun barrel pressed against his temple. Gang members encouraged the member holding the gun to "Kill the homeboy," to which Frater uttered, "Jesus is my homeboy and your homeboy, etc."[161] Gang members relented, content to leave him there beat down. Frater used the opportunity to reach out to gang members and other victims of gang violence. As the story goes, some budding entrepreneur got hold of the phrase and a screen print after the L.A. riots. They turned it into a Hollywood fad with celebrities wearing t-shirts and hats—all devoid of the original context. Someone bought my dad a hat. Homeboy Jesus became a pop icon of coolness utterly separate from the danger and risk of helping gang members.

My strongest influences early in my life were from the Greatest Generation. I suspect the Great Depression, World War II, the Korean conflict, the sixties, Vietnam, and the Cold War had worn away any emotion-based faith. They didn't tie their faith to emotional highs and lows, personal success, or health. Faith didn't rise and fall on daily circumstances. Instead, it was characterized by an abiding faith that God has a big picture, concrete dependability, practical wisdom, disciplined morality, and duty to community.

I doubt anyone will ask me to speak on spiritual disciplines. I tried a food fast for thirty hours once in Chicago. I tried hard, and the first day was tolerable after taking acetaminophen for the headache. I could think only of a chocolate shake from the nearby Burger King on the second day. In all practicality, I meditated on a milkshake. By the morning of the third day, I felt weak but made it to Burger King. On another occasion, the pastor once put incense in the offering plate for the spiritual effect. It was lost on me. I thought Floyd, the usher, was wearing cheap cologne that smelled like PineSol. Some songs I can't sing with integrity. One song poetically describes, "You're all I want. You're all I've ever needed." My analytical brain trips me up. If I'm at the 9:00 a.m. service, by 10:30, I will *need* to drain my bladder. By 11:30 a.m., I will *want* a sandwich. I feel like a constant failure because I'm not able to live in a purely spiritual state of mind as well as others.

I don't claim to hear God directly. I avoid phrases like "Jesus spoke to me" or "God put something on my heart" for several reasons. First, if I believed everyone who used those phrases, I would have a general impression that God is a schizophrenic, multiple-personality, neurotic who continually changes his mind. For another reason, I've been wrong enough not to further blame my dumb mistakes on God. If I go back to middle school, there are at least a dozen girls I had a crush on that I felt were "the one from God." When a cute Swedish exchange student came to my high school during my senior year, I thought God called me to Sweden. One of the things I most enjoy about working for government is that decisions aren't made by people claiming that God spoke to them. I can tell something about people's spirituality by their conduct and character, not how spiritual they talk.

All this is to say that I tread carefully on the subject of faith. I can understand and sympathize with those who leave organized religion. Hypocrisy, Machiavellian tactics, lack of common sense, and hatefulness are nothing new in the church. Reading Frederick Douglass's account of life as a slave is unpleasant but healthy. Take, for instance, the Rev. Rigby Hopkins.

> "Mr. Hopkins could always find some excuse for whipping a slave. It would astonish one, unaccustomed to a slaveholding life, to see in what wonderful ease a slaveholder can find things, of which to make occasion to whip a slave. ...And yet there was not a man anywhere round, who made higher professions of religion, or as more active in revivals,—more attentive to the class, love-feast, prayer and preaching meetings, or more devotional in his family—that prayed earlier, later, louder, and longer,—than this same reverend slave—driver Rigby Hopkins".[162]

In a separate parody, he wrote one verse that summed it up quite well,

> "Another preacher whining spoke
>
> Of One whose heart for sinners broke:
>
> He tied old Nanny to an oak,
>
> And drew the blood at every stroke,
>
> And prayed for heavenly union."[163]

For all the hypocritical barbarism Douglass experienced, one would not be surprised if he gave up on faith. Yet quite the opposite. He writes lovingly of the Christianity of Christ.

I was equally surprised listening to a panel at a state housing conference of four tribal chiefs among Virginia's seven federally recognized Indian tribes (2018). Chief Gerald Steward of the Chickahominy Tribe, Eastern Division, shared that despite all the injustices suffered at the English settlers' hands, the Indians on the panel abide in Christ and his big picture for them. After surviving 400 years of oppression, they still face monumental problems, but "we have a big God." It turns out that Chief Steward is also a Baptist minister. So, underneath the fraud, there is still something that people like Douglass and Indian chiefs in Virginia find authentic.

When I think about faith today, I am more attracted to behind-the-scenes faith, not the flashy. Megachurches or the latest hip churches impress me like Dolly Parton's Pirates' Voyage in Myrtle Beach impressed me. They provide an excellent, moving experience. Similarities abound. Much of church growth literature is spiritualized marketing that could just as easily apply to Panera. Have good, consistent organization and select good locations with good demographics. Hire talented staff. Spend money on the right amenities. Know the target market. Shape the product to give a great experience.

This is not to criticize large, thriving churches. They make enormous contributions, and I would be hypocritical for not admitting I enjoy churches with talent myself. The difficulty I am pinpointing is that it is difficult to tell the difference between surface appearances, like diamonds from cubic zirconia. If success is the criteria, you can't always tell what is genuinely God from what is good business sense. After a court case, it came out in the news that one large church had a tiered giving system. The higher the giving bracket, the more special privileges one received—nearly identical to hotel reward points. Through the years, I suspect God does far more than we know and far less than people take credit. This is why I am attracted to the more challenging duct-tape communities where faith is more complicated to fake.

A Ministry of Getting in the Way

When I first thought of moving to Chicago, Wilson Avenue in Chicago's Uptown neighborhood wasn't what I had in mind. It is undoubtedly the most unique place I've ever lived. It was near the height of gang warfare. In this setting, I met a church staff member named Brian Bakke from Uptown Baptist Church. Brian had a ministry of "getting in the way," as he called it. The son of Ray Bakke, he grew up in the Uptown and Edgewater area as a pastor's son at Edgewater Baptist Church. Life was rough in the neighborhood, so he finished high school at a private school in northern Virginia while living with his uncle, Dennis Bakke, the former C.E.O. of Applied Energy Services. He then went away to attend college and play football at Wake Forest in North Carolina. He was on a track to go pro. His only plans for returning to Uptown were from the back of a limo. After graduating, Uptown beckoned, and he returned not as a pro athlete but as a janitor at Uptown Baptist Church.

Once in Uptown, Bakke and his wife had a problem with graffiti tagged on their house. Youth painted graffiti. He painted back over it, which went back and forth several times. Finally, in exasperation, he beat them at their own game and painted a mural on their house. Not only did the graffiti stop, but he established a rapport and street credibility with youth in the neighborhood. This turned into a ministry. They took talent that youth would have used for vandalism and painted murals within the neighborhood. Combined with a graphic arts program at the church, this led to an agreement with Chicago officials to release juvenile graffiti offenders to their care to turn their talent positively. One of their murals was visible from the

El at the Red Line's Wilson Avenue stop. He took a neighborhood problem and turned it into an asset.

They also used their gym for sports. Gangs were so bad in Uptown at the time that the church had to pick up youth from different parts of the neighborhood separately by van. It wasn't safe for them to walk across gang lines a few blocks away. They patted down youth on their way in for weapons, but basketball took over once on the court. Bakke used sports and art to build relationships with neighborhood youth. On one occasion, he saw gang members hiding weapons and preparing for a fight, so he started sweeping the street. Over six feet tall with matching street credibility, this was his ministry of "getting in the way." It prevented the fight. The Bakkes are an amazing family propelled by faith. Bakke's dad served with the older Mayor Daley and with Mayor Washington. His uncle Dennis went on to invest his profits from A.E.S. into Imagine Schools.

Breakthrough Urban Ministry

Arloa Sutter is another one of those amazing people. She started Breakthrough Urban Ministries in 1992 with sandwiches, soup, and hot coffee for the homeless in an unused church meeting room in Chicago's Andersonville neighborhood. Today, Breakthrough and its services reside in their own $6 million multi-purpose facility. In 1993, they partnered with the Andersonville Chamber of Commerce and the Clark Street business district to pay guests to pick up litter and keep the business district clean, Cleanstreet. The first was so successful five other business associations joined, and Mayor Daley used it as a model. In 1995, they opened an overnight shelter, the Dwelling Place, with support services. Each guest met with a caseworker who helped them set regular goals. They partnered with a health care agency to assist addicts with entering treatment facilities. They also did job training for janitorial jobs.

Recognizing that street youth and youth from the church's traditional youth group were two different audiences, they began working with youth separately in a youth outreach that targeted 15 at-risk 7th-grade boys in a sports and mentoring program. In addition, they started a tutoring program that linked 25 grammar school children with adult mentors.

Through a series of partnership opportunities and the need to expand to larger facilities, they moved from Andersonville to the East Garfield neighborhood. What made them so innovative when I met Arloa was their ability to beat NIMBY. Rather than focus on large numbers, Breakthrough focused on making incremental but steady breakthroughs with a small number of homeless, thirty or fewer at a time. Other churches tried to open large, dormitory-style, hundred-bed shelters and met backlash from the community. Breakthrough was able to bypass that. Guests received strict instructions on when to arrive and leave to avoid loitering in the neighborhood. In this way, they avoided neighborhood conflict.

They begin with the premise that every person deserves to be treated with dignity and respect, including the homeless and mentally ill. During graduate school, Arloa spent time on the streets to experience shelter life firsthand as a homeless woman. Many of the larger shelters were cold and impersonal. Today, they continue this model by offering a Breakthrough Fresh Market that allows clients to "shop" for food rather than accept a pre-packaged bag of goods from a food pantry.

What also stood out to me about Breakthrough is Arloa herself. During my time in Chicago, she oversaw Breakthrough's rapid expansion, raised two teenage daughters, and attended graduate school full-time. In one of our final semesters, she experienced several personal losses in her family within a relatively short period.

Despite personal difficulties, Arloa, like my sister Beth, has the unique ability to make anyone feel like they are the most important person in the world. I remember stumbling for words to comfort her and walking away thinking, "What just happened?". She somehow left me feeling better. I do not doubt that her struggles have deepened the sense of compassion she has for others.

Looking for Faith

If faith is a substitute word for wish fulfillment, as it is among some, many of the most admired people in my life are failures. None of the previous examples started from personal ambition but emerged from sacrificial action counter to ambition. The fact that they became successful is secondary. They did what they did because it was the right thing to do. They were motivated by something higher than themselves. Faith, as defined by religions, differs from pop culture's faith. Submission is a common theme among the world's three largest religions. However, the faith of pop culture, says, "If you believe in your heart, you can do anything" or "Always be true to your dreams." It is usually internally focused on oneself.

The early seasonal episodes from *American Idol* were full of people who believed in their hearts but couldn't sing nonetheless. I always considered it a tragedy that no one bothered to tell them they couldn't sing before they went on national T.V. and embarrassed themselves. Belief in your heart alone doesn't get anyone admitted to the N.F.L., the F.B.I., or Juilliard. Faith, as defined by religions, on the other hand, is external. For the Jews tortured history or the church's first century, faith didn't place personal success as the measure of life fulfillment. Instead, religious faith holds to a big picture beyond the mountains of adversity, even when an individual's role in that big picture may not be apparent.

Luther Powell worked long hours in the garment industry during the Great Depression. He had no comprehension at the time that his self-assured manner and caring leadership to the residents of Kelly Street in the Bronx would be an inspiring example to the future Chairman of the Joint Chiefs of Staff, his son Colin.[164] Carrie Cash sang songs of faith with her children while picking cotton. She also played guitar and fiddle on the porch. When her son was interested in music, she took in schoolteachers' laundry to pay for his voice lessons. She had no comprehension that her son Johnny would become one of the best-selling musicians ever.[165]

In surroundings about as opposite in the United States as they can get, two future leaders were nourished by parents who sacrificed for an unseen but bigger picture. One was Black from the asphalt streets of the Bronx in New York City. The other was White from the black-land dirt in the rural south of Dyess, Arkansas. One of the few commonalities between the Cashes and the Powells was that their belief in a bigger picture was nourished by neighborhood churches—a Baptist church in Dyess and St. Margarets in the Bronx.

If the accomplishment of one's dreams measures success, my mother was a complete failure. Part of her dream in nursing school was to one day own a canary-yellow corvette. Instead, her first semi-new car was a red, 1990s demo-model Pontiac Grand Am that a teenager learning to drive nearly destroyed. As we began leaving home for college, she dreamed of retiring and owning a home and jet skis on Smith Mountain Lake in Virginia. Her kids and anticipated grandkids could come and play, and the family would be together. Instead, at age 59, just weeks after her first grandchildren's births, she was diagnosed with ovarian cancer. She spent her first Christmas with grandchildren in Christiana Hospital, Delaware, having a tumor removed. She spent their first birthday drugged up and nauseated after chemo. She died the same week as my nephew's third birthday and her 42nd wedding anniversary. Her "retirement" was spent in chemotherapy and paying medical bills far removed from any dream house on Smith Mountain Lake. If the accomplishment of dreams measures success or faith, she was a grand failure.

If measured by putting three kids through college debt-free, by three kids who all married terrific spouses, by all the patients for whom she cared in the E.R., by the grieving families she comforted and held, by young people and parents she counseled, by all the friends who ate at our table, then she was a remarkable success.

On one occasion, she had just bought brand-new, white, work shoes. The first day she wore them, an older woman came to the E.R. in pain. The woman had impacted bowels. That is a nice medical way of saying that Mom had to clean out the woman's rectum. Some of the contents fell on mom's new white shoes. That memory quickly dashes any sense of superiority that I have over others. What would I be doing without a mother who cleaned old women's rectums to help put me through school? She was similarly the unpleasant recipient of other people's vomit, blood, coughing, and sneezes.

Nevertheless, she provided critical but not appreciated medical care to uncooperative children, drunks, and criminals. She performed those duties because she believed she was contributing to a bigger picture. Although culture is obsessed with self, there is no shame in giving up your dreams to support someone else's. This faith, not consumed with personal success or attention, is a faith that enriches the soul of communities and fuels neighborliness.

Value - Living Above the Social Status Competition

Key Idea: Faith circumvents the fuzzy math of social status.

The number 42 tells a story. By my stride, that is the number of steps between the first door to the slave quarters and the rear door of the William McClean house in Appomattox Court House, where General Lee surrendered to General Grant during the Civil War. Forty-two steps and skin color separated a life of slavery and a life of privilege, a life of wealth and a life of poverty. The numbers are slightly different in more recent times—125 ft. That was the distance between Norfolk's Nordstrom (since closed) and the former 618 public housing units in the 44-acre Tidewater Gardens first occupied in 1955. The median household income on one side of the street was $10,000. On the other side of the street were $120 shirts and $300 dress shoes inside Nordstrom's door. Only 125 feet separated those struggling to survive and those who could afford $120 status symbols in the great American comparison contest. Residents of Tidewater Gardens and two adjacent 1940s and 1950s public housing projects passed through a world in which they could see and maybe even touch but not have.

The Fuzzy Math of Social Status

The great American comparison contest includes the fuzzy math of social status. We often measure ourselves on social status scales that fluctuate for any audience or room. Intelligence and education, for instance, are part of those scales. I have a Bachelor's degree and a Master's degree; add 25 points. They're from schools with no name recognition; deduct 10 points. I say something witty; add 5 points.

I make a lousy joke; subtract 5 points. I gain 10 points for my education in a room of blue-collar workers. I lose 10 points in a room of Ph.D's. I'm a quiet introvert; deduct 20 points in most settings where loud is proud. Physical appearance is another scale. I'm balding, have a lazy eye, uneven ears, and a crooked row of bottom teeth; deduct 20 points in most places. However, when visiting a nursing home, the ladies still think I'm a stud; add 20 points.

Like most, I prefer places where I have the most social-standing points. I like work because I make clear gains in my social-standing score. I'm a good analyst, love research, enjoy problem-solving, and am creative. Add 30 points on the job. Outside work, I hemorrhage social standing points at parties and social functions. I have little to no interest in sports, art, celebrities, or the latest about Brad Pitt or Britney Spears. Celebrity relationships and personal lives are their business, not mine. I lose points for not being up on pop culture or being prolific on social media.

I'm a White Protestant male. In some places, I gain points; in others, it costs me points. As far as I can tell, Dad's family came from the north and fought for the Union. By my calculation, I should earn some points from them never owning or supporting slavery. What points I gain on Dad's side are lost on mom's side. They descended from the Shenandoah Valley of Virginia. My great, great-grandfather was a private in the 23rd Virginia Cavalry. The church building from the 1850s, where I think my great-grandmother attended, has a loft for slaves. Although there is no evidence that they were ever wealthy enough to own slaves, some were rotten from stories I've heard. Do I lose social standing points for mom's ancestry?

Be yourself. Follow your heart. Be true to your authentic self. But which self is that? I'm familiar with the cliches, but I am unsure which self or heart they are referring to. My authentic self wants to ram the idiots' cars in our parking garage at work who drive like it's Daytona. The inclination of my heart wants to tell a few people in Norfolk where they can shove it with a few choice words. My true self and heart have led me to say many hurtful things I regret. My true self is envious of my brother's extroversion and biceps. My heart is jealous of my sister being named to the Hampton Roads 40 Under 40, and I wasn't. My authentic self has racist thoughts in moments of anger or disagreement. My true self is afraid of a long list of fears. If I were my true self and followed my heart all the time, I would be unemployed, divorced, and in jail. I'm a big mess of mixed motives.

I don't understand those who say they have no regrets. I have a dump truckload. It is hard to learn from mistakes if I can't admit I've made any. It is hard to heal relationships without saying, "I'm sorry."

Moreover, I'm not sure who I really am. Who I am today differs from a few years ago and who I will be later. Our social status score constantly fluctuates, because it is subjective and relative to our feelings and those around us. Faith offers a way to circumvent the fuzzy math of social status.

Equality of Value

Inequality has been around for millennia. The Jewish text demonstrates that societies have been wrestling with income inequality and the rich's tendency to get richer as far back as Moses, somewhere around 1400 BC.[166] In the Hebrew book of Leviticus, God gave the Israelites a mechanism for resetting their economic system every 50 years. Landowners who had accumulated land would have to return it to genealogical heirs. It would have been a colossal reset button on the economy every 50 years. Unfortunately, they weren't successful at bridging the gap from what the Hebrew prophets tell us. There is little evidence that it was ever actually implemented. The numbers never seem to balance in any age.

Children learn inequality relatively early. Nieces and nephews in elementary school are not yet contemplating concepts like democratic socialism or Esther Duflo and Abhijit Banerjee's *Good Economics for Hard Times*. They are still reading *Walter the Farting Dog* (which is much more entertaining than books on economics). By the first grade, when it comes time to choose teams for kickball, they learn that some are better athletes than others. When graded in school, they realize some are better students. When they go to birthday parties, they recognize some have wealthier parents. When they have their first swim meet or sit for their first recital, they learn some parents are more active with their kids than others. There is an inexplicable luck to the distribution of talents, health, community, and privilege.

Faith in God offers a constant value outside the great American social status competition. Neighborhood Walts are a good example. Dr. Howard Hendricks grew up in a family in a north Philadelphia neighborhood that scholars and policymakers study how to fix. He was from a broken home in a neighborhood where he didn't feel like anyone particularly cared whether he lived or died.[167]

Dr. Hendricks credits a change in his life trajectory to a man named Walt, who had only a sixth-grade education and introduced himself to Dr. Hendrick's through a game of marbles. Walt had asked to start a middle school Sunday school class at his church, but they had no students. Church leaders reluctantly agreed to let him teach if he found students. Walt went out and found some. He found 13 teen boys, nine of whom were from broken homes. He wasn't the best teacher but imparted value to their lives by caring about them. Eleven of the thirteen went on to seek the college education

Walt never received and entered full-time vocational ministry. For neighborhood Walts, it is not a policy debate or a white paper. It was an investment of the heart to pour value into thirteen "high-risk" young men because he believed that he and those 13 boys had value to God.

The religious world calls its adherents to value people because people are valuable creations, not because they fit into a treasured marketing demographic, score high on the social status scale, or because their business is desired.

Perfect equality and perfect freedom are in perpetual tension with each other. Neither exists for very long at the same time. Despite all modern efforts to the contrary, the truth that there is no perfect equality eventually becomes self-evident. The outward signs of social stratification are everywhere. They are in our job titles, clothes, transportation, parking spaces, worksites, and pay scales. If one bases their value purely on comparison with others or external circumstances, they will be doomed to despair. Someone always has more.

Faith offers a way to internalize one's value without waiting for the rest of the world to validate it. Religion has offered a level field for centuries. From towering mega-churches, tiny storefronts, synagogues, mosques, and jungle huts, children have been told by parents, grandmothers, and teachers that they are valued for no other reason than being created by God and given purpose. They have intrinsic value apart from all outward circumstances.

Martin Luther King Jr.'s speeches and writings resound with man's dignity for no other reason than being created in the image of God. Music and art in the religious world are filled with a sense of value regardless of outward circumstances. Reverend Timothy Wright's "Jesus, Jesus, Jesus" song was dubbed the Katrina song after

Hurricane Katrina. It is about an older woman who was failed by all human systems in New Orleans but was upheld by her faith. Kirk Franklin confronts disparities in the American Dream in his song "OK."

Where is the American dream?

If only one percent knows what it means

To really be ok (are y'all listening?)

Tell me is that ok? (Huh, say it again)

But he concludes it will be ok because hope is found in God's person and strength.

God has no fuzzy math of social status. Hipness, monetary resources, social status, likes on social media, or other socially acceptable measures do not determine value. Millions of the world's undervalued have identified with Jesus being born in a barn because there was no room in the inn.

I have met people in every city who believe in their value regardless of outward status symbols. Over the years, I've often preferred work in lower-income neighborhoods because of this lack of pretension. Inner security, regardless of outward circumstances, has enormous implications. One of workforce development's challenges, apart from job aptitudes, is individuals who lack inner security. Educators can teach job skills, but a person who flies off the handle at every perceived insult doesn't hold jobs long.

James McRae (a.k.a. U-Man) expresses it well. He wrote a piece called "Silent Screams of a Convict", a passionate plea to communicate worth and value to new generations.

> Consequently, while these new waves of criminals make their way behind these [prison] walls, an unpredictable number of you citizens are expected to be victimized. Under those circumstances, you cannot afford to remain uninvolved while your neighbors and loved ones are being abused or slain.
>
> I beg you to champion this call for change. Work to stop children from being attracted to violent people ... criminals. Help them to know their self-worth and the value of others.
>
> ...Your roar should echo through all social gatherings. Advertise humans as greater than lifeless concepts, verbal insults, and material objects.[168]

His word choice is impeccable. He calls on adults to roar the value of these young lives before they end up where he did.

Shopping for Love vs. Duct-tape Marriage

This ability to be secure in oneself affects how we love others and perceive marriage. The great American comparison contest extends into the search for a mate. Popular entertainment and the market have manipulated perceptions of a satisfying marriage into superficial images. Research is raising concerns about the impact of online dating. In a journal article, "Relationshopping: Investigating the market metaphor in online dating," researchers raised concerns about how the market metaphor of spouse shopping influences self-perception and objectifying others.[169] Finding a mate can be viewed like shopping for a car or a new jacket.

I've found greater wisdom from older couples in duct-tape communities than the superficial images projected by T.V., movies, and magazines. Simple, duct-tape community seniors offer a more realistic view of self, others, and a married life built on shared values.

I love to listen to my supervisor, Oneiceia Howard, talk about her grandparents, Rosa and James Key. Her Black grandparents faced harsher struggles while growing up during Jim Crow in Georgia than my White grandparents, but they weathered other struggles with similar values. Both our grandparents were raised in the country during the Depression. Both grandmothers were strict about having a clean house, loved to cook for others, were involved with their churches, loved their gardens, were frugal, and avoided extravagance. Both grandmothers' health declined after strokes.

Both couples' religious involvement was in no way disconnected from their long life together. On the contrary, their church involvement provided values, ethical standards, support systems, social integration into the community, and accountability. Oneiceia's grandparents were married 70 years before Rosa passed. My grandparents were two months shy of their 70th anniversary when my grandfather died. Their love was formidable in both cases. The Keys and the Herbsts were two couples of two races in two different locations yet had such similar values because their values were from the same source. In neither case was their love the fairytale love from movies and T.V.

Studies document the role faith communities play in marriage and families. They protect a body of ancient values. They also become informal, multi-generational mentoring peer groups. Numerous studies report the benefits of religious community involvement in marriages, families, and general well-being[170].

These studies usually come with a list of disclaimers for the divorce rate in the Bible Belt and all the maladjusted, poorly educated Billy Bobs who beat their wives and kids into "submission." Marital success and satisfaction further correlate to education, maturity, and economic well-being, not merely faith. The disclaimer list also covers the Pastor Nincompoops, who consider it an assault on their masculinity to do dishes or wash their dirty underwear. Many of their children run from the church and their father's hypocritical, tyrannical rule over the family. A 35-year generational study of faith conducted from the University of California shows that overly zealous parents often produced rebel children.[171] Instead, parental warmth was critical to transmitting faith.

Evidence supports the benefit of religious community involvement. A recent book reported that couples involved in church life "are more likely to adhere to a `code of decency' which includes hard work, temperance, obedience to the law, fidelity, care of family and personal responsibility."[172]

In communities nationwide, couples like the Keys and Herbsts model a love much different from fairy tale love. They share a commitment to values and valuing each other. The value of marriage itself is equal to and, in some cases, higher than their commitment to each other when marriage is not incredibly convenient or thrilling. They believe great marriages are made, not a product of love at first sight.

I've also observed a common thread of structured but flexible gender roles in marriage. Gender wars at the popular level are between the two extremes of rigid gender roles and complete gender role anarchy. Neither seems to be healthy. Rigid gender roles are oppressive, and anarchy leads to constant confusion and the emotional toll of negotiating every responsibility. The older couples I've observed have learned to place honoring each other above gender roles.

These marriage role models are a joy to observe and are very important to neighborhoods because they model love in realistic settings. The President's Marriage Project under President Obama asked why we should care.

> Why should we care? Marriage is not merely a private arrangement; it is also a complex social institution. Marriage fosters small cooperative unions—also known as stable families—that enable children to thrive, shore up communities, and help family members to succeed during good times and to weather the bad times. Researchers are finding that the disappearance of marriage in Middle America is tracking with the disappearance of the middle class in the same communities, a change that strikes at the heart of the American Dream.[173]

The same report quotes Andrew Cherlin, who observed that American intimate relationships are now more like a carousel, with people stepping on and off with great regularity[174].

Regarding quality marriages, the meek of the earth seem to inherit the prize. This is usually in stark contrast to the celebrities. Duct-tape couples may drive old Buicks, Cadillacs, and Chrysler 300s, not the latest luxury vehicle. Many still live in modest World War II-era cottages with only one bathroom, not The Bachelor or The Bachelorette set. A special night out may be going to Cracker Barrel, not Paris, but they are steadfastly in love just the same.

Time, values, and peer groups are the significant determiners of marriage fulfillment, not how often couples have sex a week, how toned their abs, the cost of their shoes, visiting exotic locations for anniversaries, or the other endless fluff in magazines and T.V. The demands of daily life, jobs, changing diapers, keeping house, raising teenagers, paying bills, and caring for aging parents are stressful, tedious, and monotonous. How couples choose to respond to resistance in life grows or weakens the muscle tissue of marriage. Enduring love by time-tested couples isn't revealed by having their hands all over each other like two horny teenagers but by the tenderness with which older couples care for each other: sharing meals, pushing wheelchairs, holding doors, and carrying oversized purses.

It is profound that older generations' love was so deep. All those poor, uneducated, older couples didn't have all the modern guidance of T.V. talk shows and grocery store checkout magazines to instruct them on the ways of love and sex that sizzles. Somehow, these older couples recognized love without the best-selling expert advice. Fulfillment seems to favor ancient wisdom, emphasizing values, character, and delayed gratification.

Prince Charles and Lady Diana had a fairytale wedding, which did not guarantee happiness. Some say it was the most expensive in history when adjusted for inflation.[175] It had a horse-drawn carriage, a queen, a full complement of royal uniforms, trumpets, a cathedral, a wedding dress with a 25-foot train, and a gargantuan ring. Both the wedding dress and the ring even have their own Wikipedia entries. In 2016, CNN Money calculated the average wedding cost at $33,641.[176] With the divorce rate at 50 percent, that isn't a very good return on investment.

Like neighborhoods, we chase the perfect while ignoring the beauty of the imperfect. Faith provides a constant inner value that is not dependent on external circumstances. It circumvents the fuzzy math of social status in the great American comparison contest. It also informs of a love more profound than the grocery store popcorn advice.

Grief - An Underrated Gift

Key Idea: Faith-biased grief opens the soul to grace.

Duct-tape Community is a declaration that community takes two resolves: one to make the world a fairer place and a second to be neighborly in one that isn't. Perched on a perfectly balanced fulcrum between these two resolves in girls' Mary Jane shoes, a bow in her hair, plaid dress, and tiny satchel was the nation's most famous six-year-old and her older counterparts in Norfolk.

Nearly sixty years after she first braved a simple walk to school, the story of Ruby Bridges still inspires a nation. Norman Rockwell's iconic picture of Ruby hung over my former director, Michelle Johnson's, steps. Ruby Bridges was the six-year-old who integrated the all-White William Frantz Elementary School in New Orleans in 1960. The images of a six-year-old being escorted by U.S. Marshals past violent mobs and dodging projectiles thrown at her have stuck in my mind since I first read her story during college.

She puzzled Harvard psychiatrist Dr. Robert Coles with her remarkable sense of peace through such a traumatic ordeal. The absence of trauma symptoms perplexed Coles, who had practiced psychiatry in Boston's upper-middle-class. Children and parents in well-to-do situations showed far greater anxiety, and yet Bridges's parents were impoverished.[177]

Coles' story is included in the book, *Finding God at Harvard*. He peppered Ruby and her family with questions about her psychological well-being, looking for signs of her breaking.

"How are you doing Ruby?"

"I'm OK."

He asked her parents. "She's doing fine," they said.

He asked about her appetite. She was eating just fine. He asked about her relationships with friends. She played with her friends as usual.

Her teacher, Barbara Henry, was just as perplexed. Mrs. Henry said she was happy and cheerful. Days turned into months as he studied Ruby.

After her teacher observed her talking through the mobs each day, she asked Ruby what she was saying. It turns out that Ruby was praying for them. Ruby kept a list of people and prayed for them every night, just like the church pastor did. She prayed daily for the mobs of whites who persecuted her. Her pastor had taught her that Jesus was mistreated yet practiced forgiveness, so she did likewise.

Ruby's simple, duct-tape faith shocked the experts. Her faith and inner orientation caused her to react in very different ways than expected and gave her a different reference point for processing her experience. Her reference point wasn't a philosophical argument. It was a story. In this case, it was the story of Jesus, according to Coles. It was combined with her devotion to her mother, according to Bridges's book, *Through My Eyes*.[178]

Any book concerned with the who, how, and why of neighborliness would be incomplete if ignoring two gifts tied with this simple faith: faith-biased grief and grace. The tumult of Bridges' initial year subsided. Her life was quieter and approached a more normal routine, but it was not without further heartache. Her teacher and best friend, Barbara Henry, wasn't liked by the school principal and moved back to Boston. Bridge's parents later divorced, in part due to the stress of integration. Her mom struggled financially and moved into public housing. Her brother was later killed in a drug-related shooting. As whites moved to the suburbs, the William Frantz Elementary School became re-segregated as majority Black and suffered from poverty.

During this grief, Ruby Bridges decided as an adult that her influence and purpose were not yet complete. She started the Ruby Bridges Foundation, which invested resources in her former school and other schools around New Orleans. She became an author and national speaker, and Disney produced a movie about her story. And, she reunited with Mrs. Henry.

Grief, as intended here, refers to the ability to hurt in non-destructive ways over loss, unfilled longings, and unmet expectations, especially for fairness. Whether it is the story of whites carrying a Black doll in a casket to taunt Ruby on her way into the first grade, 14-year-old Emmit Till tortured and lynched in Mississippi, the legions of family members killed by drunk drivers, losing military members in brutal wars, school shootings, or being born with severe disabilities, faith-biased grief is the ability to experience pain and hurt without losing some glimmer of hope. Faith-biased grief accepts reality for what it is without denying emotions their due course or living in fantasy land.

Faith-biased grief is overshadowed in the U.S. by the glitz and giddiness of the health and wealth gospel, but it is not absent in scripture. The Hebrew scriptures contain a book dedicated to mourning. King David put sorrow and injustice to music. Jeremiah was the weeping prophet. The shortest verse in the Christian scriptures is "Jesus wept." Jesus' most famous sermon calls the mournful blessed, and the apostle Paul commands it.

Dr. M. Scott Peck, the late psychiatrist and author of *The Road Less Travelled*, describes depression as healthy when within boundaries.

It is a giving-up process on the road to maturity of the ideas, things, and people we ultimately can't or shouldn't keep. For Peck, the list includes giving up the desire for omnipotent control over life, the "freedom" of un-commitment, possession of other people, various forms of power, and the fantasy of immortality. We become abnormal and stunted in our growth when we are "unwilling or unable to suffer the pain of giving up the outgrown which needs to be forsaken."[179] To his list, I would add the expectation that life is fair.

Faith-biased grief is a confrontation with reality, which can be hard to recognize. I shivered in disbelief the first time I came across a website in the 1990s showing celebrities without makeup or when they weren't filming. They were as saggy, flabby, and moley as the rest of us. Despite botox and saline implants, the statuesque physiques, washboard abs, perfect complexions, and youthful eyes were gone. Celebrities that I thought were sexy suddenly looked like my mom. It ruined the illusion. Grief has a way of stripping away superficial fantasy, but it nourishes the conditions for healthy neighborliness to grow.

T.V. shows like *Hoarders* or *Intervention* bring high-definition clarity to the power of self-deception. Self-deception is powerful.

Grief allows us to build community in the world as it is, not just in our idealized fantasy. Marriage is illustrative. Every marriage ends in heartache. It either ends in divorce court or the funeral home. Years of melding together a sacred union eventually lead to being torn asunder. Paradoxically, the awareness of that demise makes the present more meaningful. When I pledged vows to my Jenny, I knew that death one day awaits us. It is grievous to consider, but it offers the decision to make the present count. The first thing I often do in the morning and the last thing at night is to thank God for my beautiful, wonderful Jenny. Healthy grief is a priceless gift. It anchors us to reality and vents the soul. In many respects, prayer is a beneficial act of grief. Prayer involves a mental and spiritual release of things beyond our control.

Faith-biased grief's application to community is in its power to clarify love as the motive regardless of the outcome. Ambition may be more subdued than the corporate world, but it is an enormous driver in government and community development. In chasing grand causes, people can become less loving, thoughtful, and kind. Leaders ruin great causes when they forget to love beyond their narrow focus. Their identity becomes so entwined with achieving success that they lose love. People become the means, not the end.

Perfect equality is a mystical beast that we talk about and chase but never find. Without grief, it will drive us mad. Leaders unable to hurt healthily and who always run from pain can inflict the same cruelty on others that they abhor themselves. I can't think of anyone who loves profoundly and doesn't hurt profoundly. Healthy grieving is a profound gift that accompanies simple faith. It is faith-biased grief that permits its adherents to function in a flawed, unjust, absurd, cruel, and partially evil world.

The Un-Fixable

This gift of grief means coming to grips with our human inability to fix everything. Any time I hear speakers claim that there should be no poverty or homelessness in a nation as wealthy as the United States, it is usually a giveaway that the speaker hasn't worked closely with the poor or homeless. Wealth, or lack thereof, is usually only a fraction of the problem.

When I moved to Hazelwood, I met families and individuals for whom I had the highest hopes of helping. I was one of many. I met people with teams of social workers, therapists, educators, job trainers, and volunteers trying to help them. Despite financial assistance, a robust social service net, caring individuals, education programs, home repair assistance, financial literacy training, parenting support, and more, some were just as dysfunctional ten years later as when I came. They lived from one drama to another and expected others to bail them out.

I learned about "harm reduction strategies" from watching *Hoarders*. It is the term used when resources are exhausted trying to help people who won't cooperate. In Hazelwood, there were half a dozen people at any given time. I received one phone call for toilet paper from one frequent flier on the needy list. Although I had been in the habit of saying no, I couldn't deny a man toilet paper. One family asked for help with a move, but there was no moving truck or movers when I arrived. There were so many overflowing containers of cat litter boxes that I went into the bathroom to gag.

In the month following September 11, 2001, I received a phone call, which I first thought was a prank call from teenagers. The gentleman thought that September 11 was caused by aliens from outer space, as predicted in a comic book. The only solution was Batman. Batman would fight the aliens. He talked for about 15 minutes. I responded by doing what every good Protestant would do; I referred him to the social worker at the Catholic Church.

The severest case was a couple whose children were removed by child protective services. For two years, social workers tried to reunite the family, but the bottom line was that the couple didn't do what they were supposed to. I sympathize with the dual tragic stories of their upbringing in addicts' homes and with their addiction struggles, but they were not capable of being parents at that time. No program was able to fix them.

In all those cases, there were no solutions. There was a recurring tension between showing love and drawing boundaries. They were all worthy of love, respect, and compassion, but no amount of human effort fixed them. Cities across the country had branches known as "Office to End Homelessness," which have not, in truth, ended homelessness. A local fundraiser was dubbed "Ending Poverty." As of writing, they have not yet succeeded.

Technology, science, education, and wealth make it easy to lure us into a false sense of security that we can master unlimited solutions to everything. Both mother nature and human nature have proven otherwise. The suggestion here is not to give up but to say it is ok to grieve what we cannot fix.

Grief Through Evil

Economist Milton Friedman observed, "The typical state of mankind is tyranny, servitude, and misery."[180] Akerlof and Shiller use the phrase "phishing equilibrium" to refer to intentional deception in the marketplace to manipulate us into buying what is harmful or unnecessary.[181] Dr. Peck wrote a lesser-known but bone-chilling book, *People of the Lie*. He chronicled evil that he witnessed during years of psychiatric practice, which his scientific training from Harvard and his M.D. from Case Western Reserve could not explain. He credits this observation of evil as part of his move toward faith. It is scary partly because of the potential of evil I see within myself. I believe in sin because of my failures and willingness to blame others.

With freedom always comes its evil abuse. People often overlook evil if they get something out of it. Neither Lenin, Hitler, nor Stalin were Voldemort. None achieved power through magic. It was yielded to them because they gave people something they wanted.

Like Peck, even if I have questioned God's existence, I have never questioned the existence of evil. The Cold War thawed with the collapse of the Berlin Wall in 1989 while I was in high school. U.S. Troops steamrolled in and out of Kuwait in record time in 1991. We thought the world was headed into a new era of peace, detente, and glasnost. Unfortunately, such an expectation was not long-lasting. Since September 11, 2001, bodybags have been returning from overseas wars. In 1999, we thought the Columbine school shooting was an isolated, one-time incident. After Columbine came Virginia Tech, Sandy Hook, Parkland, Uvalde, and dozens of lesser-known school shootings.

Most may not remember the name Omran Daqneesh. He was the bloodied five-year-old covered in gray dust, whom rescuers removed from a building, another innocent victim of the civil war in Syria. The image of his little body sitting in shock with his feet hanging over the edge of an ambulance seat, covered in dust, sent shockwaves as it made its way around the globe in the 24-hour news cycle. That is until the next image replaced Omran.

Early in my career, a family called me to comfort a teenager we knew in a rural area of Harford County, Maryland. A husband doused his wife with gasoline in a drunken rage and threatened to light her. A sheriff's sharpshooter was able to shoot him before he ignited the gasoline.

As I quickly found out in Pittsburgh, the paperwork and approval process for becoming a 501(c)(3) tax-exempt designated non-profit was immense because there were so many shams. The wealthy use them as tax shields. Politicians use them to bypass campaign finance rules. Criminals use them to launder money. After Hurricane Katrina, the Government Accountability Office established a Fraud Task Force to keep up with frauds trying to cash in on the tragedy.

Grief Through Absurdity

For the better part of human history, religion has served as a coping mechanism for dealing with the disparity between the world we want versus the world as it is. Its big picture elevates hope beyond the day-to-day obstacles of life. It provides meaning and purpose. In his analysis of the Black church, Michael Battle says

> "The greatest achievement of the Black church is the awareness, in the midst of affliction and slavery, that the world is not absurd - that the harmony of divine and human work, though seemingly meaningless at times, can restore even the cruelest individual to community."[182]

Absurdity is an accurate word for navigating life. How can anyone read W.E.B. Du Bois' *The Souls of Black Folks* or J.R. Lynch and not grieve over evil and absurdity?

Technology, science, and education have changed our comfort level but not human behavior. Working in government, seeing the absurd amount of energy, time, and effort spent countering humans' bad behavior is unavoidable. I don't know how anyone can remain mentally healthy without the gift of grief. As we'll see in the next chapter, faith-biased grief opens the soul to grace.

Grace - Balancing the Math of Justice

Key Idea: Grace balances the math of justice.

From Grief to Grace

Six-year-old Ruby demonstrated another aspect of neighborliness: grace. Faith-biased grief cleans out excess baggage in the heart and makes room for grace.

Grace, though, is hard to define. M. Scott Peck described grace as a potent force that we can neither touch, see or scientifically measure but is very real and essential to spiritual growth, community, and mental health.[183] He was so fascinated by grace that it comprises the fourth and final section of his *The Road Less Travelled*.

In Norfolk, grace has a face in the person of Dr. Patricia Turner and her 16 companions. In 1959, a small group integrated Norfolk public schools, who were Ruby Bridges' older counterparts. Norfolk tried unsuccessfully to stop school integration by closing public schools, which became known as Massive Resistance. Federal courts prevailed and forced schools to reopen. Of 131 Black students who applied for the entry exams, Norfolk Public Schools only allowed 17 to enter. They became known as the Norfolk 17.

Dr. Patricia Turner and her brother James, ages 14 and 11, respectively, were among the initial students to integrate Norview Junior High School. The N.A.A.C.P. spent months preparing the Norfolk 17 academically to excel. They also did what they could to prepare them emotionally, such as not reacting when called "nigger" or spat upon.[184]

Knowing crowds of whites would be waiting at the schools, the NAACP believed that if parents of the 17 accompanied their children, it would only make the situation worse. So the Turners walked on their own. They were met with stares and pelted with items from buses as the White students passed. Old Dominion University dedicated a website to the Norfolk 17. It says of Dr. Turner:

> Ms. Turner has spoken of the fact that she couldn't make friends. No one spoke to her— except to call her names, spit on her, throw gum in her hair. But even worse than that is the behavior of her teachers. In an interview, she tells of the teachers who wore rubber gloves to receive her papers, or they had her drop her papers in a basket —but mostly they just ignored her. Even though she qualified to play field hockey and was good at it, she never got to play because no other teams would play Norview if Patricia was going to play. [185]

One teacher said she was only good at being her master's foot warmer. They made her feel like she deserved to be spat upon, pushed down the steps, and have sticks and pebbles thrown at her. She had to pass ninth and tenth-grade tests to enter the eighth grade. Then, every day for a week, she had to go to court and undergo psychiatric testing by six adult White men to see if she was normal—however they defined normal in that situation.

She eventually made friends and recalls that she and others who integrated were given a standing ovation when she graduated high school. She went on to earn degrees in Accounting, Mathematics, Nursing, and a Master of Science in Education and was awarded an honorary doctorate from Old Dominion University. After a nursing career, she became a teacher and dedicated her life to education.

She officially retired in 2008 from public schools and now directs a private Christian school. A children's book, *Today I Met a Rainbow*, tells her story.

Two things surprised me in my conversation with Dr. Turner. First, both sides rejected her. Some in the Black community treated her as an outsider. Her dad was in the Navy and helped her be strong.

The second surprise was the complete lack of bitterness. I was a White male, sitting across from a civil rights era hero who had endured some of the worst treatment from whites, yet there was not an ounce of hostility in her. When she reached for a hug on my way out, it was one of the most meaningful acts during my time with Norfolk. By all worldly standards, she deserved to have a chip on her shoulder, but it wasn't there.

Then there is Cecelia Tucker. Should you meet Mrs. Tucker, she is a hugger who knows nearly everyone in Norfolk. She spent 31 years expanding Old Dominion University's diversity. Students of color jumped from 21% to 54% during her tenure. I invited her to a lunch-&-learn session with our department. She shared about life under segregation in Virginia. Her father, a college-educated principal, was once thrown in a ditch and almost hanged. At age seven, she had her appendix removed in a makeshift operating room over a drug store because Blacks weren't allowed to go to the hospital. She was pushed, shoved, spat on, and called the N-word as a child. She had to attend graduate school in Michigan because no Virginia schools enrolled Blacks in graduate programs. She participated in peaceful protests and attended the 1963 March on Washington where Dr. Martin Luther King gave the speech that became known as the "I Have a Dream" speech. She even has a Bible he signed when he visited her college.

After describing a childhood under segregation, she said, "I don't hold Whites responsible in the present for what happened back then." She then referenced how Martin Luther King spoke about evaluating people by their worth. Race is often an elephant in the room, but what she said tamed the elephant. Her words whisked fear out of the conversation. The same is true of Shirley Butts in my neighborhood, who has the same gentleness, kindness, and lack of bitterness. All attributed their graceful attitude to their faith. I've felt it in Black churches where we have worked side by side or prayed on sidewalks together.

In contrast to the stories above, I've met individuals with far fewer burdens than Dr. Turner or Mrs. Tucker, who are far more bitter. They are addicted to it. I think of a man I'll call Georgie. When I met him, he was in his late forties. He had a tall, slender build, long, blondish-brown gray hair, and a gray beard. Something happened in his family between his brother, his dad, and the family business. Whatever it was, it left him highly bitter about his state in life. I guess it happened in the early 80s because his clothing and attitude still seemed stuck there.

He first attended our church with someone he had befriended, but it wasn't long before he burnt through that friendship with his lethal self-pity and hostility toward the world. He was offended at the slightest thing. One week, we invited him to lunch with a group, but he sat out in the church van alone because he was offended by something someone said. He was single and lonely for an attractive woman in his life. He emphasized physical attractiveness in women but became irritable when anyone questioned his disheveled appearance.

Listening to him for very long was the emotional equivalent of drinking Drano. Bitterness and jealousy are toxic to individuals, families, and communities. I've witnessed people sabotage themselves and their communities out of spite and power plays. Community organizations and government may go the extra mile to repair fractured relationships and spend millions of dollars on projects. Still, it will never be good enough if jealousy and bitterness are the real problems.

The Limitations of Justice without Grace

The word "justice" is whipped out in conversations with the frequency and familiarity of a credit card as if everyone accepted its definition. Philosophers from Plato to John Rawls have noted what is considered just and unjust is disputed. As Michael Sandel's work points out, the word is loaded with moral questions that philosophers and legal scholars have debated for millennia. The symbol for justice is a set of scales, but the math of justice is never perfectly balanced. By itself, justice has several limitations and has never been able to stand independently.

The first limitation is our human nature. When the U.S. Constitution was written, ultimate power was to rest with "the people." The framers, however, recognized the limits of human nature. Alexander Hamilton, James Madison, and John Jay wrote a series of articles now known as *The Federalist Papers* [not to be confused with the more recent magazine and website] to promote the new Constitution to the American people and hasten its adoption. They wrestled with age-old moral questions. Alexander Hamilton described human nature with words like "folly," "wickedness," and "depravity."[186] According to Hamilton, people are prone to follow leaders who tell them what they want to hear for the self-serving acquisition of power by the leader. People divide into factions, which Madison defined as "united and actuated by some common impulse of passion, or of interest, adversed to the rights of other citizens, or to the permanent and aggregate interest of the community."[187] Majorities stomp over the rights of minorities. Minorities use wealth or legal means to oppress majorities. Hamilton further summarized a significant fear: no one can be certain that those who gain justice today through some legal mechanism won't be the victim of injustice tomorrow through the same legal mechanism. [188]

During the unrest of 1969, a fired-up, idealistic University of California student wrote a passionate letter to his grandfather about how he and others were ready to burn everything down. With sage advice, the grandfather wrote back that anarchy in history usually resulted in more oppression, not less, and that younger generations should right the wrongs of former generations, including his own. He argued to his grandson that imperfection in society lies not in government alone, but in human nature itself.

> The world isn't perfect because human nature is imperfect. ... If all of these laws were obeyed, many of our problems would be solved, or at least they would be in manageable shape for solutions. But we must also take into consideration human nature.[189]

It was signed, "Affectionately, Grandpa."

The advice might not seem extraordinary were it not for the identity of the grandpa. The grandson was Jeffrey Earl Warren and the grandpa was Earl Warren, Chief Justice of the Supreme Court. He was the same Chief Justice who persuaded his colleagues to vote unanimously against segregation in the 1954 *Brown vs. Board of Education* case and presided over a court that advanced civil rights. Human nature constantly thwarts the ideal of justice. A second limitation is the tension between fairness to individuals and fairness to groups. Abe Fortas was a powerhouse attorney who argued before the Supreme Court multiple times before becoming an associate justice himself. During the civil unrest of the 1960s, he described this tension: "The story of man is the history, first, of the acceptance and imposition of restraints necessary to permit communal life, and second, of the emancipation of the individual within that system of necessary restraints."[190] There is a perpetual tug of war between what may be best for communities and what may be best for individuals.

The landmark 1966 Supreme Court case *Miranda v. Arizona* enshrined the accused's right to legal counsel during interrogation. It produced the Miranda rights that most of us recognize from T.V. shows: "You have the right to remain silent. Anything you say can and will be used against you..." It was a legal win for the masses except for one person: the woman whom Ernesto Miranda raped. He was released after the Supreme Court threw out his first conviction, and she had to endure a second trial. Fortunately, he was convicted a second time. In an ironic twist, Ernesto Miranda was later stabbed in a bar fight. His killer was read his Miranda rights, a copy of which could be found in the pocket of Ernesto Miranda's dead body.

The "system" is often blamed, but who is the system? The system is complex to identify. Sociologist Elijah Anderson ponders who the victim is in this neighborhood scenario.

> The Yuppie who is mugged and the kid who does it; the old head who loses the respect of the kid, who impregnates the teenage girl, who goes on welfare, which raises taxes, which drives out local companies, which causes unemployment, which causes homelessness, which causes crime, which depresses property values and drives

out middle-class residents, which further isolates the poor and the criminal.[191]

He goes on to say that police are also special victims in such cases because they are held responsible for providing law and order for societal issues far beyond their control.

Although often discussed as if there is good and evil system, they are frequently the same. The same system that invented a new way of governing, reduced tyranny, and pioneered new freedoms in the Bill of Rights compromised on slavery. The same system of northern industries that helped win the war against slavery abused labor and children. The same technological system that gives us modern conveniences like smart phones is the same system that steals our privacy, secretly manipulates our opinions, amplifies the great American comparison contest, and advances inequality. As flawed as the United States system is, most of us derive some benefit from living within it, and there are far worse alternatives. Talking about a perfectly fair system is much easier than making one.

A third limitation of justice without grace is the inability to untangle the past from the present. Nathaniel Bacon led a rebellion of frontiersmen, servants, and slaves against the Virginia authorities with the hope of "leveling" inequality. According to historian Howard Zinn, a portion of the White underclass who ended up on the frontier, including children, were sent to the colonies involuntarily to rid England of them. The frontiersmen, in turn, oppressed natives and Blacks. The Jamestown elite oppressed the frontiersmen, and the power in England exploited the whole colony. [192] How does anyone sort that out?

The math of justice by itself never balances. The quest for equality is a circular vortex of conflict. The Supreme Court can't find a consistent position with affirmative action, because it is difficult to reconcile the past for groups without being unfair in the present to individuals. Abhijit Banerjee and Esther Duflo tackled the case *Students for Fair Admissions Inc. v. President and Fellows of Harvard College.* Banerjee and Duflo wrote, "There is no evident solution to this problem."[193] If two Nobel-prize-winning MIT economists can't balance the math of justice, how can people like me? The argument for equity over merit struggles when based on justice alone. Grace, by contrast, offers the freedom to say, "I will have mercy on who I have mercy."

Human justice is a forever-changing, imperfect, often arbitrary, adversarial struggle. It argues endlessly over defining fairness and whose rights should take priority. Justice depends on who is in power and the most legally savvy.

Drawing from a Deeper Well of Grace

Ruby Bridges, Dr. Turner, and Cecelia Tucker show evidence of drawing from a deeper well than human justice alone. To be clear, grace without justice is cheap grace. Grace by itself doesn't mean much without a counterweight of justice somewhere else. It is a milkshake without ice cream. Something is glaringly missing.

Grace is not moral relativity. It isn't a free pass to do whatever you want. Grace is not eating five slices of pizza and a giant brownie sundae, knowing you have diabetes. That's recklessness. Grace is a stranger buying your meal. Grace always costs someone else something. Dietrich Bonhoeffer wrote about costly grace and was later hung by the Nazis for his stand against Hitler.

Julia Ward Howe, the abolitionist and women's rights advocate, described the "fateful lightening of His terrible swift sword" and "His judgment seat" when she penned the words to the poem that became The Battle Hymn of the Republic in 1861, the first year of the Civil War. More recent popular opinion conceives of God less as a sword-wielding law-giver and more of a laid-back Santa Clause who lets everyone determine what is naughty and nice on their own. This conception of God creates a problem when injustice deserves more than a frown from Santa in the sky. When grace is cheapened, so is justice.

Aleksandr Solzhenitsyn grew up adopting the atheism of the Soviet state. He served valiantly in World War II against the Germans until he was arrested for sending a private letter to a friend that criticized Stalin's war strategy. He was imprisoned for seven years and then sent into internal exile. The communist system that was supposed to end inequality had perfected 31 different forms of torture during its class war. They were ruthless in their efforts to cleanse the country of the upper classes, but it became apparent to Solzhenitsyn that "bourgeois" was used to label anyone who questioned them [one could argue it is not unlike labels thrown around in our nation].

A child of the Bolshevik revolution, he wrote about the false hope of revolutions. They destroy "the carriers of evil" but not the evil itself because we are all carriers of evil within us.[194] The strictly materialistic worldview of the Soviet state left no hope of justice. Josef Stalin, Adolf Hitler, and others responsible for the largest mass murders in history never faced human justice. He witnessed the deterioration of justice when there was no belief in ultimate accountability.

While in the gulag, he returned to the Orthodox Christianity of his parents. He saw his treatment of Germans during World War II as no better than how he was being treated. He returned to faith in part because faith was the only hope of ultimate justice and grace.

More recently, Rachel Denhollander knows something about justice as a lawyer. As a former gymnast and the first of over 200 women to publicly accuse Larry Nasser of sexual assault, she also knows something about injustice. Although Nassar received a life sentence, it still left exposed the wound of being ignored, unheard, and ultimately unvalued by so many people in positions of authority who could have stopped Nassar but did nothing. Denhollander credits her perseverance and courage to bring evil into light to her belief in a lovingly wrathful God who will ultimately hold everyone accountable.[195] Costly grace is not weakness.

How do you unravel history's oppression based of justice alone? Consider the difference between World War I and World War II. After World War I, the Allied powers tried exacting justice on Germany without grace. The humiliating punishment and insurmountable debt inflicted on the entire German people for a war caused by a relative few served to fuel the resentment that gave rise to Hitler. The U.S. took a more graceful approach after World War II. Now, Germany and Japan are some of our strongest allies. To be sure, much injustice went unpunished, but the overall effect was better. Grace offers a fresh start without having to fix everything in the past. If, there is no ultimate justice, grace makes little sense—inconsolable rage or subservient fatalism maybe, but not grace.

Expensive grace holds that higher justice is founded in a creator who sets forth perfect moral law (alternatively referred to as natural law in philosophical and legal circles). In the theoretical world, natural law provides an objective, unifying moral authority consistent over time, not subject to changing cultural whims or power structures. It is a neutral basis to assert claims of justice or injustice. It also provides universal accountability. In the real world, however, wars have been fought over who gets to interpret it.

Whereas arguments over interpreting moral law gray out its value, grace sharpens its importance in technicolor. For one, grace cancels the comparison contest. Perfect moral law establishes an objective starting point. The graceful measure themselves against perfect moral law, not other people. If the flaw is in our very nature, there is no value in the comparison contest. Good looks can't fix us. Money can't buy our way out. Whether someone is dumb as a doornail or the next Einstein, they can't fix themselves.

Grace has a way of punching envy and greed in the face. They can't be in the same heart together. A grace-filled life still passionately pursues justice but without jealousy's attitude of entitlement over others.

In today's world, Christianity seems an especially strange faith. I would like to have grace without the crucifixion of Jesus. Reading through the blood-and-guts crucifixion narratives is uncomfortable and seems so pre-Enlightenment. It seems more appropriate for the age of Attila the Hun—before deodorant, the safety razor, and toilet paper when our ancestors hunted and butchered food with their hands. It hardly seems relevant in our more genteel age of climate-controlled grocery stores, fabric softeners, and lavender-kiwi hand soap. The cross narrative is a stumbling block in our touchy-feely, feel-good world. If true, however, it solves our justice problem by balancing justice and mercy. If true, its barbarism accurately reflects the grotesque ways humans behave and treat each other. If untrue, grace is weakness in a screw-or-be-screwed world.

If true, there should be some evidence of its effects. Ruby Bridges, Dr. Turner, and CeCe Tucker are star witnesses to the impact of costly grace. The choice of forgiveness was not mere convenience-store tolerance or dollar-store acceptance. They believed in a God who issues commands and not just blows kisses. It is the costly grace of Louis Zamperini, who chose to forgive his Japanese torturers in World War II. It is the costly grace of the West Nickel Amish who took up a collection for the shooter's family after he killed their children. It is the costly grace of Sojourner Truth, who referred to her former "slaveholding master turned to a brother."[196] It is the costly grace of people who have experienced grace themselves.

Expensive grace ends the circulation of revenge and bitterness. It breaks dialectic cycles. Expensive grace can balance Michael Sandel's three-way conflict between core principles, the public good, and individual rights. Where there is contrition and repentance, grace clears the air for a fresh start. It has greater flexibility to advance equity. It recreates our individual identities into something new and different across cultures, races, and classes. The grace-empowered have greater humility, patience, gratitude, and kindness. They smile more over what others have contributed to their life than what they've attained over others. Grace can't be demanded. It isn't a right. It doesn't operate out of obligation but out of mercy. Most importantly for this book, grace gives a concrete rationale for being neighborly in a world that favors aggression and speed.

The Power of Grief and Grace

The book began with Ms. Pearl. A funny thing about Ms. Pearl is that she didn't like kids earlier in her life. Friends introduced her to the El (elevated train) as a teenager. It transported her physically beyond the confines of her parents' house and into a whole new world of hard-partying friends. One of 13 kids, she became hard for her parents to control. By 15, she was an alcoholic. She married at 17 and had her 3rd child. Alcoholism turned into drug abuse, and she bounced around from place to place. She dropped off her kids with others on a binge for weeks at a time and avoided babysitting her siblings' kids.

Her dad and mom never gave up on her. Her dad sent the church van for the kids on Sunday morning. She got mad at the van driver blowing the horn when she had a hangover. She yelled at the driver but was happy to send her kids off. The church people eventually got to her. She left her street life and became serious about faith and her kids. Not wanting them to face street dangers after dark, she began a Bible study for her kids, which others joined. With the help of others, it turned into a full-time daycare for teen moms. The Mustard Seed Foundation (funded by the Bakke family) provided $5000 to buy an abandoned property when they wanted to expand. From there, her ministry continued to grow. She started a neighborhood newsletter, one of which I still have.

When the teens fled Ms. Pearl's car, it wasn't out of fear. It was a guilty conscience in the presence of a loving, grace-filled Ms. Pearl. Such is the power of faith in shaping the souls of neighborhoods.

The truth of Jesus' statement that those who mourn are blessed is born out in the Pearls, Rubys, and Dr. Turners.[197] When combined with faith, mourning is a hidden gift bearing the fruit of a graceful life. It is the gift of helpful hurting distinguished from the counterfeits of self-pity and bitterness. Neighborhoods need more Pearls, more Rubys, and more Dr. Turners. In the field of community development, I've met many people who live bitter, some of whom are professionals. They are bitter because this world hasn't lived up to their ideals and they haven't attained the treasures they feel they deserve. The Pearls, Lois's, Ruby's, and Dr. Turners have reasons to live angry but don't. They have chosen not to store all their treasure in this world.

Conclusion
Humility Over Hubris

A resident contacted his city council member over a weekend about a sewer problem at his house on a short, little-known street. While having the councilperson's attention, he made other complaints. Orders came down that I would organize an on-site meeting on the street. The first available time on Outlook schedules for all the requisite staff was a Thursday, so I set up the meeting. The council member wanted staff from police, narcotics, code inspectors, waste management, and utilities—the whole nine yards.

In the intervening time, Utilities repaired the sewer line within two days—just as they would have done for any resident if they had called the emergency number rather than their council member. As requested, code inspectors visited the street in advance of the meeting with a zero-tolerance approach. The person who made the initial call about his sewer ended up receiving a code violation for parking on the grass in front of his house. The street at the time did not have curbs and gutters, so drivers understandably removed their cars as far out of the road as possible. I talked to the police about the narcotics complaint. They reported the problem house in question for drug dealing was already under surveillance by vice/narcotics.

It was raining the day of the meeting. I pulled up on a side street before the city council member in my personal car, a 2003 Pontiac Vibe, which happened to be white. I scanned the street and saw a line of white City of Norfolk vehicles: two patrol cars, a code inspector's car, a Tahoe from Waste Management, and a vehicle from Utilities. Because it was raining, everyone remained in their cars until the councilman arrived. When he arrived, at least seven city employees emerged from vehicles like a movie scene showing the president's motorcade coming to a stop. Doors swung open simultaneously as if on cue. Umbrellas sprung open, and we convened in the middle of the street in the rain. The councilperson made a speech about giving the street attention, returned to his vehicle, and departed. City employees did likewise. The whole thing took about five minutes.

The absurdity of the moment struck me as incredibly funny. I laughed the whole way back to City Hall. It was a classic case of someone in power seizing the opportunity to bring an M1 tank to a water balloon battle. Crews had already fixed the original sewer complaint and would have done so in the normal business course. The attention resulted in the resident reporting his sewer problem getting a code violation for parking on his grass. The police already had the suspected drug house under surveillance before the complaint. The interesting thing about covert surveillance is that it is covert. If the drug dealers hadn't known they were being surveilled before our rain visit, they certainly would have had a clue afterward. Finally, seven employees, including several mid-level managers, gave up a half hour or more to stand in the rain to hear a five-minute speech. The whole meeting was wholly unnecessary. I suppose, though, that it accomplished what was intended. It put on a nice show. People in power frequently do things because they can, not because they should.

History is partly the story of two great antagonists: hubris and humility. Hubris may shove the world forward, but humility keeps it held together. This battle plays out in the halls of the U.S. Capitol Building, corporate boardrooms, Boards of Education across the country, military units, marriages, and communities. The rain meeting harmed no one. It was more amusing than annoying. In some cases, hubris is that simple—a good show that serves no purpose other than entertaining the protagonist's ego. In other cases it is not. Hubris destroys families, communities, and even nations.

One set of researchers studied the origins of narcissism among children in Western society, where self-centeredness is rising. Children with parental overvaluation who were taught that they were more special and more entitled than other children had raised narcissism levels.[198] I doubt Ruby Bridges or Dr. Turner had that problem. Another study evaluated the role of competition and its influence on dishonesty and entitlement. They found that when one's ability to "outstrip the competition" defines success, winners show less ethical restraint, an increased sense of entitlement over others, and less honest behavior.[199] I doubt Ruby Bridges or Dr. Turner had that problem, either. Finally, a third study showed that when the wealthy reside in areas of high economic inequality, segregated in relationships from those with less, the rich were less generous, more entitled, and believed that they were more deserving than others.[200] Once again, neither Ruby Bridges nor Dr. Turner had that problem. When there was less segregation by economic status, the wealthy showed higher levels of generosity. The chase for perfect-looking neighborhoods and the self-centered, Columbus-like tendency to place ourselves at the center of a customer-oriented world in which we pay to be served has left us with less community, not more.

I first read of Blue Zones in a white paper for the Federal Reserve Bank of Dallas. Blue Zones was a research project in partnership with National Geographic to identify and study pockets of community with the highest life expectancy and longevity rates as evidenced by people living over 100. Surprising to both the researchers, sponsors, and me was that only one of the Blue Zones was in the United States, a Seventh-Day Adventist community in Loma Linda.[201] The commonalities were about their lifestyles. One factor was environments that included movement in their daily life. Three other factors were about their diet. They eat diets with less meat but rich in beans. They don't eat to be completely full. They save the smallest meal for late afternoon or early evening. They have faith, purpose, social circles, and value family.

This is astounding to me. Healthcare in the United States is a multi-trillion-dollar industry. Within a 20-minute drive from my house are a medical school, three universities, and two hospitals. The cost of one year's health insurance for my wife and me is the cost of a compact new car. In an hour of T.V. time, how many ads are for drug companies, diet plans, fitness watches, or other "healthy" goods and services for which to expend our dollars? All of this, and we only have one Blue Zone identified in the whole U.S. The most significant danger of the American marketing machine is that we believe our own hype. While we chase the latest diet craze, we're being outdone by bean eaters.

This book has been about character. "Character," said Henry Allen in 1986, "is one of those horrible Victorian virtues that makes you think of cold baths, savings accounts, the Protestant work ethic, self-sacrifice, manhood, duty, and so on in a list of everything we thought we'd ripped out of American culture like a weed."[202] The introduction identified six goals.

- Seek neighborhood character and neighborliness beyond appearances

- Value the small, humble, and kind

- Comfort the confused

- Encourage middle neighborhoods and middle voices

- Elevate the language we use about each other - especially in the urban/rural divide

- Call for humility in the gap between our stated values and actual behavior.

For these six goals, I have made the best case I can for their attention.

If I am to distill it down further and make one last effort, it comes down to what I believe is a distinctly American attribute of elevating humility over hubris. We have no kings or queens. Washington, Jefferson, and others refused regal titles for the presidency. Our most admired generals aren't known for offensive conquests of foreign peoples in the European colonial tradition. They are known for defensive stands against any powers that would set themselves against freedom, even against low odds. When Lincoln appeared in Springfield, Illinois, after being nominated as president, his friends carried in a set of rails. The audience rose to its feet and roared with approval. Lincoln quieted them only by making a joke. The object of Lincoln's previous ridicule, his lack of aristocratic breeding, his absence of formal education, and his blue-collar background became a trophy of his triumph to the northerners whom he loved and was loved.

On visiting City Point, Virginia (now Hopewell), where Grant had his headquarters during the siege of Richmond, one sees the big antebellum farmhouse with its outbuildings and easily assumes that it was Grant's headquarters. In this case, one would be mistaken. Grant established his headquarters in one of 11 small cabins, closer to his staff and soldiers.

In both Vicksburg and later when Lee surrendered at Appomattox, Grant paroled the Rebels and allowed officers to keep their sidearms. Out of his sense of respect and honoring Lincoln's wishes, he fed the starving rebel army and let those who had been enemies hours earlier keep horses and mules so they could return to their farms and sustain a living. He ordered the Union army not to celebrate their victory but to honor their former foes. He intended to cease hostility quickly and begin restoration. In a situation when it would have been easy and expected to look down on the losers, they resisted in humility.

General Sherman did likewise when Confederate General Joseph Johnston surrendered to him. Unfortunately, Johnston surrendered after Lincoln's assassination, and Andrew Johnson, taking Lincoln's place, was a much smaller leader than Lincoln. He and Secretary of War Staunton excoriated Sherman for being too kind and rescinded the terms of surrender. However, Johnston didn't forget Sherman's kindness and braved pneumonia to serve as a pallbearer during Sherman's funeral. Such is the power of humility over hubris. Ours is a special nation. Ours is a better nation when we value humility.

I love a story I heard on a Harvard Business Review Ideacast. I listen to it over and over because it makes me happy. Gerry Anderson was the C.E.O. of DTE Energy in 2008 in the Detroit area as the Great Recession hit the already imploded local economy. The company was near collapse. Executives put together a C-suite strategic plan full of the standard management tools: training, incentives, increased oversight, and a solid message to employees that the company needed to change. It did, but not much. As the financial crisis hit, their strategic plan was dead in the water, as was the company if they didn't act quickly.

He knew that employees' discretionary energy was the only resource left to cultivate. Admitting that their plan was gone, he made a promise to company employees. If they put their heart into the company and gave extra energy, creativity, and resourcefulness, he would stave layoffs as a last resort. If their company survived, they pledged to make more of a difference in the Detroit community. He understood that people only give their discretionary energy to things they believed in.

It worked. When they tallied quarterly results, they repeatedly beat their budget. My favorite part of the story is when Anderson slammed his hand on a table and told his controller to re-check his data. Their performance seemed too good to be true. There were no new programs. No new product launch. No new project. No fancy accounting tricks. They determined that performance was complicated to see because of thousands of small contributions by 10,000 employees. "So, the reason it was hard to see is that it was disaggregated. It was being carried out by 10,000 people. It was hard to put your finger on. It wasn't three, four, or five big initiatives. It was hundreds and thousands of initiatives being carried out by people."[203] As economic performance and stability improved, they preserved momentum by committing to better contributing to their city and state. The small things made the difference.

Harvard professor James Q. Wilson, generally known for the broken windows theory, authored a lesser-known but equally valuable paper in 1985 on character and its relationship to policy. It is safely assumed that good policy should come from the good intentions of policymakers. Wilson raised an equally important question, how does policy, well-intentioned or not, affect our national character? He makes the case that the federal government's rules and incentives change the national character, sometimes not for good. The belief in policy is that "All that is necessary in public policy is to arrange the incentives ... so that they [various groups] will behave in a socially optimal way."[204] Behavior does change with incentives, but frequently not in the way intended. He asked serious questions. How does government remake bad families? How does government of a free society reshape public values and still leave them free? How does government balance an ethic of self-expression with self-control? Most importantly, how do we strengthen the nation's character so that its citizens desire to do the right thing because it feels good, not because of an incentive? The paper concludes with the sentence, "In the long run, the public interest depends on private virtue."[205]

Some place their hope in public policy. It might be evident to the reader that I am not one of those people. I value good public policy. On a tiny scale, I am involved in policy recommendations in local government. I advocate for good policy. I work within it five days a week, but it is not my hope. For every progress made in public policy, there is always a new, unpredictable shock to the system that alters gains. It is a giant game of Whack A Mole. It is not enduring. People are enduring.

I saw a community development conference by a government agency in D.C. The hotel cost was $359 per night before D.C. taxes and fees. When I thought about it, I can understand the high price for two reasons. First, even if far out of my price range, this hotel is where high-level researchers, bankers, think tank executives, philanthropists and consultants are used to staying (as they talk about equity and how to help the poor). Second, few would go to a policy conference at cheap hotels. I have yet to attend a government policy conference that is so darn exhilarating without the baser attraction of visiting a different city, staying in a nice hotel, and eating at various restaurants at other people's expense. When I think about investors and policymakers staying at $359-a-night hotels trying to figure out how to juggle incentives, I also think of Pearl.

Pearl still lives in Roseland near the teen moms and their kids. The Pearls, the Lois's, the Arloa's, the Dr. Turners, the Brians, and the Provident families don't need a big, bow-wrapped box of incentives to do what is right, unselfish, loving, and kind for their community. These people are where I find my greatest hope.

In every neighborhood are neighborhood Pearls. Some are small. Some are big. Some are mild-mannered. Some are right feisty. Some are quiet. Some can be annoyingly talkative. The common denominator is that they have all earned respect and credibility in a community because they do much of the day-to-day work with love for their neighbors. They embody Lincoln's neighborliness.

When I was a young child, my second cousin Mark Frye (who was killed by a mass shooter in Smithsburg, Maryland) gave me a copy of *The Velveteen Rabbit*. For years it disappeared into toy boxes, attics, and boxes of old stuff until I discovered the book as an adult one day. Much can be learned from the wise old Skin Horse in his advice to the Velveteen Rabbit:

'What is REAL?' asked the Rabbit one day....

'Real isn't how you are made,' said the Skin Horse. 'It's a thing that happens to you. When a child loves you for a long, long time, not just to play with, but REALLY loves you, then you become Real.'

'Does it hurt?' asked the Rabbit.

'Sometimes,' said the Skin Horse, for he was always truthful. 'When you are Real you don't mind being hurt.'

'Does it happen all at once, like being wound up,' he asked, 'or bit by bit?'

'It doesn't happen all at once,' said the Skin Horse. 'You become. It takes a long time. That's why it doesn't often happen to people who break easily, or have sharp edges, or who have to be carefully kept. Generally, by the time you are real, most of your hair has been loved off, and your eyes drop out and you get loose in the joints and very shabby. But these things don't matter at all, because once you are Real you can't be ugly, except to people who don't understand.'[206]

Initially, the Rabbit did not look forward to those uncomfortable things happening to him. As time passed, though, he was loved by the boy. He was loved so much that his whiskers fell off, his fur thinned and faded, and he lost his shape. He was quite shabby looking, but he was beautiful to the boy.

Duct-tape Community is a declaration that community takes two resolves: one to make the world a fairer place and a second to be neighborly in one that isn't. In observing communities, many community Pearls are a little shabby looking and might not compare well to wealthier counterparts. They are clean-up volunteers picking up never-ending litter. They are Meals on Wheels drivers keeping seniors fed. They are recreation center aids coaching kids through life. They are code inspectors taking heat from neighbors and politicians for giving a single mother an extension on home maintenance. They are the invisible sewer supervisors who keep stuff moving. They are police officers who play chess with neighborhood kids and carry dog treats. They are church ladies who love on people no one else may notice. They are coaches with beat-up, smelly cars. They are teachers in overcrowded classrooms with leaky roofs who stay hours after paid hours helping students. They are a little shabby because they show the signs of being loved. May I close with C.S. Lewis.

"It may be possible for each to think too much of his own potential glory hereafter; it is hardly possible for him to think too often or too deeply about that of his neighbor. The load, or weight, or burden of my neighbor's glory should be laid on my back, a load so heavy that only humility can carry it, and the backs of the proud will be broken."[207]

Final Stuff
Appendix A - The Duct-tape Challenge

The Pearl Willises, George Washington Carvers, Shorty Hiltons, Ruth McBride Jordans, Provident families, Tim Smiths, McCabes, and many others are duct-tape pacesetters that I know, but they are not alone. Every locality has pockets of Duct-tape community. Each community has its pacesetters. Their chief identifier is their neighborly character. They stand out in a whiney, entitled, self-absorbed culture because they live by a different set of rules. Here are the common rules I've observed among them that are a challenge to the rest of us.

Rule #1. *They choose neighborliness.*

Humans divide and fight. After 6000 or so years of recorded history, it is dependably predictable. In a world of conflict, neighborliness is a choice. It is a decision to not view yourself or your tribe as the center of the universe. The power of Duct-tape Community is that members may be passionate defenders of their politics, but their neighborliness supersedes their politics. From their struggles, they empathize with others regardless of their race, class, political division, religion, or other identifications.

Duct-tape pacesetters feel a common compassion toward the nation's less well-off. There are 8.5 million Black people, 10.4 million Hispanic or Latino people (of any race), and 21.5 million White people living below the federal poverty line. Add to those numbers the untold Asset Limited, Income Constrained, Employed (ALICEs) not counted in the official statistics.[208] For the

Duct-tape pacesetters, it isn't a contest over who is poorer. If neighbors need help, they help them.

Duct-tape pacesetters share a frustration that something isn't right with the nation's greed but, ironically, are often the backbone of capitalism and community. They are carpenters who volunteer their expertise to Habitat for Humanity. They are local restauranteurs who give away special meals to Title I elementary schools. They are HVAC companies that sponsor local ball teams, give non-violent felons a job, or give away roofs. They are migrant workers who support their families in their home countries. They are convenience store owners who let a mother pay for diapers and canned goods when she can. They make capitalism work for their community despite its faults.

Rule #2. *They choose financial discipline.*

The last time I mowed Dad's grass (c. 2017, before he remarried and moved in with his new wife's family), he used my grandfather's push mower, who died in 1988. The muffler was completely rusted, and you could hear it in the next county over. He could afford a new mower, but the discipline to make equipment last was standard operating procedure. Choosing financial security over appearances was more important.

Being poor is not an automatic qualifier for Duct-tape pacesetters. I've worked among people with low incomes long enough to know some can't afford rent but pay for premium cable subscriptions. Some lease expensive luxury vehicles and buy name-brand clothes for appearances' sake. Some seniors wasted their income earlier in life or underreported their income to the IRS and now don't have enough savings or Social Security Income, respectively. *Duct-tape Community* is not a tribute to them. It is a tribute to the mamas who work their butts off for their kids and teach their children financial discipline.

Rule #3. *They can find joy in the simple.*

My favorite cooking show is a YouTube channel named Great Depression Cooking, about Clara Cannucciari, a woman in her nineties. Her grandson captured Clara's Depression-era recipes and advice in a beautiful tribute until her death at 98. They are far more memorable than anything on cable T.V. Judging from the millions of views, I am not the only one so moved. Her recipes are simple, un-doctored by professional photographers, and there is no staff to do all the prep and cleanup work. What is relevant to this book is the number of times she describes growing up in the Great Depression, "We were poor, but we had a good time as children." There was a sense of rich community despite the depressed economy.

A hard life is not always a bad life. Duct-tape pacesetters can be content being together without exotic vacations or 5000-square-foot houses.

Rule #4. *They use their grit to raise others and themselves (in that order).*

Ruth McBride Jordan is a stellar example of this rule, but there are others. *Mr. Holland's Opus* is a movie about a music teacher who spends his career mentoring youth rather than using his talent to become famous. *Mr. Holland's Opus* is fictional, but thousands of real-life examples exist. A friend of the family, Bob Thompson, was one such music teacher in Cumberland, Maryland. He and his family were always running with the school band, the show choir, a school musical, or a performance at a church. The lifestyle must not have bothered his children any. Both his son and daughter became music teachers. The daughter provided music lessons to our program in Pittsburgh while her husband was in graduate school; the son became teacher of the year for his home county. There are thousands of other inspiring Bob Thompsons. A defining characteristic of Duct-tape pacesetters is that they use their grit to rise and take others with them.

Although the uber-successful benefit from intelligence, talent, opportunities, or luck, they aren't criteria for Duct-tape pacesetters. Grit, perseverance, hard work, and un-selfish ambition are the markers of Duct-tape pacesetters. Duct-tape pacesetters may include doctors and lawyers who overcame significant obstacles. But just as valuable, it may consist of first-generational immigrants whose work as janitors helps their children be the first in their families to graduate from college or a trade school.

Rule #5. *They give until it hurts.*

As they rise, they never take sole credit. Instead, they attribute their rise to others who helped them. Like Evvie McKinney, they view life with gratitude and give back.

While it is commendable that billionaires have pledged to live on half their wealth or even one percent, one percent of $1 billion is still $10 million. It is hard to imagine anyone suffering with $10 million or that giving up a big yacht for a smaller one counts as a sacrifice.

A sad tragedy of American history is that George Washington and Thomas Jefferson both saw slavery as a moral problem. Still, they were never willing to pay the cost of giving up slavery on their plantations. How would American history be different if they had paid the moral cost then? In contrast, Duct-tape pacesetters give until it hurts as a moral exercise. And unlike the Rockefellers and Carnegies of the world, they don't plaster their name everywhere to draw attention to themselves.

Rule #6. *They speak the language of sacrifice.*

Members of the Duct-tape Community speak the language of sacrifice, not just the language of take. Jefferson biographer Jon Meacham wrote of Jefferson after the Stamp Act crisis, "Leadership, Jefferson was learning, meant knowing how to distill complexity into a comprehensive message to reach the hearts as well as the minds of the larger world."[209] He must have learned the lesson. The last sentence of the Declaration of Independence reads: "And for the support of this Declaration, with a firm reliance on the protection of Divine Providence, we mutually pledge to each other our Lives, our Fortunes, and our sacred Honor."

The language of Parliament was the language of take. "We, in London, have a problem, so we are going to take from you, in the colonies, to fix it." The Declaration of Independence balanced the language of take with the language of shared sacrifice: "This is a list of our rights of which we are taking back, but this is what we pledge to give. We mutually pledge to each other our lives, our money, and our honor."

The language of shared sacrifice may never be the norm. Washington, Adams, and Jefferson were at odds within a few years of the Declaration of Independence. It turns out that dreaming about a country was easier than running one, but there are glimpses of hope.

A few years ago, the Kettering Foundation conducted a series of national public conversations about the federal debt. They reported two encouraging takeaways from their discussions.

- Citizens from different walks of life could have serious, thoughtful conversations given the right set of non-partisan circumstances.

- Most participants agreed that shared sacrifice was the basis of tackling the national debt, but they are sensitive to the sacrifice being shared equally.[210]

Behavioral economists call these "conditional cooperators."[211] People are willing to contribute to the public good only as long as others do likewise. When contributors feel that others are free-riding, contributions decrease.

These two aspects are woven into the DNA of our American character and perhaps as humans. When a few people step forward to sacrifice for a good cause, more will follow if we can do it together, but we rebel like hell when someone tries to take something from us involuntarily. Indeed, U.S. History has born this out: community in the U.S. is stronger when a crisis warrants sacrifice.

Despite rising levels of selfishness, there are signs of hope across the income spectrum. Abigail Disney and 200 millionaires asked to pay more taxes to fund affordable housing, infrastructure, and other efforts.[212] At the other end of the spectrum, comedian Jeff Foxworthy experimented while volunteering at a homeless shelter in Atlanta. One Christmas, he gave out $50 to each homeless guest, but he also told them about a big fire that affected families and children. Without exception, every homeless guest gave up their $50. Some reached into their pockets and gave what other little cash they had. [213] If the homeless are willing to sacrifice, what does that say about the rest of the country's character?

Will you accept the Duct-tape Community challenge?

Appendix B - Money and Happiness

Psychologists, sociologists, and economists have all studied the relationship between money and happiness. They have found variations in the correlation between money and happiness. Scholars have developed a specialized vocabulary in an attempt to explain variations.

The Easterlin Paradox - The Easterlin Paradox refers to how the rich as individuals report higher levels of happiness, but happiness in society as a whole, notably in the U.S., does not increase with rising incomes and national Gross Domestic Product (GDP).[214]

Veblen Status Effects - This term refers to how people can measure their sense of well-being by ranking their status against others. It originates from the term "Veblen Good," which is a good whose value increases because of its appeal as a status symbol.[215]

Hedonic Treadmill - Two scholars, Philip Brickman and Donald Campbell coined this term in 1971 to "describe this tendency of expectations to increase along with possessions, resulting in no permanent gain in happiness."[216] More recent scholars offer adaptations when this isn't always the case.

Habituation Effect - Habituation refers to decreased responsiveness among humans and animals to repeated stimuli over time. Desensitization is a more commonly known related term. It takes more and newer toys to keep us happy.

Multiple papers support a consensus that the relationship betwen money and happiness is absolute and relative. It is absolute in the way that money can bring more choices, more control over time, more to give away (thereby enhancing satisfaction), less stress about basic survival, and a higher social status.[217] Money can also buy safer neighborhoods, better education for children, healthier eating options, and more toys.

The money-happiness relationship is also relative in several ways. The more we have, the more materialistic we can become. Some research shows that younger generations have become more materialistic since the 1970s, with a somewhat alarming reduction in willingness to work for nice things.[218] Even when incomes rise, if there is a high degree of income inequality, there is more perceived competition and status anxiety.[219] Happiness partially depends on comparisons and ranking independent of actual well-being. Firebaugh and Schroeder conclude that Americans tend to be happiest when living in wealthier neighborhoods but near poor ones. [220]

All this is to say, Americans are addicted to the Great American Comparison Contest.

Acknowledgements

This book contains dozens of people's stories who have taught me neighborliness from demographically different areas across the country. I am forever grateful to them. To stay focused on neighborliness, I had to resist turning the book into a tribute to all the other people who positively influenced my life. I have left out entire swaths of my life to stay focused on my goals. I could fill a chapter about teachers and professors alone. When thinking about writing, I pulled out an encouraging note from a professor, Don Green, from twenty-five years ago. Coworkers would warrant another chapter. I owe so much to many more people than are included here.

Above all, I'm thankful to God. He blessed me with wonderful relationships. Among the first is my wife. How often I've wondered if she didn't wish she had married someone more talkative and exciting than someone who comes home, eats, does dishes, and retreats into the spare bedroom to study or write. My wife is the only person who will be happier than me when this book is finished. Please tell all your friends to buy this book so I can take Jenny somewhere special to eat. This book is about the importance of small things, and none are more important than how my wife has supported me.

Second, I couldn't ask for a better, more neighborly family. They are or were all people-oriented and integrated into their various communities. I'm grateful for my parents, brother and sister, grandparents, in-laws, nieces, and nephews.

Third, I'm grateful to the readers who waded through the early drafts, which were more accurately described as a wandering stream of consciousness: my dad, Eddie and Marissa Provident, Dr. Robin Underhill, Steve Robison, Oneiceia Howard, and colleagues at work who pointed me in the right direction.

Fourth, I could fill other chapters about church folk from Winifred Road, Creswell, Northside, Hazelwood, and Avalon. I've never moved anywhere without an instant church family who welcomed me with open arms: White, Black, Hispanic, Filipino, and more.

Finally, I'm grateful to live in the United States and for our armed forces and law enforcement who protect our way of life. Even Duct-tape communities are rich compared to much of the world. We owe much of that wealth to the security we enjoy. Pundits have the freedom to discuss the world as it should be. Law enforcement and our service men and women confront the world as it is. Thank you!

C.Y.A. Statement

Every seasoned government employee knows the importance of C.Y.A. (cover your a$$). First, the opinions and observations expressed in this book are mine and do not reflect the City of Norfolk. Second, for the sake of my own conscience and to protect against critics, I was careful not to use taxpayer resources. Not one page of this book has ever been printed on a City of Norfolk copier. When printing more than my home printer could handle, I paid to use Copy Connection in downtown Norfolk or took it to Office Depot. Third, one of many reasons it has taken me eight years to finish this book is that I was also careful not to write or research while on taxpayer time.

Pictures

THE WAR MEMORIAL MAINTAINED BY THE PERRIS FAMILY
IN THE HAZELWOOD NEIGHBORHOOD OF PITTSBURGH IN

DISABLED VEHICLES OFF 2ND AVENUE IN THE HAZELWOOD
NEIGHBORHOOD OF PITTSBURGH IN 2002.

CORN DAY AT THE RINGGOLD RURITAN IN THE 1950S NEAR SMITHSBURG, MARYLAND.

A MEMORIAL TO " SHORTY" HILTON IN THE FIVE POINTS INTERSECTION OF NORFOLK.

MY MATERNAL GRANDPARENTS' TRAILER AFTER IT
FLOODED IN 1972.

PART OF THE FIVE POINTS DRIVE THROUGH ART GALLERY
IN NORFOLK. CREATED BY KAREN RUDD.

DR. PATRICIA TURNER, THE AUTHOR, AND GARNZIE WEST.

A MURAL IN THE UPTOWN NEIGHBORHOOD OF CHICAGO
CREATED BY UPTOWN BAPTIST CHURCH IN THE 1990S.

Bibliography

Akerlof, George A., and Robert Shiller. *Phishing for Phools: The Economics of Manipulation and Deception.* Apple Books. Princeton: Princeton University Press, 2015.

Allen, Henry. "Character Takes on Personality." *Washington Post,* January 5, 1986. https://www.washingtonpost.com/archive/opinions/1986/01/05/character-takes-on-personality/d15aeae3-d266-4c8b-a7c2-77cbcbdcb3b6/.

Amato, Paul R., and Alan Booth. *A Generation at Risk: Growing Up in an Era of Family Upheaval.* Cambridge: Harvard University Press, 1997. https://books.google.com/books?id=qp4DmQEACAAJ.

Anderson, Elijah. *Code of the Street.* New York: W.W. Norton, 2000.

———. *Streetwise: Race, Class and Change in an Urban Community.* Chicago: University of Chicago Press, 1990.

Associated Press. "Man Sues Church for $2.5M After Being 'Felled by Holy Spirit' | Fox News." *Foxnews.Com,* July 10, 2008. https://www.foxnews.com/story/man-sues-church-for-2-5m-after-being-felled-by-holy-spirit.

———. "Small Alabama Town Raises Big Stink about Abandoned NYC 'Poop Train.'" *USA Today,* April 18, 2018. https://www.usatoday.com/story/news/nation/

2018/04/18/small-alabama-town-raises-big-stink-abandoned-new-york-city-poop-train/527364002/.

"Atlas of the St. Clair Village and Mt. Oliver Neighborhoods of Pittsburgh 1977." Accessed March 10, 2022. https://historicpittsburgh.org/islandora/object/pitt%3A31735070288059/viewer#page/1/mode/2up[1].

Banerjee, A., and E. Duflo. *Poor Economics: A Radical Rethinking of the Way to Fight Global Poverty*. New York: Public Affairs, 2012.

Banerjee, Abhijit V., and Esther Duflo. *Good Economics for Hard Times*. New York: Hatchett Book Group, 2019.

Battle, Michael. *The Black Church in America: African American Christian Spirtuality*. Religious Life in America. Malden: Blackwell Publishing, 2006.

Being Generous | Jeff Foxworthy and Andy Stanley, 2017. https://www.youtube.com/watch?v=UZiHJ5wWkvU.

Bengston, Vern, Norella Putney, and Susan Harris. *Families and Faith: How Religion Is Passed Down Across Generations,*. New York: Oxford University Press, 2013.

Blackwell, Angela. "America's Tomorrow: Race, Place and the Equity Agenda." In *Investingi n What Works for America's Communities*. San Francisco: Federal Reserve Bank of San Francisco & Low-income Investment Fund, 2012.

---

1. https://historicpittsburgh.org/islandora/object/pitt%3A31735070288059/viewer#page_6666cd76f96956469e7be39d750cc7d9_1_6666cd76f96956469e7be39d750cc7d9_mode_6666cd76f96956469e7be39d750cc7d9_2up

Blazer, Dan German, II. "Empirical Studies About Attendance at Religious Services and Health." *JAMA Internal Medicine* 176, no. 6 (June 1, 2016): 785–86. https://doi.org/10.1001/jamainternmed.2016.1626.

Blum, Elizabeth Sobel. "Healthy Communities: A Framework for Meeting CRA Obligations." Dallas: Federal Reserve Bank of Dallas, March 2014. https://www.dallasfed.org/~/media/documents/cd/healthy/CRAframework.pdf.

Boehlke, David. "Strategies to Improve Middle Neighborhoods." *Community Development Investment Review* 11, no. 1 (2016). https://www.frbsf.org/community-development/publications/community-development-investment-review/2016/august/strategies-to-improve-middle-neighborhoods/.

Boyte, Harry C. "Reinventing Citizenship as Public Work: Citizen-Centered Democracy and the Empowerment Gap." The Kettering Foundation, 2013. art[2].

Bridges, Ruby, and Margo Lundell. *Through My Eyes: Ruby Bridges.* New York: Scholastic Press, 1999.

Brooks, David. *The Road to Character.* Apple Books. New York: Penguin Random House, 2015.

Brummelman Eddie, Thomaes Sander, Nelemans Stefanie A., Orobio de Castro Bram, Overbeek Geertjan, and Bushman Brad J. "Origins of Narcissism in Children." *Proceedings of the National Academy of Sciences* 112, no. 12

---

2. https://doi.org/art

(March 24, 2015): 3659–62. https://doi.org/10.1073/pnas.1420870112.

Buffet, Warren. "2017 Letter to Shareholders," February 24, 2018. https://www.berkshirehathaway.com/letters/2017ltr.pdf.

Buki, Charles. "CZB, Llc. Final Report." A Report Prepared for the City of Norfolk. Norfolk, VA: CZB, Llc., October 2010.

Burns, Christopher, and James M. MacDonald. "America's Diverse Family Farms: 2018 Edition." USDA, December 2018. http://www.ers.usda.gov/publications/pub-details/?pubid=90984.

Buttrick, Nicholas, and Shigehiro Oishi. "Money and Happiness: A Consideration of History and Psychological Mechanisms." *Proceedings of the National Academy of Sciences* 120, no. 13 (March 28, 2023): e2301893120. https://doi.org/10.1073/pnas.2301893120.

Callard, Benjamin. "Be Real: Knowing and Expressing the Authentic Self in a Performative Age." Vertitas Forum Podcast, n.d. https://www.digitaltheology.net/video/VWmEpXzDY2w.

Cash, Johnny. *Cash*. New York: Harper Collins, 1997.

Chen, James. "Veblen Good: Definition, Examples, Difference from Giffen Good." Investopedia. Accessed January 1, 2024. https://www.investopedia.com/terms/v/veblen-good.asp.

City of New York. "A Stronger, More Resilient New York." New York, June 11, 2013. https://www1.nyc.gov/site/sirr/report/report.page.

Coles, Robert. "The Inexplicable Prayers of Ruby Bridges." In *Finding God at Harvard*, edited by Kelly Monroe, 33–40. Grand Rapids: Zondervan, 1996.

Collier, Paul. *The Future of Capitalism: Facing the New Anxieties*. Apple Books. London: HarperCollins, 2018.

Collins, Jim. *Good to Great: Why Some Companies Make the Leap...And Others Don't*. Good to Great. New York: Harper Collins, 2001.

Columbus, Christopher. *American Journeys: Journal of the First Voyage of Columbus*. Edited by Julius E. Olson and Edward G. Bourne. New York: Charles Scribner's Sons, 1906. https://www.americanjourneys.org/aj-062/index.asp.

Colvin, Leonard. "Part 2 School Desegregation in Norfolk in 1959; When 17 Brave Students Stood Tall." *New Journal and Guide*, July 7, 1999.

"Community Rhythms: The Five Stages of Community Life." The Harwood Institute for Public Innovation, 2013. https://theharwoodinstitute.org/news/1999/12/1/community-rhythms-the-five-stages-of-community-life.

Côté Stéphane, House Julian, and Willer Robb. "High Economic Inequality Leads Higher-Income Individuals to Be Less Generous." *Proceedings of the National Academy of Sciences* 112, no. 52 (December 29, 2015): 15838–43. https://doi.org/10.1073/pnas.1511536112.

Cromartie, John. "Rural America at a Glance, 2017 Edition." USDA. Accessed March 12, 2022. http://www.ers.usda.gov/publications/ pub-details/?pubid=85739.

De Tocqueville, Alexis. *Democracy in America*. Edited by Eduardo Nolla. Translated by James T. Schleifer. Vol. 2. Indianpolis: The Liberty Fund, 2010.

Denhollander, Rachel. "Can Faith Reconcile Justice and Forgiveness?" Vertitas Forum Podcast, n.d. https://app.resonaterecordings.com/hosting/the-veritas-forum-podcast/e5b7589c-6254-41ff-aaeb-469003c55207.

DiAngelo, Robin. "White Fragility." *The International Journal of Critical Pedagogy* 3, no. 3 (May 16, 2011). http://libjournal.uncg.edu/ijcp/article/view/249.

Douglas, Frederick. "A Parody." In *The Norton Anthology of World Masterpieces*, 5th ed. Vol. 2. New York: W. W. Norton, 1985.

———. "The Narrative of the Life of Frederick Douglas, An American Slave." In *The Norton Anthology of World Masterpieces*, 5th ed. Vol. 2. New York: W. W. Norton, 1985.

Federal Reserve Bank of San Francisco. "Middle Neighborhoods." *Community Development Investment Review* 11, no. 1 (2016). https://www.frbsf.org/

community-development/publications/community-development-investment-review/2016/august/middle-neighborhoods/.

Firebaugh, Glenn, and Matthew B. Schroeder. "Does Your Neighbor's Income Affect Your Happiness?" *AJS; American Journal of Sociology* 115, no. 3 (November 2009): 805–31. https://doi.org/10.1086/603534.

Fortas, Abe. *Concerning Dissent and Civil Disobedience.* New York: Signet, 1968.

Friedman, Milton. *Capitalism and Freedom.* Chicago: University of Chicago Press, 1962.

Gillum, Richard, and Kristen Dodd. "Book Review of Soul Mates: Religion, Sex, Love, and Marriage among African Americans and Latinos." *Journal of the National Medical Association* 108 (September 1, 2016). https://doi.org/10.1016/j.jnma.2016.08.007.

Gimpel, James, and Kimberly Karnes. "The Rural Side of the Urban-Rural Gap." *PS: Political Science & Politics* 39, no. 3 (July 1, 2006): 467–72. https://doi.org/10.1017/S1049096506060859.

Goad, Jim. *The Redneck Manifesto.* New York: Simon & Schuster, 1997.

Gordon, Wayne L., and Randal Frame. *Real Hope in Chicago.* Chicago: Zondervan Publishing House, 1995.

Grant, Ulysses. *Personal Memoirs of U.S. Grant.* Libravox. New York: Charles L. Webster and Company, 1885.

Grogan, Paul. "The Future of Community Development." In *Investing in What Works for America's Communities*, edited by Nancy O. Andrews, David J. Erickson, Ian J. Galloway, and Ellen Seidman. San Francisco: The Federal Reserve Bank of San Francisco and the Low-Income Investment Fund, 2016.

Gundersen, Craig, and Susan Offutt. "Farm Poverty and Safety Nets." *American Journal of Agricultural Economics* 87, no. 4 (2005): 885–99.

Hamilton, Alexander. "The Federalist No. 78," n.d.

———. "The Federalist No. 78," n.d.

Hansen, Marty, and Sam Hong. *Behind the Golden Door: Refugees in Uptown*. Chicago: HH Communications, 1991.

Hartley, Eric. "Norfolk Church's Popular Pumpkin Sale Leads to City Council Voting on New Gourd Rule." *The Virginian-Pilot*, October 28, 2016. https://www.pilotonline.com/government/local/article_844a9321-216d-5f8f-99e6-6cf63b705693.html.

Harvard Business Review Ideacast. "Turning Purpose Into Performance." Accessed March 17, 2022. https://hbr.org/podcast/2018/07/turning-purpose-into-performance.

Havel, Vaclav. "Speech to the U.S. Congress," February 2, 1990. https://www.vhlf.org/havel-quotes/speech-to-the-u-s-congress/.

Heino, Rebecca, Nicole Ellison, and Jennifer Gibbs. "Relationshopping: Investigating the Market Metaphor in Online Dating." *Journal of Social and Personal Relationships* 27 (June 9, 2010): 427–47. https://doi.org/10.1177/0265407510361614.

Helliwell, John, Richard Layard, and Jeffrey Sachs. "World Happiness Report 2016." New York: Sustainable Development Solutions Network, 2016. https://worldhappiness.report/ed/2016/.

Hendren, Nathaniel, and Ben Sprung-Keyser. "A Unified Welfare Analysis of Government Policies Executive Summary." Opportunity Insights at Harvard University, July 2019. https://opportunityinsights.org/wp-content/uploads/2019/07/welfare-executive-summary.pdf.

Hendricks, Howard G. *Teaching to Change Lives*. Multnomah: Multnomah Press, 1987.

Hendrickson, Mary K., and Harvey S. James Jr. "The Ethics of Constrained Choice: How the Industrialization of Agriculture Impacts Farming and Farmer Behavior." University of Missouri Department of Agricultural Economics Working Paper No. 2004-3, 2004. https://doi.org/10.22004/ag.econ.26040.

Hitchens, Peter. *The Rage Against God: How Atheism Led Me to Faith*. Grand Rapids: Zondervan, 2010.

Holland, John. "A Flying Book. A Call to Police. A Civic League Spiraling." *The Virginian-Pilot*, August 4, 2014, sec. News, News. https://www.pilotonline.com/news/article_235eec2b-45a3-5b3a-916e-6bc4d56bfec7.html.

Howard, Spencer. "Kicking off a Presidential Campaign — Herbert Hoover's 1928 Acceptance Speech." *Hoover Heads* (blog), August 11, 2020. https://hoover.blogs.archives.gov/2020/08/11/kicking-off-a-presidential-campaign-herbert-hoovers-1928-acceptance-speech/.

Hughes, Louis. *Thirty Years a Slave: From Bondage to Freedom. The Institution of Slavery as Seen on the Plantation and in the Home of the Planter.* Available as an audiobook on Librivox. South Side printing Company, 1896. https://librivox.org/thirty-years-a-slave-by-louis-hughes/.

Hvidberg, Kristoffer, Claus Kreiner, and Stefanie Stantcheva. "Social Positions and Fairness Views on Inequality." Cambridge, MA: N.B.E.R., November 2020. https://doi.org/10.3386/w28099.

Isenberg, Nancy. *White Trash: The 400-Year Untold History of Class in America.* New York: Viking, 2016.

Jacobs, Harriet A., L.M. Child, and Boston Stereotype Foundry. *Incidents in the Life of a Slave Girl.* Apple Books. Pub. for the Author, 1861.

Jacobs, Jane. *The Death and Life of Great American Cities.* New York: Random House, 1961.

Jesus Is My Homeboy. "The Story." Accessed March 15, 2022. http://www.jesusismyhomeboy.com/the-story.

Johnson, Jean. "No Easy Way Out: Citizens Talk About Tackling the Debt." The Kettering Foundation, 2012.

https://www.kettering.org/catalog/product/no-easy-way-out-citizens-talk-about-tackling-debt.

Justice Marshall Receives National Bar Association Award, 1988. https://www.c-span.org/video/?3962-1/justice-marshall-receives-national-bar-association-award.

Kageyama, Peter. *For the Love of Cities: The Love Affair Between People and Their Places*. St. Petersburg: Creative Cities Productions, 2011.

Kahneman Daniel and Deaton Angus. "High Income Improves Evaluation of Life but Not Emotional Well-Being." *Proceedings of the National Academy of Sciences* 107, no. 38 (September 21, 2010): 16489–93. https://doi.org/10.1073/pnas.1011492107.

King, Martin L., and Clayborne Carson. *The Essential Martin Luther King, Jr.: "I Have a Dream" and Other Great Writings*. Apple Books. King Legacy. Beacon Press, 2013.

Kozol, Jonathan. *Amazing Grace: Lives of Children and the Conscience of a Nation, The*. New York: Harper Perennial, 1995.

Langlois, Shawn. "Disney Heiress: Jesus Christ Himself Doesn't Deserve This Much Money." MarketWatch. Accessed March 13, 2022. https://www.marketwatch.com/story/disney-heiress-jesus-christ-himself-doesnt-deserve-this-much-money-2019-03-07.

Lewis, C.S. *The Weight of Glory*. Harper Collins edition 2001. New York: Harper San Francisco, 2001.

London School of Economics and Political Science. "Parents, Poverty and the State," n.d. https://www.lse.ac.uk/Events/2019/10/ 20191010t1830vHKT/parents-poverty-and-the-state.aspx.

Lubin, Gus. "The 12 Most Expensive Weddings In History." *Business Insider*, April 28, 2011. https://www.businessinsider.com/most-expensive-weddings-in-history-2011-4.

Luttmer, Erzo F.P. "Neighbors as Negatives: Relative Earnings and Well-Being | N.B.E.R." *N.B.E.R. Working Paper*, no. working paper #10667 (2014). https://doi.org/10.3386/w10667.

Lynch, John R. *The Facts of Reconstruction*. Apple Books. Neale Publishing Company, 1913. https://books.google.com/ books?id=JlZLAAAAMAAJ.

Madison, James. "The Federalist No. 10.," n.d.

Manning, Brennan. *The Ragamuffin Gospel*. Sisters: Multnomah Publishing, 2000.

Markovits, Daniel. "The Meritocracy Trap." London School of Economics and Political Science, n.d. https://www.lse.ac.uk/Events/2019/05/ 20190508t1830vOT/The-Meritocracy-Trap.aspx.

Marshall, Cynt. *You've Been Chosen: Thriving Through the Unexpected*. Kindle. New York: Random House Publishing Group, 2022.

Marshall, Thurgood. *Thurgood Marshall: His Speeches, Writings, Arguments, Opinions, and Reminiscences*. Edited by Mark V. Tushnet. Apple Books. Chicago: Lawrence Hill Books, 2001.

Martela, Frank. "I'm a Psychology Expert in Finland, the No. 1 Happiest Country in the World—Here's the Real Meaning of Life in 5 Words." CNBC, June 9, 2023. https://www.cnbc.com/2023/06/09/psychology-expert-from-finland-the-worlds-happiest-country-shares-the-meaning-of-life-in-5-words.html.

Martela, Frank, Bengt Greve, Bo Rothstein, and Juho Saari. "The Nordic Exceptionalism: What Explains Why the Nordic Countries Are Constantly Among the Happiest in the World." In *World Happiness Report 2020*, 128–46, 2020. https://worldhappiness.report/ed/2020/the-nordic-exceptionalism-what-explains-why-the-nordic-countries-are-constantly-among-the-happiest-in-the-world/.

McBride, James. *The Color of Water: A Black Man's Tribut to His White Mother*. 2006 Edition. New York, 1996.

McCabe, Margaret Sova. "Cooperation or Compromise? Understanding the Farm Bills Omnibus Legislation." *Journal of Food Law & Policy* 14, no. 1 (Spring 2018). https://scholarworks.uark.edu/jflp/vol14/iss1/5.

McClaughry, Robert. "Crime and Its Causes." *Public Opinion*, November 7, 1891, Public Opinion 12, no. 5 (Washington and New York, November 7, 1891), 106. edition.

McComas, Katherine, John C. Besley, and Laura W. Black. "The Rituals of Public Meetings." *Public Administration Review* 70, no. 1 January/February (2010): 122–30. https://doi.org/10.1111/j.1540-6210.2009.02116.x.

McIntosh, Peggy. "White Privilege: Unpacking the Invisible Knapsack," 1989. https://psychology.umbc.edu/files/2016/10/White-Privilege_McIntosh-1989.pdf.

McKnight, John L. "Re-Functioning: A New Community Development Strategy for the Future (Learning Nine)," August 16, 2019. https://johnmcknight.org/re-functioning-a-new-community-development-strategy-for-the-future-learning-nine/.

McRae, James. "Silent Screams of a Convict," n.d.

Meacham, Jonathan. *Thomas Jefferson: The Art of Power*. New York: Random House Publishing Group, 2013.

Meraji, Shereen Marisol. "'Hispanic,' 'Latino,' Or 'Latinx'? Survey Says ..." *NPR*, August 11, 2020, sec. Hispanic Heritage Month. https://www.npr.org/sections/codeswitch/2020/08/11/901398248/hispanic-latino-or-latinx-survey-says.

Miller, Christian B. *The Character Gap: How Good Are We?* New York: Oxford University Press, 2018.

Miller, Luke C. "A First Look at Teacher Retention in Virginia." Presented at the 2018 Teacher Retention Summit, October 23, 2018. https://curry.virginia.edu/sites/default/files/uploads/epw/Teacher_Retention_PPT_Slides2.pdf.

Mills, Edwin S., and Bruce W. Hamilton. *Urban Economics*. 5th ed. New York: Harper Collins College Publishers, 1994.

Miranda v. Arizona: Earl Warren's Letter to Grandson, 2015. https://www.c-span.org/video/?401974-1/miranda-v-arizona-earl-warrens-letter-grandson.

Morton, Lois Wright, Ella Annette Bitto, Mary Jane Oakland, and Mary Sand. "Accessing Food Resources: Rural and Urban Patterns of Giving and Getting Food." *Agriculture and Human Values* 25, no. 1 (January 1, 2008): 107–19. https://doi.org/10.1007/s10460-007-9095-8.

Moyo, Dambisa. *Dead Aid: Why Aid Is Not Working and How There Is a Better Way for Africa*. New York: Farrar, Straus and Giroux, 2009.

New Journal and Guide. "Police Absent, Vandals Follow Dynamiters." September 18, 1954. Sargeant Memorial Collection at Slover Library.

Nicolay, John G., and John Hay. *A Short Life of Abraham Lincoln*. 2014 reprint. New York: The Century Company, 1914.

"Norfolk Redevelopment and Housing Authority Report 1957." Norfolk, VA: Norfolk Redevelopment and Housing Authority, April 1957. Available at the Sargeant Memorial Collection at Slover Library, Norfolk Public Libraries.

Obama, Barak. *Dreams from My Father*. Apple Books. New York: Crown Publishing, 1995.

Obama, Michelle. *Becoming*. Apple Books. New York: Crown, 2018.

Oishi, Shigehiro, Youngjae Cha, Asuka Komiya, and Hiroshi Ono. "Money and Happiness: The Income-Happiness Correlation Is Higher When Income Inequality Is Higher." *PNAS Nexus* 1, no. 5 (November 2022): pgac224. https://doi.org/10.1093/pnasnexus/pgac224.

Olsen, Marvin, Harry Perlstad, Valencia Fonseca, and Joanne Hogan,. "Participation in Neighborhood Associations." *Sociological Focus* 22, no. 1 (1989): 1–17.

Ostrom, Elinor. "Constituting Social Capital and Collective Action." *Journal of Theoretical Politics* 6, no. 4 (October 1, 1994): 527–62. https://doi.org/10.1177/0951692894006004006.

Pacyga, D.A., and E. Skerrett. *Chicago, City of Neighborhoods: Histories & Tours*. Chicago: Loyola University Press, 1986.

Patricia Turner · School Desegregation in Norfolk, Virginia. "Patricia Turner · School Desegregation in Norfolk, Virginia · ODU Libraries Online Exhibitions." Accessed March 17, 2022. https://exhibits.lib.odu.edu/exhibits/show/sdinv/the-norfolk-17/turnerpatricia.

Peck, M. Scott. *People of the Lie*. New York: Simon and Schuster, 1983.

———. *The Road Less Traveled: A New Psychology of Love, Traditional Values, and Spiritual Growth*. Touchstone Book. New York: Simon and Schuster, 1978.

Perez-Truglia, Ricardo. "The Effects of Income Transparency on Well-Being: Evidence from a Natural Experiment." *N.B.E.R. Working Paper*, no. working paper 25622 (2019). https://doi.org/10.3386/w25622.

Perloff, Jeffrey. *Microeconomics*. 5th ed. Boston: Pearson, Addison Westley, 2009.

Perry, James L. "Measuring Public Service Motivation: An Assessment of Construct Reliability and Validity." *Journal of Public Administration Research and Theory* 6, no. 1 (1996): 5–22.

Perry, James L., and Lois Recascino Wise. "The Motivational Bases of Public Service." *Public Administration Review* 50, no. 3 (1990): 367–73. https://doi.org/10.2307/976618.

Peterman, William. *Neighborhood Planning and Community-Based Development: The Potential and Limits of Grassroots Action*. Thousand Oaks: Sage Publication, 2000.

Porter, Michael E. "Inner-City Economic Development: Learnings From 20 Years of Research and Practice." *Economic Development Quarterly* 30, no. 2 (2016): 105–16. https://doi.org/10.1177/0891242416642320.

———. "The Competitive Advantage of the Inner City." *Harvard Business Review*. Accessed March 6, 2022. https://hbr.org/1995/05/the-competitive-advantage-of-the-inner-city.

Powell, Colin L., and Joseph E. Persico. *My American Journey*. New York: Ballantine Books, 1995.

Public Opinion. "A Southern Opinion of Confederate Flags." November 7, 1891.

Public Opinion. "Packers Tar Soap Advertisement." November 7, 1891.

Putnam, Robert D. *Bowling Alone: The Collapse and Revival of American Community*. New York: Simon and Schuster, 2000.

———. *Our Kids: The American Dream in Crisis*. New York: Simon & Schuster, 2015.

Putnam, Robert D., and David E. Campbell. *American Grace: How Religion Divides and Unites Us*. New York: Simon & Schuster, 2010.

Putnam, Robert D., and Shaylyn Romney Garrett. *The Upswing: How We Came Together a Century Ago and How We Can Do It Again*. New York: Simon and Schuster, 2020.

Reis, Jacob. *How the Other Half Lives*. New York: Charles Scribner's Sons, 1890.

"Resolute." Resolute Definition & Meaning at Merriam-Webster.com. Accessed March 6, 2022. https://www.merriam-webster.com/dictionary/resolute.

Ringelstein, Kevin. "Residential Segregation in Norfolk, Virginia: How the Federal Government Reinforced Racial Division in a Southern City, 1914-1959." Old Dominion University, 2015. https://digitalcommons.odu.edu/history_etds/1.

Rivlin, By Gary. "In Silicon Valley, Millionaires Who Don't Feel Rich." *New York Times*, August 5, 2007.

Robinson, Alyssa I, and Nicolas M Oreskovic. "Comparing Self-Identified and Census-Defined Neighborhoods among Adolescents Using GPS and Accelerometer." *International Journal of Health Geographics* 12, no. 1 (December 10, 2013): 57–57. https://doi.org/10.1186/1476-072X-12-57.

Roch, Christine H., and Theodore H. Poister. "Citizens, Accountability, and Service Satisfaction: The Influence of Expectations." *Urban Affairs Review* 41, no. 3 (January 1, 2006): 292–308. https://doi.org/10.1177/1078087405281124.

Roosevelt, Theodore. *An Autobiography of Theodore Roosevelt*. 2019 Edition. Digireads Publishing, 2019.

———. "Citizenship in a Republic Speech." The Sorbonne, Paris, April 23, 1910. https://theodoreroosevelt.org/content.aspx?page_id=22&club_id=991271&module_id=339364.

Sanchez-Jankowski, Martin. *Cracks in the Pavement: Social Change and Resilience in Poor Neighborhoods*. Berkeley: University of California Press, 2008.

Sandel, Michael. *Justice: What's the Right Thing to Do?* New York: Farrar, Straus and Giroux, 2009.

Schmeichel, Susan. "Church Whips Up Controversy." *Pittsburgh Tribune-Review*, April 8, 2004.

Schurr, Amos, and Ilana Ritov. "Winning a Competition Predicts Dishonest Behavior." *Proceedings of the National Academy of Sciences* 113, no. 7 (February 16, 2016): 1754–59. https://doi.org/10.1073/pnas.1515102113.

Shiller, Robert J. "The Negative Transformation of the American Dream." *The National Post*, August 8, 2017. https://nationalpost.com/opinion/robert-j-shiller-the-transformation-of-the-american-dream/wcm/f375f709-031b-4f8d-ba7a-bf83b7ad167a/amp/.

Simon, Harvey. "Norfolk's Police Assisted Community Enforcement (PACE): The Bay View and East Norview Neighborhoods." John F. Kennedy School of Government, Harvard University, 1998. https://case.hks.harvard.edu/norfolks-police-assisted-community-enforcement-pace-the-bay-view-and-east-norview-neighborhoods/.

Solzhenitsyn, Aleksandr. *The Gulag Archipelago*. Apple Books., 1973.

"Sonia Sotomayor." In *Wikipedia*, December 19, 2023. https://en.wikipedia.org/w/index.php?title=Sonia_Sotomayor&oldid=1190781600.

Stipak, Brian. "Citizen Satisfaction with Urban Services: Potential Misuse as a Performance Indicator." *Public Administration Review* 39, no. 1 (1979): 46–52. https://doi.org/10.2307/3110378.

Stock, Paul, and Jérémie Forney. "Farmer Autonomy and the Farming Self." *Journal of Rural Studies* 36 (October 1, 2014): 160–71. https://doi.org/10.1016/j.jrurstud.2014.07.004.

Su, Francis Edward, and Shira Zerbib. "Piercing Numbers in Approval Voting." *Mathematical Social Sciences* 101 (2019). https://doi.org/10.1016/j.mathsocsci.2019.06.007.

Thaler, Richard H., and Cass R. Sunstein. *Nudge: The Final Edition*. New York: Penguin Books, 2021.

"The Batten Surveys: A Regional Civic Capital Assessment 2008-2009"." The Hampton Roads Center for Civic Enagagement, n.d. formerly at www.hrcce.org[3].

---

3. https://doi.org/formerly%20at%20www.hrcce.org

The Long, Long Trailer. Movie. Los Angeles: Metro-Goldwyn-Mayer, 1954.

"The Model Cities Program Questions and Answers." US Department of Housing and Urban Development, 68 1967. Sargeant Memorial Collection at Slover Library.

The Nation. "A Criticism of Our Schools." June 11, 1866.

The Nation. "To Govern Well, Govern Little." June 11, 1866.

"The Stamp Act | Colonial Williamsburg." Accessed March 13, 2022. https://www.colonialwilliamsburg.org/learn/deep-dives/stamp-act/.

"The State of Our Unions 2012: The President's Marriage Agenda." Charlottesville: University of Virginia: The National Marriage Project and the Institute for American Values, 2012. http://www.stateofourunions.org/2012/SOOU2012.php.

"The War on Poverty: 50 Years Later." Washington D.C.: U.S. House of Representatives (Republicans). Accessed March 15, 2022. https://republicans-budget.house.gov/initiatives/war-on-poverty/.

Theatre Historical Society of America. "Chicago's Once-Grand Movie Palaces." Accessed March 5, 2022. https://historictheatres.org/blog/2016/03/28/chicagos-once-grand-movie-palaces/.

Thompson, Curt. "Shame and Spirituality: Living as a Whole Person in a Disembodied World." Vertitas Forum.

Accessed September 1, 2021. https://soundcloud.com/ user-248999605/shame-spirituality-living-as-a-whole-person-in-a-disembodied-world-curt-thompson?utm_source=clipboard&utm_medium=text&utm_campai

Trueblood, Elton. *A Place to Stand*. Apple Books. Harper & Row, 1969.

Truth, Sojourner. *Narrative of Sojourner Truth*. New York: Barnes and Noble Books, 2005.

Twenge, Jean M., and Tim Kasser. "Generational Changes in Materialism and Work Centrality, 1976-2007: Associations With Temporal Changes in Societal Insecurity and Materialistic Role Modeling." *Personality and Social Psychology Bulletin* 39, no. 7 (July 1, 2013): 883–97. https://doi.org/10.1177/0146167213484586.

Uptown United. "History." Accessed March 5, 2022. https://exploreuptown.org/explore-uptown/history/.

US Census Bureau. "American Community Survey (ACS)." Census.gov. Accessed March 12, 2022. https://www.census.gov/programs-surveys/acs.

US Department of Agriculture. "FY2017 Budget Summary." Accessed March 12, 2022. https://www.usda.gov/obpa/budget-summary.

Vale, Lawrence J. *From the Puritans to the Projects: Public Housing and Public Neighbors*. Cambridge: Harvard University Press, 2000.

Vasel, Kathryn. "Couples Are Spending More than Ever to Get Hitched." *CNNMoney*, April 6, 2016. https://money.cnn.com/2016/04/05/pf/ average-wedding-costs/index.html.

Washington, Booker T. *The Negro Problem*. 2015 reprint. New York: Fireworks Press, 1899.

———. "To Would Be Teachers." In *Character Building*, Audiobook on Librivox., 1902. https://librivox.org/ character-building-by-booker-t-washington/.

West, Cornel. *Race Matters*. New York: Random House, 1993.

Weston, George M. "Poor Whites of the South." Buell and Blanchard, 1856. https://credo.library.umass.edu/ view/full/murb003-i342.

Williams, Margery. *The Velveteen Rabbit*. New York: Doubleday, 1922.

Wilson, James Q. "The Rediscovery of Character: Private Virtue and Public Policy." *The Public Interest*, Fall 1985. https://www.nationalaffairs.com/public_interest/detail/ the-rediscovery-of-character-private-virtue-and-public-policy.

Woodring, Frank. "Ringgold Community Provides Insights Into Life's Complexities." *Maryland Cracker Barrel*, December 2007.

Woods, Robert A. "The Neighborhood in Social Reconstruction." *American Journal of Sociology* 19, no. 2 (March 1914).

Zarrella, John, and Patrick Oppmann. "Pastor with 666 Tattoo Claims to Be Divine." *Cnn.Com*, February 19, 2007. https://www.cnn.com/2007/US/02/16/miami.preacher/.

Zinn, Howard. *A People's History of the United States*. New York: Harper Collins, 2003.

Notes

[1] Cynt Marshall, *You've Been Chosen: Thriving Through the Unexpected* (New York: Random House Publishing Group, 2022), chap. 2, Kindle.

[2] David Brooks, *The Road to Character* (New York: Penguin Random House, 2015), chap. 3: Self Conquest, Apple Books.

[3] "Sonya Sotomayor," Wikimedia Foundation, last modified December 19, 2023, 20:30, https://en.wikipedia.org/wiki/Sonia_Sotomayor

[4] John G. Nicolay, *A Short Life of Abraham Lincoln* (Lexington: 2014 reprint), 231. Condensed from the ten-volume *Abraham Lincoln: A History* co-authored with John Hay (New York: The Century Company, 1914).

[5] I'm a fan of Raj Chetty, the Opportunity Insights team, Robert Putnam, Robert Shiller, Daniel Markovits, Esther Duflo and Ahbijit Banerjee who have written extensively about inequality.

[6] Kristoffer Hvidberg, Claus Kreiner, and Stefanie Stantcheva, "Social Positions and Fairness Perceptions of Inequality," NBER working paper 28099, (November 2021), http://www.nber.org/papers/w28099.pdf. I

reference Stefanie Stantcheva, because I first heard about the paper on and HBR Ideacast podcast (number 835).

[7] Robert Putnam, *Our Kids: The American Dream in Crisis* (New York: Simon and Schuster, 2015), 9.

[8] Barak Obama, *Dreams from My Father* (New York: Crown Publishing, 1995, 2004) chap. 11, Apple Books.

[9] Aleksandr Solzhenitsyn, *The Gulag Archipelago*, Part IV, Chap. 2, "Or Corruption?", Apple Books. Originally published 1973.

[10] Robert J. Shiller, "The Negative Transformation of the American Dream," reprinted in the *The National Post*, August 8, 2017, https://nationalpost.com/opinion/robert-j-shiller-the-transformation-of-the-american-dream/wcm/f375f709-031b-4f8d-ba7a-bf83b7ad167a/amp/

[11] Edwin S. Mills and Bruce W. Hamilton, *Urban Economics*, 5th ed. (New York: HarperCollins College Publishers, 1994) 256.

[12] Brennan Manning, *The Ragamuffin Gospel* (Sisters: Multnomah Publishing, 2000), 15.

[13] Associated Press, "Small Alabama Town Raises Big Stink: Abandoned New York City Poop Train," (April 4, 2018), https://www.usatoday.com/story/news/nation/2018/04/18/small-alabama-town-raises-big-stink-abandoned-new-york-city-poop-train/527364002/

[14] John Cromartie, "Rural America at a Glance", U.S. Department of Agriculture report, 2017 Edition, 3, https://www.ers.usda.gov/webdocs/publications/85740/eib-182.pdf?v=5256.7

[15]London School of Economics Public Lectures and Events podcast, "Parents, Poverty and the State", October 9, 2019, featuring Naomi Eisenstadt, Carey Oppenheim, Ryan Shorthouse, and Matthew Taylor, https://www.lse.ac.uk/Events/2019/10/20191010t1830vHKT/parents-poverty-and-the-state.

[16] Ulysses S. Grant, *Personal Memoirs of U.S. Grant* (New York: Charles L. Webster and Company, 1885), Librivox edition; George M. Weston estimated that just less than one third of White families in the south were slaveholders in his 1856 antislavery pamphlet *Poor Whites of the South* available at http://credo.library.umass.edu/view/full/murb003-i342.

[17] Louis Hughes, *Thirty Years a Slave: From Bondage to Freedom. The Institution of Slavery as Seen on the Plantation and in the Home of the Planter,* (Southside Printing Company, 1897), available as an audiobook on Librivox.

[18] James McBride, *The Color of Water*, (New York: Penguin, 2006), 290, 294.

[19] Michelle Obama, *Becoming* (New York: Random House, 2018), chap. 13, Apple Books.

[20] Thurgood Marshall in a speech given to the American Bar Association on August 10, 1988. Recording titled "Justice Marshall Receives National Bar Association Award" available from C-span at https://www.c-span.org/video/?3962-1/justice-marshall-receives-national-bar-association-award.

[21] Brooks, *The Road to Character*.

[22] Gary Rivlin, "In Silicon Valley, Millionaires Who Don't Feel Rich," *New York Times*, August 5, 2007, http://www.nytimes.com/2007/08/05/technology/05rich.html.

[23] Alexis De Tocqueville, *Democracy In America*, trans. James T. Schleifer, ed. Eduardo Nolla (Indianpolis: The Liberty Fund, 2010), Vol. 2, 316.

[24] Alexis De Tocqueville, *Democracy In America*, Vol. 4, 1070.

[25] This is reference to Book V of Aristotle's *Politics*. I used multiple English and Greek sources.

[26] Frank Martela, Bengt Greve, Bo Rothstein, Juho Saari, "The Nordic Exceptionalism: What Explains Why the Nordic Countries are Constantly Among the Happiest in the World", World Happiness Report 2020. ed. John F Helliwell, Richard Layard, Jeffrey D Sachs, Jan-Emmanuel De Neve, (New York, 2020) 128-146. https://worldhappiness.report/ed/2020/the-nordic-

exceptionalism-what-explains-why-the-nordic-countries-are-constantly-among-the-happiest-in-the-world/

[27] Frank Martela, "I'm a psychology expert in Finland, the No. 1 happiest country in the world—here are 3 things we never do," CNBC, January 5, 2023, https://www.cnbc.com/2023/06/09/psychology-expert-from-finland-the-worlds-happiest-country-shares-the-meaning-of-life-in-5-words.html.

[28] Ricardo Perez-Truglia, "The Effects of Income Transparency on Well Being: Evidence from a Natural Experiment," NBER working paper 25622, (September 2019), https://www.nber.org/papers/w25622.

[29] Erzo F.P. Luttmer, "Neighbors as Negatives: Relative Earnings and Well Being," NBER working paper 10667, (August 2004), https://www.nber.org/papers/w10667.

[30] Daniel Kahneman and Angus Deaton, "High income improves evaluation of life but not emotional well being," *PNAS,* 107, no. 38, (September 7, 2010), https://doi.org/10.1073/pnas.1011492107.

[31] The journal I used is available at http://www.americanjourneys.org/pdf/AJ-062.pdf. It is attributed to Christopher Columbus, *American Journeys: Journal of the First Voyage of Columbus,* eds. Julius E. Olson and Edward G. Bourne (New York: Charles Scribner's Sons, 1906), 87-258.

[32] Theodore Roosevelt, *An Autobiography of Theodore Roosevelt,* (Digireads Publishing, 2019 edition), 117-118.

[33] Paul Grogan, "The Future of Community Development," in *Investing in What Works for America's Communities*, eds. Nancy O. Andrews, David J. Erickson, Ian J. Galloway, and Ellen Seidman, (San Francisco: The Federal Reserve Bank of San Francisco & the Low-income Investment Fund, 2016), 186.

[34] Nancy Isenberg, *White Trash: The 400 Year Untold History of Class in America,* 18-19.

[35] Cornel West, *Race Matters* (New York: Random House, 1993), 27.

[36] Robert A. Woods, "The Neighborhood in Social Reconstruction," *American Journal of Sociology*, 19, no. 5 (March 1914).

[37] Herbert Hoover as quoted by Spencer Howard, "Kicking off a Presidential Campaign — Herbert Hoover's 1928 Acceptance Speech" available at https://hoover.blogs.archives.gov/2020/08/11/kicking-off-a-presidential-campaign-herbert-hoovers-1928-acceptance-speech/. Accessed April 18, 2022.

[38] Shereen Marisol Meraji, "'Hispanic,' 'Latino,' Or 'Latinx'? Survey Says ...," *NPR*, August 11, 2020. Accessed on May 8, 2022 at https://www.npr.org/sections/codeswitch/2020/08/11/901398248/hispanic-latino-or-latinx-survey-says.

[39] Michael Sandel, *Justice: What's the Right Thing to Do?* (New York: Farrar, Straus and Giroux, 2009), chap. 5, Apple Books.

[40] Francis E. Su and Shira Zerbib, "Piercing Numbers in Approval Voting," *Mathematical Social Sciences* 101 (2019): 65-71, https://www.sciencedirect.com/science/article/abs/pii/S016548961930054X.

[41] Richard H. Thaler and Cass R. Sunstein, *Nudge: The Final Edition* (New York: Penguin Books, 2021), Chap. 2 - Resisting Temptation, Apple Books.

[42] Robert Putnam with Shaylyn Romney Garrett, *Upswing* (New York: Simon and Schuster, 2020), chap. 5, Apple Books.

[43] Curt Thompson, "Shame and Spirituality: Living as a Whole Person in a Disembodied World" (March 9, 2021) *Veritas Forum* Podcast, Apple Podcasts. https://podcasts.apple.com/us/podcast/the-veritas-forum/id1210782509?i=1000512230363.

[44] I should note that the bundle of joy who knocked me off my throne and the little princess who came three years later worked out in my favor. I look up to them and want to be more like them, not less. They also produced offspring who are much cooler than they ever were.

[45] "Chicago's Once-Grand Movie Palaces," Archives of the Theatre Historical Society of America found at

https://historictheatres.org/blog/2016/03/28/chicagos-once-grand-movie-palaces/

[46] Pacyga, Dominic A., and Skerrett, Ellen, *Chicago, City of Neighborhoods Histories and Tours* (Chicago: Loyola University Press, 1986), 110.

[47] http://exploreuptown.org/uptown-history/

[48] Hansen, Marty, and Hong, Sam, *Behind the Golden Door: Refugees in Uptown* (Chicago: HH Communications, 1991), 10.

[49] Hansen and Hong, *Behind the Golden Door*, 10

[50] Martin Sanchez-Jankowski, *Cracks in the Pavement - Social Change and Resilience in Poor Neighborhoods* (Berkeley: University of California Press, 2008).

[51] *Merriam-Webster.com,* s.v. "resolute," accessed 2017, www.merriam-webster.com/dictionary/resolute.

[52] William Peterman, *Neighborhood Planning and Community Based Development,* (Thousand Oaks: Sage Publication, 2000), 153.

[53] West, *Race Matters,* 17-31.

[54] Harvey Simon, "Norfolk's Police Assisted Community Enforcement (PACE): The Bay View and East Norview Neighborhoods," John F. Kennedy School of Government, Harvard University, 1998, 32-44.

[55] I learned that government consultants have at least one of two roles. Some are hired because of specific skills for a specific, short-term project. Others are hired to say what most already know but no one wants to say out loud.

[56] Abhijit Banerjee and Esther Duflo, *Good Economics for Hard Times* (New York: Hatchett Book Group, 2019), chap. 5, Apple Books.

[57] Jim Collins, *Good to Great: Why Some Companies Make the Leap and Others Don't* (New York: Harper Collins Publishers, 2001), 86.

[58] Collins, *Good to Great*, 69.

[59] Warren Buffett's letter to Shareholders of Berkshire Hathaway, Inc., February 24, 2018 available at http://www.berkshirehathaway.com/letters/2017ltr.pdf

[60] Abhijit Banerjee and Esther Duflo, *Poor Economics: A Radical Rethinking of the Way to Fight Global Poverty* (New York: Public Affairs Publishing, 2012), chap. 7, Apple Books.

[61] Banerjee and Duflo, *Poor Economics*, 264.

[62] Michael Porter, "The Competitive Advantage of the Inner City," *Harvard Business Review* May-June 1995.

[63] Michael Porter, "Inner-City Economic Development: Learnings from 20 Years of Research and Practice",

Economic Development Quarterly 2016, Vol. 30(2), 1-5-116.

[64] Porter, "The Competitive Advantage of the Inner City," 70.

[65] Perloff, *Microeconomics*, 2.

[66] Daniel Markovits, *The Meritocracy Trap* lecture at the London School of Economics, May 8, 2019, Apple Podcasts. Available at https://www.lse.ac.uk/Events/2019/05/20190508t1830vOT/The-Meritocracy-Trap.

[67] John Holland, "A Flying Book. A Call to Police. Civic League Spiraling," *The Virginian-Pilot*, August 4, 2014.

[68] Katherine McComas, John Beasley, and Laure Black, "The Rituals of Public Meetings," *Public Administration Review*, January/February 2010, 122-130.

[69] Marvin Olsen, Harry Perlstadt, Valencia Fonseca, and Joanne Hogan, "Participation in Neighborhood Associations," *Sociological Focus*, 22, no. 1 (February 1989): 1-17.

[70] *A Stronger, More Resilient New York*. A 438 page report released by New York City on June 11, 2013 in response to Hurricane Sandy.

[71] Available at https://www.pps.org/article/the-power-of-10

[72] Federal Reserve Bank of San Francisco, "Middle Neighborhoods," *Community Development Investment Review* 11, no. 1 (2016), https://www.frbsf.org/community-development/wp-content/uploads/sites/3/cdir-middle-neighborhoods.pdf

[73] David Boehlke, "Strategies to Improve Middle Neighborhoods," *Community Development Investment Review* 11, no. 1 (2016): 90, https://www.frbsf.org/community-development/wp-content/uploads/sites/3/cdir-middle-neighborhoods.pdf.

[74] Allyssa I. Robinson and Nicolas M. Oreskovic, "Comparing Self-Identified and Census-defined Neighborhoods Among adolescents Using GPS and Accelerometer," *International Journal of Health Geographics* 12, no. 57 (December 2013), https://doi.org/10.1186/1476-072X-12-57

[75] The technical term for this is filtering.

[76] McComas, Besley, and Black, "The Rituals of Public Meetings," 126.

[77] Dambisa Moyo, *Dead Aid: Why Aid Is Not Working and How There is a Better Way for Africa* (New York: Farrar, Straus and Giroux, 2009), Apple Books.

[78] Elijah Anderson, *Code of the Street* (New York: W.W. Norton, 2000), 34, 47.

[79] Jane Jacobs, *The Death and Life of Great American Cities* (New York: Random House, 1961), 114.

[80] Colon Powell and Joseph Persico, *My American Journey* (New York: Ballentine Books, 1995) 97.

[81] Powell and Persico, *My American Journey*, 141.

[82] Brian Stipak, "Citizen satisfaction with urban services: Potential misuse as a performance indicator," *Public Administration Review* 39 (1979): 46-52 quoted in Christine H. Roch and Theodore H. Poister, "Citizens, Accountability, and Service Satisfaction: The Influence of Expectations," *Urban Affairs Review* 41 (2006): 292. http://jar.sagepub.com/content/41/3/292

[83] Luke C. Miller, "A First Look at Teacher Retention in Virginia." A presentation given on October 23, 2018 at the 2018 Teacher Retention Summit. Available at https://curry.virginia.edu/sites/default/files/uploads/epw/Teacher_Retention_PPT_Slides2.pdf. Accessed on November 10, 2021.

[84] London School of Economics podcast, "Parents, Poverty and the State", October 9, 2019.

[85] James L. Perry and Lois R. Wise, "The Motivational Basis of Public Service," *Public Administration Review* 50, no. 3 (May - Jun., 1990): 367-373, http://www.jstor.org/stable/976618

[86] James L. Perry, "Measuring Public Service Motivation: An Assessment of Construct Reliability and Validity," *Journal of Public Administration Research and Theory* 6, no. 1 (January 1996): 5–22.

[87] Perry and Wise, "The Motivational Basis of Public Service," 372.

[88] Eric Hartley, "Norfolk church's popular pumpkin sale leads to city council voting on new gourd rule," *The Virginian-Pilot*, October 28, 2016.

[89] I owe a great deal to the volunteers at Libravox, the free book app, who opened the door to Booker T. Washington, W.E.B. Du Bois, Charles Chesnutt, J.R. Lynch, Harriet Beecher Stowe, Louis Hughes, Grant's memoirs, and John Nicolay's biography of Lincoln.

[90] Booker T. Washington, ed., *The Negro Problem* (New York: Fireworks Press, 2015 reprint of the original 1899 book).

[91] I confirmed that information at http://jimcrowlivedhere.org/exhibits/show/vaconstitution.

[92] Norfolk Redevelopment and Housing Authority Report published in April 1957, p. 6. Available at the Sargeant Memorial Collection at Slover Library, Norfolk Public Libraries, Norfolk, VA.

[93] Lawrence J. Vale, *From the Puritans to the Projects* (Cambridge: Harvard University Press, 2000).

[94] Kevin L. Ringelstein, "Residential Segregation in Norfolk, Virginia: How the Federal Government Reinforced Racial Division in a Southern City, 1914-1959" (Masters thesis, Old Dominion University, 2015),14,17, https://digitalcommons.odu.edu/history_etds/1/

[95] Kevin L. Ringelstein, "Residential Segregation in Norfolk, Virginia", 3.

[96] "Police Absent, Vandals Follow Dynamiters," *New Journal and Guide* (September 18 1954), C1.

[97] Jacobs, *The Death and Life of Great American Cities*, 122.

[98] James Q. Wilson, "The Rediscovery of Character: Private Virtue and Public Policy," *The Public Interest*, no. 81 (Fall 1985): 11,14.

[99] Harry C. Boyte, "Reinventing Citizenship as Public Work; Citizen-Centered Democracy and the Empowerment Gap", A Study by the Kettering Foundation, (2013).

[100] John McKnight, "Re-functioning: A New Community Development Strategy for the Future," (August 16, 2019), https://johnmcknight.org/re-

functioning-a-new-community-development-strategy-for-the-future-learning-nine/.

[101] Elinor Ostrom, "Constituting Social Capital and Collective Action," *Journal of Theoretical Politics* 6, no. 4, (1994): 527-562.

[102] Booker T. Washington, *Character Building,* (1902), a compilation of his speeches to students at Tuskegee Institute from a chapter titled "To Would Be Teachers" available as audiobook on Librivox.

[103] This is not my observation alone. Esther Duflo and Abhijit Banerjee note that economists use models that are based on assumptions: Duflo and Banerjee, *Good Economics for Tough Times*, chap. 1.

[104] Peterman, *Neighborhood Planning and Community Development*, 155.

[105] Charles Buki, "CZB, Llc. Final Report," Vision and Engagement Project (Norfolk: October 2010).

[106] It was a classic example of the parable of the Blobs and Squares found on Vimeo or YouTube from Edgar Cahn and David Mathews.

[107] Robert Putnam, *Bowling Alone* (New York: Simon and Shuster, 2000), 205.

[108] "The Batten Surveys: A Regional Civic Capital Assessment 2008-2009", Published by the former Hampton Roads Center for Civic Engagement.

[109] Vaclav Havel addressed a joint session of Congress on February 2, 1990. The text of his speech may be found at https://www.vhlf.org/havel-quotes/speech-to-the-u-s-congress/.

[110] Jacob Reis, *How the Other Half Lives* (New York: Charles Scribner's Sons, 1890).

[111] Jon Meacham, *Thomas Jefferson: The Art of Power* (New York: Random House, 2013), 295.

[112] "An Atlas of the St. Clair Village and Mt. Oliver Neighborhoods of Pittsburgh 1977". Part of the Pittsburgh Neighborhood Atlas completed by the University Center for Urban Research at the University of Pittsburgh, http://ucsur.pitt.edu/wp-content/uploads/2014/11/St.-Clair-Village-Mount-Oliver.pdf

[113] James G. Gimpel and Kimberly A. Karnes, "The Rural Side of the Urban-Rural Gap," *PS: Political Science and Politics* 39, no. 3 (July 2006): 467-468.

[114] Robert Putnam, *Bowling Alone*, 205

[115] Lois Wright Morton et al., "Accessing food resources: Rural and urban patterns of giving and getting food" *Agriculture and Human Values* 25, no.1 (2008): 107.

[116] Frank Woodring, "Ringgold Community Provides Insights Into Life's Complexities," Reflections column, *Maryland Cracker Barrel*, Ringgold Edition (December 2007/January 2008), 3.

[117] Gimpel and Karnes, "The Rural Side of the Urban-Rural Gap," 467-468.

[118] Craig Gundersen and Susan Offutt, "Farm Poverty and Safety Nets," *American Journal of Agricultural Economics* 87, no. 4 (November 2005): 886.

[119] Paul V. Stock and Jeremie Forney, "Farmer Autonomy and the Farming Self," *Journal of Rural Studies* 36 (October 2014): 169-171.

[120] Christopher Burns and James M. MacDonald, *America's Diverse Family Farms, 2018 Edition* (December 2018) https://www.ers.usda.gov/publications/pub-details/?pubid=90984

[121] Mary Hendrickson and Harvey S. James, Jr., "The Ethics of Constrained Choice: How the Industrialization of Agriculture Impacts Farming and Farmer Behavior," Department of Agricultural Economics Working Paper No. AEWP 2004-03, College of Agriculture, Food and Natural Resources at the University of Missouri, https://ageconsearch.umn.edu/record/26040/files/wp040003.pdf.

[122] Margaret Sova McCabe, "Cooperation or Compromise? Understanding the Farm Bills Omnibus

Legislation," *Journal of Food & Law Policy* 14, no. 1 (Spring 2018): 4.

[123] Roosevelt, *An Autobiography of Theodore Roosevelt,* 185-197.

[124] Jim Goad, *The Redneck Manifesto* (New York: Simon and Shuster, 1997), 34.

[125] Goad, *The Redneck Manifesto,* 32.

[126] John R. Lynch, *The Facts of Reconstruction* (1913) is in the public domain and is available through the Librivox app or at https://librivox.org/the-facts-of-reconstruction-by-john-r-lynch/

[127] Obama, *Becoming,* chap. 19.

[128] Obama, *Becoming,* chap. 23.

[129] The Peggy McIntosh article, "White Privilege: Unpacking the Invisible Knapsack" is available at https://psychology.umbc.edu/files/2016/10/White-Privilege_McIntosh-1989.pdf. the "White Fragility" article by Robin DiAngelo is from the *International Journal of Critical Pedagogy* 3, no. 3 (2011), https://libjournal.uncg.edu/ijcp/article/viewFile/249/116.

[130] Theodore Roosevelt, "Citizenship in a Republic" speech (Paris: April 23, 1910),

https://theodoreroosevelt.org/
content.aspx?page_id=22&club_id=991271&module_id=339364

[131] Romans 12:9:18 (NIV)

[132] Harriet Jacobs (under the pen name of Linda Brent), *Incidents in the Life of a Slave Girl*, (Boston, 1861), Chap. 9, Apple Books.

[133] Elton Trueblood, *A Place to Stand* (New York: Harper Collins, 1969), chap. 1, Apple Books.

[134] Robert D. Putnam and David E. Campbell, *American Grace* (New York: Simon & Schuster, 2010), 3.

[135] Peter Hitchens, *The Rage Against God: How Atheism Led Me to Faith* (Grand Rapids: Zondervan, 2011).

[136] *Oxford Dictionary* declared post-truth to be the word of the year in 2016 and *The Economist* made it a cover article the same year.

[137] Booker T. Washington, *Character Building*.

[138] Martin Luther King, Jr., "The Power of Non Violence" a 1958 address compiled in *The Essential Martin Luther King, Jr.* (Boston: Beacon Press, 2013), Apple Books.

[139] D. Elton Trueblood, *A Place To Stand* (New York: Harper Collins, 1969, 2014), chap. 1, Apple Books.

[140] Putnam and Garrett, *The Upswing*, chap. 1.

[141] Benjamin Callard, "Be Real: Knowing and expressing the authentic self in a performative age", *Veritas Forum* Podcast (University of Chicago: April 21, 2022), https://podcasts.apple.com/uz/podcast/can-anyone-know-your-authentic-self-university-of-chicago/id1210782509?i=1000585745102

[142] Wayne Gordon and Randal Frame, *Real Hope in Chicago* (Grand Rapids: Zondervan Publishing House, 1995), 73-97.

[143] Robert Putnam, *Bowling Alone*, 66.

[144] Robert Putnam, *Bowling Alone*, 66.

[145] Putnam and Campbell, *American Grace*, 444-452.

[146] Jonathan Kozol *Amazing Grace: Lives of Children and the Conscience of a Nation* (Harper Perennial,1995), 78.

[147] Dan G. Blazer, "Empirical Studies About Attendance At Religious Services and Health," *JAMA Internal Medicine* 176, no. 6 (June 2016): 785.

[148] John Helliwell, Richard Layard, and Jeffrey Sachs, *World Happiness Report 2016, Update* (Vol. I). (New York: Sustainable Development Solutions Network: 2016).

[149] Peter Kageyama, *For the Love of Cities: The Love Affair Between People and Their Places* (St. Petersburg: Creative Cities Productions, 2011), 44.

[150] Packers Tar Soap ad, *Public Opinion* 12, no. 5 (Washington and New York: November 7, 1891), 6.

[151] "A Southern Opinion of Confederate Flags", *Public Opinion* 12, no. 5 (Washington and New York, November 7, 1891) 101.

[152] Robert McClaughry, "Crime and Its Causes," *Public Opinion* 12, no. 5 (Washington and New York, November 7, 1891), 106.

[153] "A Criticism of our Schools", *The Nation* 2, no. 56 (New York, Monday evening, June 11, 1866), 741.

[154] "To Govern Well, Govern Little" *The Nation* 2, no. 56 (New York, Monday evening, June 11, 1866), 745.

[155] Angela Glover Blackwell, "America's Tomorrow: Race, Place and the Equity Agenda", *Investing in What Works for America's Communities* (San Francisco: Federal Reserve Bank of San Francisco & Low-income Investment Fund, 2012), 137

[156] President Harry Truman as quoted by Lawrence Vale, *From the Puritans to the Projects*, 237.

[157] "The Model Cities Program Questions and Answers", Norfolk Model City Program brochure from

the U.S. Department of Housing and Urban Development, Washington D. C., circa 1967 or 1968.

[158] Nathaniel Hendren & Ben Spring-Keyser, "A Unified Welfare Analysis of Government Policies Executive Summary," a report by Opportunity Insights at Harvard University (July 2019), https://opportunityinsights.org/wp-content/uploads/2019/07/welfare-executive-summary.pdf.

[159] Associated Press, "Man Sues Church for $2.5M After Being 'Felled by Holy Spirit,'" *Fox News*, July 10, 2008, https://www.foxnews.com/story/man-sues-church-for-2-5m-after-being-felled-by-holy-spirit; John Zarrella and Patrick Oppmann, "Pastor with 666 tattoo claims to be divine," *CNN.com*, February 19, 2007, https://www.cnn.com/2007/US/02/16/miami.preacher/.

[160] Susan Schmeichel, "Church Whips Up Controversy," *Pittsburgh Tribune-Review*, April 8, 2004.

[161] http://www.jesusismyhomeboy.com/the-story

[162] Frederick Douglass, *The Narrative of the Life of Frederick Douglass, An American Slave.* (1845) as contained in *The Norton Anthology of World Masterpieces, Fifth Edition*, Volume 2, 693.

[163] Frederick Douglass, "A Parody," (1845) as contained in *The Norton Anthology of World Masterpieces, Fifth Edition*, Volume 2, 719.

[164] Powell and Persico, *My American Journey*, 15.

[165] Johnny Cash, *Cash,* (New York: Harper Collins, 1997), 71.

[166] See Leviticus 25 and the concept of "The Year of Jubilee".

[167] Howard Hendricks, *Teaching to Change Lives,* (Multnomah: Multonmah Press, 1987), 21.

[168] James McRae, *Silent Screams of a Convict.*

[169] Rebecca D. Heino, Nicole B. Ellison, and Jennifer L. Gibbs, "Relationshopping: Investigating

the market metaphor in online dating," *Journal of Social and Personal Relationships* 27, no. 4, (2010): 427, https://doi.org/10.1177/0265407510361614.

[170] See Paul Amato and Alan Booth, *A Generation At Risk* (Cambridge: Harvard University Press, 1997), 123.

[171] Vern L. Bengtson, with Norella Putney and Susan C. Harris, *Families and Faith: How Religion Is Passed Down Across Generations* (New York: Oxford University Press, 2013), Chap. 10: Conclusion: What We Have Learned and How It Might Be Useful, Apple Books.

[172] Richard F. Gillum and Kristen D. Dodd, review of *Soul Mates: Religion, Sex, Love and Marriage among African Americans and Latinos* by W.B. Wilcox and N.H.

Wolfinger in the *Journal of the National Medical Association* 108, no. 4 (Winter 2016): 244.

[173] The National Marriage Project. "The State of Our Unions 2012: The President's Marriage Agenda," 2012, 12. A paper by The Institute for American Values and the National Marriage Project located at the University of Virginia as part of the President's Marriage Project. Accessible at http://www.stateofourunions.org/2012/SOOU2012.php Last accessed on December 3, 2021.

[174] Andrew Cherlin as quoted in "The State of Our Unions." From Andrew J. Cherlin, *The Marriage-Go-Round: The State of Marriage and Family in America Today* (New York: Alfred A. Knopf, 2009).

[175]Gus Lubin, "The 12 Most Expensive Weddings in History," *Business Insider*, April 28, 2011, http://www.businessinsider.com/most-expensive-weddings-in-history-2011-4

[176]Kathryn Vasel, "Couples are spending more than ever to get hitched," *CNN Money*, April 6, 2016, http://money.cnn.com/2016/04/05/pf/average-wedding-costs/

[177] Coles, Robert, "The Inexplicable Prayers of Ruby Bridges" in *Finding God at Harvard,* ed. Kelly Monroe (Grand Rapids: Zondervan, 1996), 33-40.

[178] Ruby Bridges and Margo Lundell, *Through My Eyes* (New York: Scholastic Press, 1999).

[179] M. Scott Peck, *The Road Less Travelled* (New York: Simon and Schuster, 1978), 69.

[180] Milton Friedman, *Capitalism and Freedom.* (Chicago: University of Chicago Press, 1962), 9.

[181] Akerlof and Shiller, *Phishing for Phools.*

[182] Michael Battle, *The Black Church in America. African American Christian Spirituality* (Malden: Blackwell Publishing, 2006), 44.

[183] Peck, *The Road Less Traveled*, 261.

[184] Leonard Colvin, "Part 2 School Desegregation in Norfolk in 1959; When 17 Brave Students Stood Tall," *New Journal and Guide*, Jul 7, 1999.

[185] "Patricia Turner," "School Segregation in Norfolk" series of webpages through Old Dominion University Libraries, https://exhibits.lib.odu.edu/exhibits/show/sdinv/the-norfolk-17/turnerpatricia.

[186] Alexander Hamilton, *The Federalist No. 78.*

[187] James Madison, *The Federalist No. 10.*

[188] Alexander Hamilton, *Federalist No. 78.*

[189] "Miranda v. Arizona: Earl Warren's Letter to Grandson" video recording, https://www.c-span.org/

video/?401974-1/miranda-v-arizona-earl-warrens-letter-grandson, accessed October 9, 2022.

[190] Abe Fortas, *Concerning Dissent and Civil Disobedience*, (New York: Signet, 1968), 117.

[191] Elijah Anderson, *Streetwise: Race, Class and Change in an Urban Community* (Chicago: University of Chicago Press, 1990), 250-251.

[192] Howard Zinn, *A People's History of the United States* (New York: Harper Collins, 2003), 42.

[193] Banerjee and Duflo, *Good Economics for Hard Times*, chap. 4.

[194] Solzhenitsyn, *The Gulag Archipelago*, Part IV, Chap. 1, "The Ascent."

[195] Rachel Denhollander, "Can Faith Reconcile Justice and Forgiveness" (October 28, 2018) *Veritas Forum* Podcast, Apple Podcasts. https://app.resonaterecordings.com/hosting/the-veritas-forum-podcast/e5b7589c-6254-41ff-aaeb-469003c55207.

[196] Sojourner Truth, *Narrative of Sojourner Truth* (New York: Barnes and Noble Books, 2005), 92 (first published in 1850).

[197] Matthew 5:4

[198] Eddie Brummelman et al, "Origins of Narcissism in Children," *PNAS* 112, no. 12 (March 24, 2015): Abstract, https://doi.org/10.1073/pnas.1420870112.

[199] Amos Schurr and Ilana Ritov, "Winning a Competition Predicts Dishonest Behavior," *PNAS,* 113, no. 7 (February 16, 2016): 1, https://doi.org/10.1073/pnas.1515102113.

[200] Stephane Cote, Julian House, and Robb Willer, "High Economic Inequality Leads Higher-income Individuals to Be Less Generous," PNAS 112, no. 52 (December 29, 2015):1, https://doi.org/10.1073/pnas.1511536112.

[201] Elizabeth Sobel Blum, "Healthy Communities: A Framework for Meeting CRA Obligations" (Dallas: Federal Reserve Bank of Dallas, March 2014): 3-4, https://www.dallasfed.org/~/media/documents/cd/healthy/CRAframework.pdf

[202] Henry Allen, "Character Takes on Personality," *The Washington Post,* January 5, 1986, https://www.washingtonpost.com/archive/opinions/1986/01/05/character-takes-on-personality/d15aeae3-d266-4c8b-a7c2-77cbcbdcb3b6/.

[203] "Turning Purpose Into Performance" HBR (Harvard Business Review) *Ideacast* 639, July 24, 2018. Transcript available at https://hbr.org/ideacast/2018/07/turning-purpose-into-performance.html

[204] Wilson, "The Rediscovery of Character: Private Virtue and Public Policy," 4.

[205] Wilson, "The Rediscovery of Character: Private Virtue and Public Policy," 16.

[206] Margery Williams, *The Velveteen Rabbit* (New York: Doubleday, 1922), 5-8.

[207] C.S. Lewis, *The Weight of Glory* (San Francisco: HarperSanFrancisco, 2001), 45.

[208] American Community Survey, 2022 Five-year estimates. Available at www.data.census.gov. Poverty statistics used here are in full recognition that the traditional federal poverty measures underestimate the true cost of living.

[209] Meacham, *Thomas Jefferson The Art of Power*, 35.

[210] Jean Johnson, "No Easy Way Out: Citizens Talk about Tackling the Debt", a report prepared for the Kettering Foundation, November 2012, https://www.kettering.org/catalog/product/no-easy-way-out-citizens-talk-about-tackling-debt.

[211] Thaler and Sunstein, *Nudge: The Final Edition*, Chap. 14 - Saving the Planet.

[212] Shawn Langlois, "Disney Heiress: "Jesus Christ Himself Doesn't Deserve This Much Money," *MarketWatch*, March 3, 2019,

https://www.marketwatch.com/story/disney-heiress-jesus-christ-himself-doesnt-deserve-this-much-money-2019-03-07.

[213] Andy Stanley and Jeff Foxworthy, "Being Generous," North Point Community Church, YouTube, November 13, 2017, 31:11 to 33:38 https://www.youtube.com/watch?v=UZiHJ5wWkvU.

[214] Glenn Firebaugh and Matthew B. Schroeder, "Does Your Neighbor's Income Affect Your Happiness," *AJS; American journal of sociology* 115, no. 3 (2009): 805-31, https://pubmed.ncbi.nlm.nih.gov/20503742/.

[215] James Chen, "Veblen Good: Definition, Examples, Difference from Giffen Good," *Investopedia.com*, updated June 29, 2023, https://www.investopedia.com/terms/v/veblen-good.asp

[216] Firebaugh and Schroeder, "Does Your Neighbor's Income Affect Your Happiness," 4.

[217] Nicholas Buttrick and Shigehiro Oishi, "Money and happiness: A consideration of history and psychological mechanisms," PNAS 120, no. 13 (March 28, 2023): https://doi.org/10.1073/pnas.2301893120.

[218] J. M. Twenge and T. Kasser, "Generational changes in materialism and work centrality, 1976-2007: associations with temporal changes in societal insecurity and materialistic role modeling," *Personality & social psychology bulletin* 39, no.7 (May 2013: 883–897,

https://doi.org/10.1177/0146167213484586. Available at https://pubmed.ncbi.nlm.nih.gov/23637277/.

[219] Shigehiro Oishi, Youngjae Cha, Asuka Kamiya, and Hiroshi Ono, "Money and happiness: the income-happiness correlation is higher when income inequality is higher," 1, 1-12, PNAS Nexus. 2022 Oct 8;1(5):pgac224. doi: 10.1093/pnasnexus/pgac224. Available at https://pubmed.ncbi.nlm.nih.gov/36712361/

[220] Firebaugh and Schroder, "Does Your Neighbor's Income Affect Your Happiness," 15.

About the Author

Jim started life on his grandparents' dairy farm in Smithsburg, Maryland, before his parents settled in the beautiful mountains of Cumberland, Maryland. He left Cumberland after high school to pursue a Bachelor of Arts in Biblical Studies from Lincoln Christian University—East Coast. From there he moved to the Uptown neighborhood of Chicago where he earned an interdisciplinary Master of Arts that covered urban studies, leadership, and theology from Lincoln Christian University's Chicago satellite office. In 2000, he moved to the Hazelwood neighborhood of Pittsburgh. With his church, he started a non-profit, special event coffee house that provided job training and skill development to neighborhood teens. He wrote winning grants from Operation Weed and Seed, The Pittsburgh History and Landmarks Foundation, Compassion Allegheny, and Hunter Memorial Trust. After moving to Hampton Roads in 2010 to be closer to family, he became a Neighborhood Development Specialist with the City of Norfolk and now serves as Programs Manager with Norfolk's Department of Neighborhood Services.